Sport in the Global Society

General Editor: J. A. Mangan

THE FIRST BLACK FOOTBALLER

SPORT IN THE GLOBAL SOCIETY

General Editor: J. A. Mangan

The interest in sports studies around the world is growing and will continue to do so. This unique series combines aspects of the expanding study of *sport in the global society*, providing comprehensiveness and comparison under one editorial umbrella. It is particularly timely, with studies in the political, cultural, social, economic, geographical and aesthetic elements of sport proliferating in institutions of higher education.

Eric Hobsbawm once called sport one of the most significant practices of the late nineteenth century. Its significance is even more marked in the late twentieth century and will continue to grow in importance into the next millennium as the world develops into a 'global village' sharing the English language, technology and sport.

Other Titles in the Series

Scoring for Britain
International Football and International Politics, 1900–1939
Peter J. Beck

Sporting Nationalism
Identity, Ethnicity, Immigration and Assimilation
Edited by David Mayall and Michael Cronin

Footbinding, Feminism and Freedom
The Liberation of Women's Bodies in Modern China
Fan Hong

The Games Ethic and Imperialism
Aspects of the Diffusion of an Ideal
J. A. Mangan

The Race Game
Sport and Politics in South Africa
Douglas Booth

Rugby's Great Split
Class, Culture and the Origins of Rugby League Football
Tony Collins

THE FIRST BLACK FOOTBALLER

Arthur Wharton 1865–1930

An Absence of Memory

PHIL VASILI

FRANK CASS
LONDON • PORTLAND, OR

First published in 1998 in Great Britain by
FRANK CASS PUBLISHERS
Newbury House, 900 Eastern Avenue
London, IG2 7HH

and in the United States of America by
FRANK CASS PUBLISHERS
c/o ISBS, 5804 N.E. Hassalo Street
Portland, Oregon 97213-3644

Website: http://www.frankcass.com

Reprinted 1999

British Library Cataloguing in Publication Data

Vasili, Phil
The first black footballer – Arthur Wharton, 1865–1930 : an absence of memory. – (Sport in the global society)
1. Wharton, Arthur 2. Soccer players – England – Biography
3. Athletes, Black – England –Biography
I. Title
796.3'34'092

ISBN 0-7146-4903-1 (cloth)
ISBN 0-7146-4459-5 (paper)
ISSN 1368-9789

Library of Congress Cataloging-in-Publication Data

Vasili, Phil, 1956–
The first black footballer, Arthur Wharton, 1865–1930 : an absence of memory / Phil Vasili.
p. cm. – (Sport in the global society, ISSN 1368-9789 ; vol. 11)
Includes bibliographical references and index.
ISBN 0-7146-4903-1 (cloth). – ISBN 0-7146-4459-5 (pbk.)
1. Wharton, Arthur, 1865–1930. 2. Soccer players–Ghana–Biography. 3. Athletes, Black–Ghana–Biography.
4. Discrimination in sports–Great Britain. 5. Race discrimination–Great Britain. I. Title. II. Series: Cass series–sport in the global society ; 11.
GV942.7.W425V37 1998
796.334'092–dc21
[B] 98-27690
CIP

Typeset by Vitaset, Paddock Wood, Kent
Printed in Great Britain by
Bookcraft (Bath) Ltd, Midsomer Norton, Somerset

Dedicated to the Memory of

RAY JENKINS

who started Arthur running again

Contents

List of illustrations

25 Alwyn Tatum.
26 Spot the mistake! Arthur died on 12 December, not the 13th.
27 The dedication ceremony, Edlington, 8 May 1997.

Illustrations 2, 3, 4, 5, 6, 13, 19, 22, 23 and 24 are courtesy of Sheila Leeson; 8, 9, 10 are reproduced by permission of the Syndics of Cambridge University Library; 14 is reproduced by permission of the Football Museum, Preston; and 18 is reproduced by permission of the Tameside Local Studies Library.

Foreword

Arthur Wharton is hardly a household name, but perhaps he should be. Objectively his sporting achievements elevate him way beyond many far better known and more celebrated figures. A world sprint champion and professional footballer who played at the highest level, as a remarkable sporting all-rounder he could well be spoken of in the same breath as the Compton brothers. So why so little mention of him?

Racism is obviously a key reason. There is an assumption implicit in British culture and history that the United Kingdom of Great Britain and Northern Ireland was a homogeneous, and above all, a White society before large-scale immigration from the New Commonwealth in the 1950s and 1960s. This view denies the existence of the long-established Black communities in British cities like Cardiff, Bristol and Liverpool.

The second and related reason for Arthur Wharton's lack of status, is to do with the class nature of British society. Wharton was lionised by a defiant, radical section of the British working-class community and in the process became wilfully proletarianised. Photographs of Arthur show his metamorphosis from African aristocrat to Yorkshire miner. In spite of his background, Arthur Wharton chose to become and remain part of that community.

I remember having a discussion with a publisher for whom I have a great deal of respect. He talked about the number of manuscripts he received and how the good ones always got published. Yes, there were a lot of angry and paranoid failed writers (I know, I've been reviewed by most of them) but publishing was largely effective at representing the lives, cultures and experiences of a socially diverse society. This seemed like a load of old bollocks to me. Go into the British Fiction section of your local bookshop and see how many books are written in the same narrative style.

About this time, the Scottish writer, Tom Leonard, during his period as writer-in-residence at Paisley Libraries, unearthed writings of publishable standard by local working-class poets. These were ignored in their time and place but were edited by Tom Leonard in a book entitled *Radical Renfrew*.

Class bias is always found in the writing of history. To use John Lydon's memorable phrase, 'history is the winners telling the losers how bad they are'. We have to fall back on a truism; any society is a society in conflict. Different groups and individuals are in competition for resources. The object of the conflict is for the usual winners, the dominant sections of society, to maintain their position of dominance. Inequalities in society are what the rich reward themselves with. And these inequalities not only have to be maintained but justified.

John King's excellent book *England Away* describes the liberating effect that being in another country had on working-class people who travelled *en masse* beyond end-of-the-tube-line package resorts through football in the eighties. He mentions how 'cool' things seemed when you escaped from one-sided class propaganda, which was so persuasive that you often did not even notice it was all around you. I've heard this point made time and time again by friends who've followed their teams in Europe or left these shores in search of clubbing highs. I certainly noticed this myself when I lived in Amsterdam.

The point is that while a well-funded cultural system exists to spew out ruling-class culture, any culture, art and history promoted outside of this system relies largely on concerned maverick groups or individuals. The society is only 'liberal' or 'pluralist' to the extent that it tolerates those different voices which are generally let in to spice up the mainstream only when it becomes intolerably bland. In the meantime, we lose so much of our culture. Nobody is going to tell me that there isn't the same talent, and tales to be told, in Skye, or Manchester or Bournemouth as there is in Renfrew. The only difference is that there is no Tom Leonard in those places to unearth them.

Thankfully, for the sake of Arthur Wharton's memory, and for working-class and Black culture in Britain there is Phil Vasili. Wharton deserves to have his story told. He was a remarkable athlete who led a remarkable life through one of the most turbulent periods in British history. Had Wharton been white and Oxbridge-educated, it is very doubtful whether Phil's biography of him would have been the first. We can rest assured that his reputation would have been looked after by the cultural system. Phil has done the business for Arthur, but how many more Arthurs are there out there? This book, however, goes a long way to reclaiming history. Young, working-class and Black kids in Britain now at least have the opportunity of celebrating this true sporting hero.

There is still a generation of Black people which has been driven out of football by overt racism. As a kid I remember seeing Leith's Sikhs attending Hibernian games in numbers, with not a maroon turban in sight. Why is it that Arsenal-daft Black kids in Finsbury Park, unlike their white counterparts, do not attend Highbury games *en masse* when they grow big enough to go with their mates? British football has worked harder than most institutions to tackle racism, not for idealistic reasons, but to sanitise the game to make it appeal to more consumers and sponsors and thus make more money for clubs. However, this anti-racism effort is one welcome by-product of the sanitising process. Nevertheless there is still a lot of work to be done, as the recent controversy involving Collymore and Harkness reminds us, and I see this book as an important contribution to it. Arthur Wharton was a great working-class Black British hero. We should know about him.

Phil is a driven man. He was part of the Football Unites – Racism Divides group who campaigned to have Arthur Wharton's grave marked with a commemorative headstone. His enthusiasm for putting the record straight is formidable. I know that enthusiasm first hand: he got me drunk in Amsterdam and enlisted me in co-writing the screenplay based on Arthur's life for Channel Four. He's a genuine football lover as well, and not a bad player either.

When we were doing the screenplay for *The Gold Coast Showman*, we were struck by the parallels between the game then and now. In spite of all its fashionable hype these days, many long-standing, working-class genuine fans are more alienated from the game than ever. But look on the bright side: when the avaricious, egotistical chairmen, the opportunistic sponsors and the ex-public school Mockney pundits, who discovered the game in their thirties, have jumped ship, deciding that football is not profitable, the Phil Vasilis and Arthur Whartons will still be there, because they love it. They really do.

Irvine Welsh
May 1998

Series Editor's Foreword

Edmund Burke, that most mature of commentators, in *Reflections on the Revolution in France*, wrote: 'The nature of man is intricate; the objects of society are of the greatest possible complexity; and therefore no simple disposition or direction of power can be suitable either to man's nature, or to the quality of his affairs.' There are two enmeshed themes in this intriguing biography of Arthur Wharton which, on occasion, seems to raise more questions than it answers: invisibility in history and victimisation in history. Both must be approached with caution: as John M. MacKenzie, the distinguished historian of British imperialism, has recently written:

> The concept of the eternal victim fits ill with the recent reaction against viewing the indigenous peoples of the Empire, or for that matter the subordinate classes of Britain, as essentially passive. The notion that such people are always the objects of dominant behaviour, the absorbers of a superior culture doomed to twitch to the electrodes of imperial energy, has been rejected. The idea that they meekly respond to the images imposed upon them by copying the stereotype itself is to stretch the concept of self-oppression beyond credulity.

Wise words.

To a considerable degree, as this book reveals, Wharton made his own bed and chose to lie on it – in more senses than one. He chose Europe, he chose sport, he chose his career. He was much more than the unfortunate recipient of xenophobic racism; he was quite evidently a strong-minded, self-assertive, enormously talented sportsman. He walked his own road – out of a restrictive middle-class milieu, out of teetotal Methodism – into a more vibrant, sensual way of life of physical exuberance, release and reward. There is always the danger that must be resisted, of taking from his dignity, his vitality and his talent and making him more cipher than man.

Wharton's story is one of ironies, paradoxes and contradictions; a striking irony is that his claim to fame, certainly as a footballer, is based in fact on his colour; he was, after all, a very good, rather than excellent, games (football and cricket) all-rounder. And as a goalkeeper reaction to him was mixed – some emphatically thought him brilliant, others strongly disagreed. However, as a Black goalkeeper – in his time he was unique; a legacy left to biography. And a paradox? Wharton's unequivocal claim to fame is as the AAA sprint record holder for forty years, an astounding achievement, and this record is written down for all to see and as such has always been acknowledged. As AAA record holder his achievements are no more forgotten (or remembered) than those of all the others, from all classes and of any colour, whom it is now difficult to recall: *sic transit gloria mundi*.

With the virtues and vices of a member of the human race, Wharton comes to vivid life in the following pages. His humanity is his attraction. In the light of history, no doubt when the dust of the fashionable cause has settled, he will be seen even more clearly as an extraordinarily gifted man of action who, to a marked extent, made his own destiny rather than acted out a role as passive recipient of racial prejudice. The finest irony, perhaps, is that in this committed biography his humanity, rather than others' inhumanity, has been brought to the fore. For this reason he lingers long in the memory – a man of outstanding natural abilities who gained, and gave, enormous satisfaction from them and through them.

And the fascinating questions for the future? To what extent did Wharton hasten his own social demise through drink, to what extent was his lack of favour in the South (he was loved in the North) a typical illustration of the classic North/South divide which has blighted the careers of many Northern sportsmen and women? To what extent was Wharton an erratic performer, a Best rather than a Compton, who sowed at least some of the seeds of his own decline into obscurity? And then there is that sharp question raised so eloquently by Harry Edwards, Black athlete and academic, in that famous television documentary defence of the Black athlete in the 1980s: 'How Black is Black?' To what extent was Wharton, the Euro-African with Scottish grandfathers on both the paternal and maternal side, Black? To what extent is Black in the eye of the beholder, in the prejudice of the individual, in the pen of the recorder? The English historian H.A.L. Fisher once remarked with perfect truth that European purity of race does not exist. Europe is a continent of energetic mongrels. Harry Edwards would understand that remark. It might be a happier world if more people did.

Incidentally, caution should be exercised over the iconolatry of the athlete – the athlete as role model. The gentle and dignified Arthur Ashe, before his too early and tragic death, warned unceasingly, a warning that has been issued unremittingly also by Harry Edwards, of the dangers to the young Black of the projection of the athlete as a preeminent icon – too much competition and far too little opportunity, and consequently, too many failures who end up, unqualified and unemployable, in poverty! Sense not soundbite and gravitas not glibness are required by the commentator. Such issues require mature perception, not naïve passion.

Wharton, a wonderful athlete and a fascinating man, has a story well worth the telling, and although it is not yet all told, what we now know through this appealing biography is well worth knowing. Dwight Morrow, the experienced and realistic American banker, lawyer and diplomat, once advised his son that the world was divided into those who do things and those who get the credit, and he would be well advised to belong to the first group – there was far less competition. In the North, Wharton in his lifetime, happily, was a member of both groups. This biography will ensure that North *and* South and beyond, after his lifetime, he will also be in both.

J.A. Mangan
International Research Centre for Sport, Socialisation and Society
University of Strathclyde
June 1998

Acknowledgements

There are many, many people to whom I am in debt over the completion of this book. But there are some whose persistent love, encouragement and help provided me with the means to see the work through and deserve special mention. So, heartfelt thanks and apologies to: Carrie MacArthur, my wife, who earned the bacon while I enjoyed myself; my children Andrea, Fionnulla, Alex and Louisa, who put up with a grumpy father whose mind was on other things; Howard Holmes of Football Unites – Racism Divides for believing in me and cajoling FURD to put their money where his mouth was; Sheila Leeson, Arthur's grandniece (or granddaughter), and her family for welcoming me despite my prying questions; Tony Whelan, once a great player and now a great friend; Irvine Welsh, who is just, well, great; Andy Ward and Tony Mason for reading and bettering the manuscript; Trisha Rawson for proof-reading the first draft; Alan Harman for suggesting Arthur had a fondness for the odd pint or five; Harry Berry for his information on Preston North End and Arthur's running career; my editor, Jonathan Manley, for pushing this project forward at a pace Arthur would have been proud of; Jackie Jenkins, the widow of Ray Jenkins, for allowing me unlimited access to Ray's research. An immense debt is owed to you all for your unique contributions.

This book is dedicated both to Ray's memory, Carrie's perseverance and to all those who have fought against racism and died in the struggle.

To all of you who have taken part and not been mentioned, I owe you. Thanks.

Preface

At the close of the 1995–96 football season viewers of BBC 1's 'Match of the Day' highlights programme voted Goal of the Season – a spectacular 25 yard volley – to Anthony Yeboah, a Ghanaian international playing for Leeds United. Another of his goals was also in contention. Exactly 110 years earlier the first Ghanaian footballer was about to sign for Preston North End, considered by one contemporary sportswriter to be 'the best team in the world'.[1] The 'Invincibles' were certainly Britain's most professional side, winning the first division unbeaten in 1888–89 – in its inaugural season – and the FA Cup without conceding a goal. Perhaps then, the marriage of the world's first Black footballer with the world's first professional club had a poetic symmetry. When he joined Preston he was, for the second successive year, Amateur Athletic Association 100 yards champion of England. Arthur Wharton's reputation as *the* Black sportstar of late-Victorian Britain was beginning to unfold.

In an interview given to the *Athletic Journal*, 26 June 1888 – a national circulation sports paper – Wharton recalled an incident at an athletics meeting in Yorkshire. After winning the heat of a race he was resting out of view of two competitors but he could not help overhearing the comment: 'Who's he, that we should be frightened of him beating us? We can beat a blooming nigger any time.' The 'dark un', as the reporter described Arthur, offered to box them. The 'terror stricken friends' got out of his reach quickly.

The incident and his direct, defiant response tells us much about the man and how Britain was becoming increasingly racialised. As a Black man in an environment where people were being categorised through the colour of their skin, Wharton was not judged by his actions alone. Yet his triumphant survival in battles of the fittest represented a paradox: through them he became a national celebrity; because of them he is portrayed to the public as different – a 'nigger'; 'darkey'; 'walnut visaged'. As his success grew, so did the conflict intensify to own and control his image of himself – his identity. The span of his sports career coincided with the scramble for Africa. Against this imperial backdrop Arthur's contests on track and field can be seen as symbolising the struggle of Africans for dignity in the face of denigration.

While in public Arthur raged against those who raged against him, his private life was characterised by grief and turmoil that was largely self-imposed. His relationship with his wife, Emma, was turbulent. When he closed the door on (the love of?) his adoring public, he entered a private domain of anguish, bereft of the interrupting calm of love. It was as if his fame, despite the hard graft necessary in its creation, came at a vastly inflated price. Indeed, when (if?) Arthur did find love it was not comfortable and accessible but subversive, forbidden and ultimately destructive.

His dedication to active participation in sport also distanced him from his family in Ghana, then the Gold Coast. Their intention was for him to follow in his father's footsteps and preach the Methodist gospel. The prodigious yet prodigal son had no inclination for this spiritual path. He ran away to the physical embrace of a more worldly culture. In so doing the distance he covered became irretraceable. He never returned to the Gold Coast. Nor did his West African family members rejoice out loud in his ascendancy.

Wharton's tale encapsulates those contradictions found in life but writ large. He was famous, but for being 'darkey' as much as sportsman; he was loved but not always by those whose love he wanted; he gave love but often not to those to whom he had promised, and to whom it was needed – in particular his 'bastard' children; he was the fittest and fastest around but had a weakness for cigars and a thirst for alcohol; he ran and played for charity but died penniless; enjoyed fame and was on hand-shaking terms with controversy yet could underline the following ode to humility, from Book 2 of Corinthians, chapter 12, verse 7 in his Bible. 'And lest I should be exalted above measure through the abundance of the revelations, there was given to me a thorn in the flesh, the messenger of Satan to buffet me, lest I should be exalted above measure.' His life had three consistent and intertwining themes: love, sport and politics. It was a Victorian melodrama with concerns that are relevant today.

The struggle against racism was the overarching context of Arthur's life. During the last three decades of the twentieth century there have been numerous anti-racist campaigns focusing on sport. In Britain these began with mass demonstrations against the Springbok rugby tour in 1969–70. A current initiative concerned with soccer 'Kick It Out', stems from supporters, players and anti-racist groups' reactions to growing activity by right-wing parties such as the National Front and British National Party in the 1980s. Both sold papers and attempted to recruit members at club grounds. Another group, 'Football Unites – Racism Divides', based in Sheffield, funded the writing of this book. Their aim is to foster a more accessible, welcoming and friendly football environment for ethnic minorities in the Sharrow district of the city where Sheffield United are based.

It is timely, then, to remind ourselves of the experiences of Britain's first Black sprint champion and professional footballer who, for 66 years lay anonymously in a mining village in the North of England. His grave, unmarked and indistinguishable from the numerous other nameless resting places dotted around, was found by his grandniece – or possibly granddaughter – Sheila Leeson in the spring of 1996. Remarkably, she too was unaware of the historic importance of his athletic and footballing achievements. This lack of a physical memorial mirrored, with eerie coincidence, the absence of memory of this Victorian sports star from the histories of athletics and football in particular and the historiography of sport in Britain in general.

NOTE

1. *Athletic News*, 8 March 1887.

Phil Vasili
March 1998

Introduction

I came to know about Arthur Wharton when I received a letter from Phil Vasili in February 1996. He was seeking to interview me as part of his research for a PhD on the history of Black professional footballers in Britain 1886–1970. I remember being quite stunned, because until Phil's letter I had absolutely no idea that the history of Black footballers in Britain stretched back so far.

I was somewhat ashamed that I had no idea of the existence and prominence of such luminaries as Arthur Wharton, Walter Tull (Spurs 1909–11) and numerous others. I should not have felt so bad because I was to find out that even Arthur's relatives – notably his grandniece Sheila Leeson – only 'discovered' his achievements after following up a letter by Phil to the *Rotherham Advertiser* seeking information about Arthur for his research. Although she knew him as her great-uncle she had no idea about his exploits as an all-round sportsman. It occurred to me that if his blood relatives did not know his story, how could the wider sporting world be expected to know? It made me feel a good deal better. Simon Turnbull, writing in *The Independent on Sunday*, called the Arthur Wharton story: 'The most conspicuously absent volume from the library of British sport' (1 June 1997). In the light of Arthur's extraordinary achievements described so admirably in this book, who would deign to disagree?

Arthur's story would have remained hidden in the vaults of history were it not for Phil's endeavours to excavate it. This biography is the result of long and prodigious research and deserves a wide readership as it makes a substantial contribution to the story of Black footballers in Britain. It shows Arthur to be the first Black pioneer in the sphere of professional football. The wagon train that he first rode led ultimately to the modern day Black British superstars such as Paul Ince and Ian Wright. His initial prospecting was to yield many other gold nuggets along the way; but more than this, Arthur is shown to be a multi-talented sportsman *par excellence*.

When considering Arthur's professional achievements I couldn't help but pause to reflect on my own career and compare my experience with his, all but a generation earlier. The problems and difficulties I had to overcome given the colour of my skin, pale into insignificance (relatively speaking) compared to what Arthur must have endured living in an age where concepts such as equal opportunity and racial equality held no sway.

Arthur's career fell within the orbit of Lancashire football, playing as he did for both Stockport County and Stalybridge Celtic. In this respect we had something in common, because during my own career in England (1968–77) I played for three Lancashire clubs: Manchester United, Manchester City and Rochdale. Coincidentally, I was married on the 110th anniversary of Arthur's birth, 28 October 1975.

Throughout my schoolboy football days (1963–68) in which I captained both my school and local town team (Stretford schools, now Trafford schools) I cannot recall playing either with or against another Black player. I did have a Lancashire schoolboy trial (November 1967) but failed to make the final squad. Despite that disappointment I was invited to train with Manchester United by Joe Armstrong (the legendary scout) and eventually went on to sign schoolboy, apprentice professional, and finally, full professional forms with the club (1968–73). During my time at the club I had an England youth trial and had the privilege of being selected to go on the club's senior tour to Bermuda, Canada and the USA (May 1970). I was 17 years of age. During this tour I played against the Bermudan national team, which included Clyde Best. On leaving England I went to play in the now defunct North American Soccer League (NASL) before retiring in 1984 after playing professionally for 16 years.

Throughout my career I undoubtedly experienced racism in its myriad guises. There was sometimes direct abuse, but mostly stereotype views about the ability of Black players were expressed covertly. For example: they had a bad attitude; couldn't play in the cold weather; were injury prone; lacked character; they couldn't defend. Some of these views sadly still prevail despite a mountain of contradictory evidence. Needless to say, I was determined, like Arthur and others before me, to carve out a career in professional football whatever the obstacles I encountered.

I vividly recall having progressed through the club's junior teams, making my debut for Manchester United reserves against Leeds at Old Trafford (10.12.70). I was selected at outside left (to use the old terminology). Appearing on the opposite wing in the same position was the Black South African Albert Johanneson. Albert, now sadly deceased (1996), was the first Black player to feature in an FA Cup Final (Leeds v. Liverpool, 1965). He was the first Black player I can remember playing against. There is irony here also, because at that time I considered him to be the first Black professional footballer. I find this quite embarrassing now especially in the light of this book.

I actually didn't play with or against many Black players during my career in England; there simply weren't that many around. Players I do recall playing against were Clyde Best (West Ham), Brendon Batson (Cambridge Utd), and Cecil Podd (Bradford City). However, I did have the privilege of playing with Stan Horne (ex Manchester City) when I was at Rochdale. I remember Stan as a superb professional as well as a very good player. We, and others, were all at a particular point in a lineage that led from Arthur Wharton down to the Black players who are now playing in the modern game in England.

Anybody who examines the career of Arthur with only a minimum degree of objectivity would see that his achievements were immense by any standards. These are all fully described in the book including his remarkable achievement of being the first man to run the 100 yard event in 10 seconds flat in a major championship (AAA, Stamford Bridge 1886). He was a nationally known and acclaimed sportsman, and he clearly enjoyed his celebrity. Arthur was affectionately described by newspaper pundits as the 'Dark Un', 'best goalkeeper in the north' and 'coloured gentleman'. Phil encapsulates Arthur's bravery as a goalkeeper in the epithet 'El Loco'. Arthur's grace and speed on the track described in the book in turn reminds me of the epithet Homer ascribes to the hero Achilles in the *Iliad* 'Swift Footed'. Such epithets are a mark of the affection and esteem in which he was held in the Victorian sporting world.

For all his achievements in the world of sport Arthur was essentially a working-class man, and carried within his being the social consciousness mirrored by his class. He was, as Phil points out, no paragon of virtue, but rather an ordinary man trying to make his way in life in the hard world of Victorian society.

Phil eloquently recounts the story of Arthur's birth in Accra on the

Gold Coast (now Ghana), West Africa and his coming to England to study for the ministry at the Weslyan College in Darlington. This episode gives an insight into Arthur's intellectual abilities for he was quite clearly an able scholar indeed as well as an athlete, and we can only speculate as to what kind of minister he would have made if the world of sport had not claimed him.

Despite Phil's extensive research, inspired by the pioneering work of Ray Jenkins, there is a singular lack of evidence of *all* the facets of Arthur's life and so much must be assumed. What is documented, however, are the humanitarian aspects of his character which are beyond dispute. The book is replete with examples of Arthur's compassion for his fellow man notably demonstrated by his appearance in numerous charity matches for fellow professionals. Arthur's celebrity and popular appeal helped to increase attendance, and of course, gate receipts. He also displayed great dignity in supporting the NUM during the general strike of 1926. What is sad is the poor response to his own testimonial witnessed by only a small crowd. Phil describes this episode as 'A Pathetic Affair'. I personally view this as somewhat tragic and can only guess how slighted Arthur himself must have felt given the public response, or lack of it. Arthur's services to football and humanitarian concern for the plight of his fellow man deserved better recompense than this. What is abundantly clear, however, is that throughout the travails of his life Arthur always remained a thoroughly decent human being.

The author makes it clear throughout the book that Arthur's life was set within a specific political, cultural and social milieu – mid-Victorian Britain. A Britain which was experiencing a vibrant working-class movement for social change such as Chartism while at the same time expanding her colonies at the expense of the indigenous population. Phil goes to some length in the book to explain the concept of scientific racism, an ideology which permeated Victorian intellectual life and provided the framework for institutionalised racism to exist. The writings of Charles Darwin and Herbert Spencer did much to disseminate negative views about black- and brown-skinned people among the wider population. 'Theories' such as natural selection and the distinct racial origins of humankind (polygenesis) were gaining wide credence. No less an authority than the renowned *Encyclopaedia Britannica* (1884) incredibly expounded these views in stating that 'no full-blooded Negro has ever been distinguished as a man of science, a poet, or an artist'. Given these views, how could one fail to agree with the author's unequivocal assertion that the reason that Arthur didn't play for an England representative side was due to 'The Pigmentation of his skin'. Arthur's personal and professional life can be understood only within this social context.

An important part of Victorian social life was of course sport. Phil explains such conventions as the Sheffield System, pedestrianism, handicapping and roping, which were a feature of Victorian sports and make interesting reading. We are also introduced to such characters as Spank Smith and Tom Botts, Arthur's coach and financial backer respectively. We are also given a glimpse of Willie Suddell, the chairman of Preston North End and a forerunner of the modern-day chairman/director. Other characters include the sprinter Frank Ritchie, Arthur's great rival and *bête noire*. Their intense rivalry is reminiscent of the classic track jousts of Coe and Ovett, Johnson/Lewis and more recently Johnson/Bailey. Such rivalry had a long tradition.

Phil also points to the origins of the commercialisation of sport which is such a feature of the modern sports world; he refers to Arthur's talent being sold as a commodity or 'proletarianised'. Thus we get further insight into Arthur's working-class background. However, Phil teasingly asserts that Arthur was extremely clever in his financial affairs, so that it was often difficult to determine precisely who was exploiting whom.

In the light of Arthur's huge success and national recognition why was he forgotten for so long? Phil argues persuasively that the prime reasons he was forgotten were his working-class origins and his skin colour; there seemed to be a conspiracy to omit him from the records. His omissions from *Football Who's Who 1900–1* and *1901–2* are cited as just one example.

Phil makes a fascinating comparison with the career of K.S. Ranjitsinhji, the aristocratic Indian prince who was a contemporary of Arthur's. His name has always been high in the pantheon of cricketing heroes. Phil argues that unlike Arthur, Ranjitsinhji was not forgotten because not only was he considered to be an 'upper class gentleman', but he also derived from a purer racial stock. This was partly because the Victorians considered the Sanskrit language of India, spoken by Ranjitsinhji, more sophisticated and intellectually superior to the languages of Black Africa, Arthur's home continent. Ranjitsinhji's achievements were therefore considered worthy of propagation.

Chapter 13 of the book is an exquisite exposition of the reason why the achievements of Black sportsmen were expurgated from the records. Black achievement embodied by people like Arthur had serious consequences for notions of white supremacy and the systematic racism which was a thread running through Victorian society.

The story of Arthur's life is in many respects a sad one; sad because he never really received the rewards in life his talents deserved. The last years of his life were spent in relative obscurity working as a haulage hand at the Yorkshire Main Colliery, Edlington, until his death in 1930 from cancer.

A memorial to his memory was unveiled at Edlington cemetery on 8 May 1997 to which I was invited. As I stood by Arthur's grave that day I felt so privileged to have been invited to attend such a memorable occasion. It was a simple ceremony, but Arthur's relatives were immensely proud of him and what he had achieved. They were so elated that at last his achievements were being recognised. I was deeply moved.

Phil Vasili has written an eminently readable biography of Arthur Wharton which I commend to you because it truly honours his memory. It is written with passion and erudition and football owes him a debt of gratitude for bringing to the fore such a remarkable story. I hope this book is read by anyone who is interested in the history of sport in general and football in particular so that the story of Arthur Wharton, The Quintessential Victorian Sportsman, will no longer remain absent from memory!

Tony Whelan
Staff Coach Manchester Utd
Centre of Excellence
May 1998

1 *Rising North Star: Darlington and football 1884–88*

The first mention of Arthur Wharton in the English press was to record his performance as a reader at the Wesleyan Sunday School in Cannock in February 1884. He provided a recitation at an evening event for the Wesleyan Band of Hope. Three months later the *Cannock Advertiser* (11 May) reported his appearance for the town's cricket club. He scored a duck (0)! Despite this ignominious batting debut the 19-year-old all-rounder went on to play 11 games, captaining the side at least once, scoring a total of 93 runs and taking at least 4 wickets. George Grant, his cousin, also played. In a game that June the pair scored 31 out of the team total of 54. While these public references were the first of many, neither pursuits were to act as the primary tributaries of his excellence, although Arthur did become a professional cricketer. In fact it was Cannock and Cannock White Cross Football Clubs, for whom he played during the 1883–84 football season, that provided the springboard for Arthur's career as a sportsman.

The summer of 1884, while it marked the beginning of Arthur's public life as a sportsman, was his last at Shoal Hill College, Cannock, Staffordshire. He had spent two years at the Methodist institution. The ill-health of the principal, Samuel G. Gwynne, had forced its closure in July. The teenager moved further north to enrol at Cleveland College, Darlington in County Durham. (His cousins George and Josiah Grant returned to the Gold Coast having 'succeeded' in their exams at Shoal Hill. It is not known what happened to Justin, the youngest of the three Grants who was also a pupil at Cannock.) As was not uncommon in such circumstances the Methodist network of friends, contacts and colleagues had been utilised. Timothy Laing junior, editor of the *Gold Coast Times*, the newspaper owned by F.C. Grant, Arthur's uncle, patron and father of George, Josiah and Justin, was an ex-pupil of Cleveland College. The principal there was Henry Brooks. Both he and Gwynne had been born at Nailsea, Somerset in 1827 and had probably attended Wesley College, Taunton together. (Gwynne later became a teacher there.) Their parallel lives included dual roles as Wesleyan lay preachers, members of the Liberal Party and local School Board officers. Even their educational enterprises had like-minded aims and objectives: with emphasis on moral discipline, Wesleyan Methodist religion and an orthodox academic curriculum designed to prepare students for entry into the professions and higher education.

It was in the North East that Wharton came to be more widely recognised for his prowess at sport. His aptitude and skills were applied to athletics, association and rugby football and cricket with differing degrees of success. It could be argued that in sprinting and the position of goalkeeper, for a time, he was without equal.

'Best goalkeeper in the North': Football 1885–86

During this season Wharton established himself as first choice goalkeeper for Darlington Cricket and Football Club. They played – and still do – at the Feethams ground. The arena was also the venue of many of his early, reputation-building athletic triumphs. The club had been formed in 1883 after a meeting at Darlington Grammar School. There was no Football League at this time; that began in 1888. The premier competition in the 1880s was the Football Association Challenge Cup, begun in 1872. There were also important regional competitions organised by local County Football Associations. For Darlington CFC these were the Cleveland and Durham County Challenge Cups. The latter had begun in the year of the club's formation. Prior to 1885–86 the furthest the 'Skernesiders' had progressed in any competition was to the third round of the Durham Cup, where they lost after a replay to the team with a feared reputation in the North East, Bishop Auckland Church Institute.

Arthur's ability and unusual style as a goalkeeper soon became noticed. His 'fisting out' of the ball over a long distance – 'the goalkeeper with the prodigious punch'[1] – became a characteristic feature of his play; as was his outstanding agility. Reporters frequently marvelled how the novice often stopped goalbound shots that would have beaten other custodians. The father of Herbert Burgin

> used to talk enthusiastically about the exploits of 'Darkie' Wharton … in the Darlington goalmouth … he was a very athletic and energetic goalkeeper, and … became famous for crouching in the corner of the goal until the last minute when he would literally spring into action, diving across the goal to make fantastic saves.[2]

In short – he was worth a goal or two start. The first team played 32 matches in 1885–86 – Arthur's first full season – winning 18, losing 8 and drawing 6. The West African played in over 20 cup, charity and friendly fixtures. In those he did not play in he was often 'sorely missed'.[3]

He was also selected to play for the representative sides of Newcastle and District, Northumberland and Durham, Durham, and Cleveland. It was in the matches for the first and last mentioned that he played against the elite 'amateurs' of the football establishment, the Corinthians, containing four England internationals. This team of mostly Oxbridge Blues had been established by N. Lane Jackson with the primary purpose of bringing together amateur England internationals in an attempt to improve the poor record of the national team against Scotland. (The designation 'amateur' was, in fact, more a signifier of the bourgeois background of the players rather than a reference to not being paid for playing. The Corinthians often charged more in expenses than the weekly wage bill of their professional opponents. A joke doing the rounds at the time went: 'Why is the Prince of Wales [the future Edward VII] like the Corinthians when on tour? Because, before agreeing to turn up, he bargains for the whole of the "gate".') These gentlemen toured the country indulging in their favourite winter pastime, sustained by having their expenses covered more than adequately by their opponents. Some football reporters and writers, usually London-based, thought the Corinthians the most accomplished players in England.

The Newcastle and District side lost 8–2 to their robust, physical opponents; the gate receipts of £50 no doubt providing the gentlemen tourists with the petty cash for a refined, post-match jolly-up. To put this figure in perspective, Darlington's receipts for the 1885–86 season were £69. This helps us understand why Corinthians' opponents were willing to accept such high expense claims. The Cleveland XI, with the 'wonderful defence of Wharton',[4] managed to keep the deficit to half that of their neighbours north of the Tyne, but failed to score.

A week later, he played again for Newcastle and District against Preston North End. This fixture came at the tailend of the season in which the Lancastrians had played 54 games undefeated. Most northern football correspondents felt they had the beating of any team. True to form, PNE defeated the select XI 3–0 with a swift, accurate passing style of play characteristic of Scottish football. Through their collective and *professional* approach of organised teamwork they were making anachronistic the orthodox individual-dribbling style favoured by the southern 'amateurs'. The match report in the *Newcastle Weekly Chronicle* made particular mention of Wharton's excellent display in goal. However, before then, another local reporter had already labelled Arthur as the 'best goalkeeper in the North'.[5] The 'Preston players [too] were very much taken with his play'.[6] The ambitious, forward thinking Preston chairman/manager Major Sudell, the key figure in forcing the FA to accept professionalism, wasted no time in persuading the young Black student to sign – as an amateur – for his equally ambitious team of working professionals.

The iron and coal trades – both large employers of labour – were in depression during the mid-1880s in the North East. Lay-offs and reductions in wages were common at such times, making worse what was an already meagre existence for these toilers in foundry, shipyard and mine and their families. The greater part of the abundance of wealth that was produced in the region tended to be concentrated in the hands of a few land and factory owners. 'To relieve the distress which exists' Arthur played for 'a team selected from the best clubs in Durham and Northumberland'[7] in a charity match against Bishop Auckland Church Institute, holders of the Durham Cup. It took place in April in the park of Durham Castle, in front of the Bishop of Durham. Participation in such events was a noticeable feature of Wharton's sports career. His readiness to lend his fists and feet went beyond that necessary to garner and sustain communal respect. His consistent involvement in charity events testifies to a genuine concern with the poverty around him.

By the close of the 1885–86 season Arthur had amassed a dressing-room full of superlatives for his outdoor triumphs, thrown at him by admiring scribes: he was 'magnificent', 'invincible', 'unapproachable', 'superb', 'wonderful'. His excellence at goalkeeping had followed in the wake of his successful athletics season of 1885 and by the spring of 1886 he was no longer a sportsman of regional renown, but a nationally known minor celebrity. The following football season, 1886–87, saw his desirability as a player surge.

Local hero: 1886–87

At the beginning of the season Arthur promised PNE he would play football for them only. At this time footballers, in particular amateurs, were able to play for more than one club but not in the same competition. He could have turned out for Darlington in local matches and for the 'Invincibles' in FA Cup games. His decision to sever his ties with the football (and athletic) branches of the Darlington club soured relations for a time between Wharton and his Feetham colleagues. In fact Arthur was too busy running for Birchfield Harriers to play much football in September, the tail-end month of the athletics calendar. His first game for Sudell came in the latter part of that month. But, by the turn of the year Wharton was once again also wearing the black and white of Darlington CFC. The resumption of Arthur's football career at Darlington was helped enormously by the wonderful reception he received at the club's annual dinner in December 1886. The genuine show of affection for their local hero – now the AAA 100 yards champion of England – paved the way for an amicable reunion.

A toast was given to his health and a song, 'Wharton of Darlington' composed by ex-trainer Manny Harbron, its first (and possibly only) airing. Sadly, the words have been lost. The tremendous warmth that in an instance destroyed the antagonism of the previous months dazzled the young man of 21.

> When he rose to respond to the improvised demonstration which had taken place, he was received with cheers of the heartiest, the loudest, most enthusiastic in character, which rose and rose again as the youth stood half-dazed before the reiterated volleys of the guests. It was the reception of an athlete by athletes, and I do not think any prize could be dearer to the hero than such unstinted recognition of his qualities by those best able to appreciate them.[8]

He returned to Feethams for Darlington's Cleveland Association Cup game against Redcar Crusaders on 8 January 1887. The bad weather reduced the status of the game to a friendly, which the home side won

4–2. The cup-tie was rearranged for the following month and again Wharton played. The match was a violent, ill-tempered confrontation. The Darlington captain, Smeddle, was accused of punching an opponent. Their protective instincts excited, Redcar supporters invaded the pitch and surrounded the ball-playing pugilist. Only the intervention of police saved Smeddle from a thrashing. On the call of time it was the turn of the Redcar players to be attacked by Darlington supporters! The 'Skernesiders' managed to battle through to the semi-final, but with just a 1–0 win this time. The Darlington-based *Northern Echo* reporter thought Redcar, members of the Cleveland Football Association based in Middlesbrough, a rough, tough side but nevertheless unlucky not to win. Only 'the clever play of Wharton in goal'[9] had stopped them. An inquiry into just the Smeddle incident was held ten days later at the Imperial Hotel, Middlesbrough. The Darlington man argued that the punch was an accident and his plea was upheld.

A week after the replayed Redcar tie the 'Skernesiders' played their semi-final against South Bank. In front of an estimated 1,500 at Feethams, Arthur's entry onto the pitch brought a great cheer. Eager not to disappoint his supporters he responded in kind with an 'excellent' performance in a 2–0 win.

As North End had no FA Cup matches in February Wharton was available for Darlington's Durham Cup third-round tie against local club Brankin Moor. The score was an historic 3–0 in the 'Skernesiders' favour. They had now progressed further in any challenge cup than ever before, and they went on to reach the final of both the Durham and Cleveland Cups. Arthur's goalkeeping record in these provincial cup-ties was, so far, as good as that for the national competition. In all official cup-ties to date, for Darlington and Preston, he had not conceded a goal. However, in this last game against Brankin Moor he had played as inside right in the first half and right wing in the second.

> Twenty minutes of the second half had been expended when Wharton caught up the ball in midfield. He dribbled forward, and the centre half in endeavour to save, fell. To pass him and Henderson was the work of a moment. Garbutt made a commendable run out; but Wharton was too much for him, and amid much enthusiasm the ball went within the post.

The same report details the speed of Darlington's attack; how most of the action was in Brankin's half of the pitch; Wharton's 'first class' tackling and second 'brilliant' goal. Unfortunately he 'shot wide on several occasions' after and was unable to get his hat-trick.[10]

In fact, this was his second game in three days as an outfield player. On the previous Wednesday Arthur had played for his college against a Fred Ibbotson XI. He had rehearsed for the Brankin game by scoring two goals in a 3–3 draw. In March he would again play outfield – for the second half only – against Stockton. A one-sided first-half yielded just four shots for Arthur to save. The half-time score was 2–0. On resumption he joined the forwards. The final score was 8–0. The goalie/attacker managed one disallowed 'goal'. He also played outfield for Preston during this period. This was his experimental phase: with boredom; cold – did he just want to keep warm?; and trying to get on the scoresheet.

Between the posts Arthur's excellent form continued. 'The feature of the [friendly against Durham College] was the defence of Wharton in goal. Shot after shot was put in, but each was cleverly stopped – indeed a better display of goalkeeping has rarely been witnessed.'[11] The score of 2–0 represented yet another game without a goal conceded. 'Offside', football correspondent of the *Northern Echo* and outspoken admirer of Arthur, made it clear he did not fancy Darlington CFC's chances against Darlington St Augustine's in the forthcoming final of the Cleveland Cup if Wharton was called by PNE to play in their FA Cup semi-final. He was.

Before the Cleveland Cup final, the 'Skernesiders' had to play Sunderland to decide the winners of the Durham Cup. Arthur missed this as well because of illness. There was rumour he was suffering from scarlet fever. Fortunately, it was not true. (Just what was the cause was never made clear. As we will see, Arthur's resistance to periodic bouts of illness – 'indisposition' – declines as his career develops. However, the ambiguity surrounding the reason remains constant. Drink?) After the hectic match for Preston, with matches in London, Nottingham and Darlington, his body may have been exhausted. The 'Wearsiders' were considered one of the few teams in the North East able to stand as equals with Darlington. The referee, 'Mr Bastard of Middlesbrough'[12] had officiated at the 1878 FA Cup final. The report does not mention whether he wore black. There were two sporting icons on the pitch that day. Sunderland won 1–0.

'Offside's' prediction that without Wharton in goal victory would be difficult proved correct. Darlington did well in three cup competitions – the FA, Cleveland and Durham Challenges – reaching the semi-final of the former and the final of the latter two. However, the 21-year-old student almost missed playing in both finals owing to administrative ineptitude and exhaustion. Disaster was only averted by Darlington drawing with St Augustine's in the semi-final of the Durham Cup and refusing to play extra-time. (The longer daylight hours of March would have enabled the players to continue had both sides agreed.) One could cast a shadowy conspiratorial light over events by suggesting that this was gamesmanship to forgo another half an hour's play. Why carry on now without Arthur when he might be fit again for the replay? If so, the ploy was an apposite reminder of his importance to the team. In cup games Arthur had built an excellent goalkeeping record. According to some observers he was the principal architect of Darlington's success. No doubt all Darlington's players and supporters cheered inwardly and outwardly when the refreshed West African strolled out for the second match at Middlesbrough on 2 April.

The railway company provided two special excursion trains from Darlington. The good weather seems to have swelled the attendance, and by kick-off at 3.30 it was estimated at over 6,000. (Gate receipts eventually totalled £98. The figure did not include women and members of the Middlesbrough club who were admitted free.) Darlington were at full-strength and up for it. Merely having the Cleveland College man in the team was 'a decided acquisition and one which perhaps more than anything else tended to decide the contest'.[13] Darlington were a goal in front after seven minutes but it was not long before the 'Saints' levelled the score in a game that went from goalmouth to goalmouth. A combination of 'miraculous' goalkeeping, a 'brilliant' individual goal and a serious injury to a Saints forward produced a flattering 4–1 win in Darlington's favour. After receiving their gold medals from the mayoress of Middlesbrough, Darlington captain Smeddle suggested both teams amalgamate for next year's competition, in order that the town of Darlington field a side capable of matching any in the competition. The two teams then dined together before returning home.

Of the winners, Miller, the full-back and Wharton were considered the outstanding players. Both easily 'coped with their charges … Wharton proved impassable'. This last point was not literally accurate. He had misjudged the shot that led to the Saints equaliser. Perhaps the reporter's mind was fresh with an incident in the final minutes when a Saints forward broke free of Darlington defenders and had only the goalkeeper to beat. 'Wharton proved impassable and saved a low shot in a miraculous manner.'[14] The main features of Arthur's play – his fisting out, which broke up attacks and started counter-attacking movements; his speed in coming out of goal; and his agility – were by now becoming routinely characteristic.

So ended a very successful football season for the national amateur sprint champion: he had played outstandingly for PNE, arguably the best team in Britain; won a gold medal with Darlington, making them the official champions of Cleveland; helped them to another final, and had been recommended for an England cap (which will be discussed more fully in Chapter 7). Unfortunately his representative career with Newcastle and District had come to an abrupt, controversial end in January after a confrontation with the organising secretary, Mr Phillips, of the Northumberland FA. (This will be discussed in Chapter 5.)

These football legislators … a delightful set': 1887–88

Arthur was linked to three clubs at the beginning of the season – Middlesbrough, PNE and Darlington. In September the *Northern Echo* reported that Wharton had apparently 'promised' A. Borrie, the Middlesbrough captain and goalkeeper, that he would play for them when not with PNE. This arrangement may have been 'agreed' to at the Scarborough Festival held that month. A number of players, including Wharton and several from Middlesborough, had been invited to play PNE under the title of a 'Northeast District XI'. To strengthen their team, the Teesside club had signed three other notable players by, among other inducements, arranging the 'best list of fixtures in the district'.[15] Clubs scheduled to visit included Glasgow Rangers, Bolton Wanderers, Blackburn Rovers and Hibernian of Edinburgh. The ambition of Borrie's club was not threatened by the alternative game of rugby football, either. This had no real presence in the area. Neither did Wharton – his 'promise' to them unfulfilled.

Arthur played for Preston North End on two consecutive Saturdays in early September. This had the effect of obscuring his relationship with Darlington who were again unsure as to where they figured in the plans of the sprinter-cum-goalie. It was not until 29 November that the *Athletic News* was able to report that Wharton had 'pretty well ceased his connection' with PNE. The same issue noted that his display against Northumberland Cup holders Shankhouse in Darlington's third round FA Cup-tie was his best of the season (so far). This inspired performance – there was little of the 'clowning' that irritated some and amused others – and the perspective of a settled future were maybe not unconnected. Perhaps the conclusion of the 'will he – won't he play for PNE?' saga allowed him to unclutter his mind and concentrate upon the precise application of his skills. Despite his heroics the Cleveland Cup holders lost 2–0, and with it their chance to retain their crown.

Wharton had been joined at Darlington by Withington, a left-winger from Walsall. The two were probably mates; certainly old acquaintances. Withington had been organiser of Cannock White Cross and Cannock Football Clubs: his decision to sign for Darlington may have come out of a visit to Cannock Arthur made in October to play in a Wakes (charity) match. There would have been no lucrative financial offer luring the Midlander North. Withington would have been reimbursed his expenses only as the North East club was still amateur. (It did not turn professional until 1908.) His friendship with Arthur seems to have been the determining influence upon his move.

Once again Darlington had entered for three cup competitions: the English FA Challenge Cup, the Durham County FA Challenge Cup, and the Cleveland FA Challenge Cup. However, they were disqualified from the semi-final of the last named because of a dispute between their local Durham County Football Association and Cleveland FA. At the heart of the dispute was Darlington secretary and founder member C.S. Craven. Darlington had been drawn away to Stockton in this semi-final of the Cleveland Challenge Cup. The 'Skernesiders' had arrived late, much to the annoyance of their hosts and the large crowd of over 3,000. Both were annoyed further by losing 4–2. The home side subsequently penned an official complaint to the Challenge Cup organising committee of the Cleveland Association. After an enquiry by the organisers on 20 February it was decided that the tie should be replayed on 25 February. This angered Craven who felt the original result should have been left to stand. It also produced fixture difficulties for his club as they had a Durham Cup quarter-final against Port Clarence scheduled for the same day. (Darlington had in fact tried to play the tie on 18 February but the sudden arrival of a snowstorm during the game led to the abandonment of the status of the fixture. The contest itself was continued as a friendly.) A few days after the Cleveland enquiry the Durham Cup committee met with Craven. The latter pointed out that the referee of the Port Clarence match had ordered that tie to be replayed on 25 February. In light of this, the Darlington secretary continued, the Durham Cup quarter-final, not the Cleveland Cup semi-final, should go ahead on that day. The Durham FA agreed. They sanctioned the club's refusal to agree with the demands of the Cleveland Association to replay Stockton on 25 February. Darlington played Port Clarence on that date, winning 5–0. To add to the farce and prolong the confusion, Port Clarence now appealed to the Cup committee of the Durham FA, complaining that the Darlington ground had been under five inches of snow and unfit for play. The Durham committee refused the appeal. Yet at the same time they had allowed an appeal by Darlington Athletic to replay their home match with Bishops Auckland Church Institute second team because of snow covering the pitch!

'Offside' thought the bias and hypocrisy shown by the Durham Cup committee 'characteristic'. They had put personal, regional and club rivalries before principle. The secretary of the Durham Association was a committee member of Darlington and his brother was captain of the first team. There was also a Darlington member, J. Glover, on the Cup committee. Consequently, argued 'Offside', the Darlington club had a corrupting influence on Durham FA affairs. The obstinate self-interest of this incestuous cabal seems to be confirmed by P. Huntingdon, the secretary of the Port Clarence club. He argued Craven had actually told him, before the meeting of the Cleveland Association on 20 February which Huntingdon attended, that the Darlington v. Port Clarence tie would be replayed on 3 March, and, in light of this, not to suggest any players for the Cleveland v. Northumberland representative match scheduled for the same day. Thus it was not until after the decision of the Cleveland Association that the Stockton v. Darlington tie should be replayed on 25 February had been made, that the Durham committee decided to confront them. Responding, the Cleveland Association awarded the semi-final to Stockton. They would now meet Middlesbrough – who were powerfully represented on the Cleveland Association – in the final. Craven kicked the spite ball back. He chided the Cleveland Association, arguing that the disqualification had more to do with Middlesbrough's reluctance to meet his team than any matter of principle or organisation. And who was better in recognising the lack of principle in decision making?

On such occasions of administrator in-fighting players could only act as bystanders as the drama unfolded. (A similar bungle had happened some months before between PNE and Renton, which will be discussed below.) For his part, Wharton may have felt controversy followed him like a virus sure of a victim. His athletics career was pitted with off-track confrontations – not all of them racial in nature. Unsurprisingly 'Offside' had little time for Craven. In his end of season round-up of Darlington CFC the *Northern Echo* football corespondent repeated his charge made earlier that the club were badly run by the autocratic secretary. Referring to the Darlington–Stockton affair, the inflated pride and personal jealousies of 'these football legislators ... [who were] a delightful set'[16] had once more harmed the footballers more than themselves. It was an experience Arthur would have to suffer many times.

Sunderland were the 'Skernesiders' opponents in the semi-final of the Durham Cup. (In the third round Arthur had played as a forward, scoring an undeclared number of goals in the 10–0 win over Springfield at Feethams.) The tie was to be played at the ground of Bishops Auckland Church Institute. Darlington took this game very seriously and actually did some preparatory training. Arthur had not been in best form recently, noted 'Offside', yet his mere presence was a 'tower of strength' to his team-mates. A crowd of around 5,000 produced receipts of £80. The 'Wearsiders' played sophisticated football, but they faced a goalkeeper who put in 'one of his best games ... The champion dodged and saved beautifully'.[17] Frustratingly, the outfield players could not build on this firm foundation, despite having controlled the latter stages because of their greater fitness. The final score was 1–1 and no extra time was played. The replay two weeks later was not such a close affair. The bigger, quicker thinking and faster moving Sunderland men won 2–1. Time was called also on Darlington's hope of finishing the season with any trophies.

There is little doubt that Wharton enjoyed his fame, performing in benefit and charity matches, though this social duty was a double-edged sword. The organisers and beneficiaries were aware that his inclusion would have popular appeal, adding considerably to the receipts. As a member of fellow Darlington sprinter T.H. Mountford's Select Team, Arthur played rugby to raise funds for a Christmas tree for the 'inmates' of Stockton hospital. Such was the frugality of the Victorian hospital budget, with its reliance upon charity and voluntarism.

There was a depressed economic climate for much of the 1880s.

This made 'stale, flat and unprofitable'[18] the main trades in the North East – iron, coal and steel. This harsh economic environment and the *laissez-faire*, minimalist begging-bowl approach of providing for the needy and poor of late-Victorian Britain put moral pressure upon personalities like Arthur – sensitive to the wider social responsibilities and demands of his status – to 'volunteer' their services to aid the cause of the sick and hungry. What may have incensed him – as a sporting visitor to the proletarian districts of Victorian society – was that the vast majority of charity organisers had failed to attend to the economic and social misery that afflicted these neighbourhoods. Indeed, these bourgeois philanthropists were usually the recipients of the abundant and luxurious resources that flowed from the very social class they were seeking to 'help'.

The definition of charity and what constituted a charitable cause was often stretched to its limits. Over the Christmas period of 1887 Wharton played seven matches in ten days. For most workers, especially workaday footballers, the last week in December was not a break from the toils of labour. Games arranged by team secretaries for Christmas and New Year tended to be done for the benefit of the local association and club finances, and to the detriment of the players' bodies. This time of year presented a commercial opportunity; a chance to rejuvenate the health of the balance sheet. Durham County played, without Arthur, against the Corinthians at Sunderland in front of 4,000 – though it is not known how much of the gate receipts the local association kept, if any! Club fixtures were equally prestigious, usually against first-class, often Scottish, opposition. Darlington's opponents included two from north of the border: Partick Thistle, who had reached the fifth round of the English FA Cup the previous season; and Dumbarton Athletic, who impressed the Feethams crowd of 2,000 with their short passing game winning 4–1 in stylish comfort.

Wharton also made one appearance for Sheffield Wednesday in the testimonial of their England international Billy Mosforth, the 'Little Wonder'. It was indicative of Arthur's reputation that he was invited by Mosforth, which was itself indicative of Mosforth's financial acumen! It was not a memorable debut for 'the dark-skinned gentleman' against his former colleagues PNE. A freezing Monday afternoon at 'the world-famed Bramall Lane Ground' on a snow covered pitch were not the most ideal conditions for a player of Arthur's exuberant style. It was none too pleasant for the spectators either.

> There was a glorious unanimity as to keep their hands out of sight, and it was most amusing to notice how, if a hand was drawn out of its pocket to rub a red nose or touch the pipe in the mouth, it was quickly returned to its previous warming place.

Though he made several fine saves to keep the half-time score at 1–1, a number of the seven goals scored after the tea-and-cigarette-break were blamed on the guest celebrity. He was booed at the close 'for his ineffective goalkeeping' and there were no further offers to play for Sheffield's premier club. Away from the crowd of 4,000 that had braved the hostile weather, 'including a lot of the devotees of St Monday',[19] Mosforth may have had a chuckle to himself. Though he and his colleagues had been on the wrong end of an 8–1 thrashing he took home £96 to stuff under the mattress. Arthur took home de-frosting limbs and a deflated ego to lay upon his.

Though Darlington CFC had a comparatively unsuccessful season, Arthur had played for PNE, in District and Durham County representative matches, captaining the latter on at least one occasion. He even fielded his own select XI, losing 5–2 to Cockerton A team. And during midweek, when his calendar allowed, he played for Darlington Wednesday. In fact, over the season, Arthur had worn the colours of seven different teams. One shirt which he did not wear, had never worn, was that of the North representative XI. Perhaps he was just not good enough – though his playing record shouts a different refrain. It was only in the North East that his skills were recognised at representative level. Interestingly, it was in this region also that the epithet 'Darkie', so willingly employed by hacks outside, was less frequently prefixed to Wharton.

Arthur did not play for the 'Skernesiders' again after this season. By April 1888 he had moved to Sheffield. (Coincidentally Darlington's penultimate game was against the Sheffield club – now the oldest association football team in the world. There was rumour also that he might soon be returning to West Africa.) He left the club in a very healthy financial state. The football team had played a total of 39 games, winning 20 and losing 14. The total income from football had been £487.8s.0d (£487.40p). After expenditure there was a net profit of £164.18s.6d (£164.93p) given to the cricket club. This may have rankled with Arthur in years to come. Of the clubs he played for in the 1890s, only Sheffield United were underpinned with a bank balance sound enough to pay all players throughout the season the wages promised at the start.

He moved to Sheffield to try his feet at professional running. This effectively severed his academic and domiciliary ties with the North East. The allure of the South Yorkshire city was due primarily to its status as the capital of pedestrianism (professional running). Tom Bott, a Sheffield sports entrepreneur, invested his money and time to facilitate the move. He was involved in other sports as well, including football and cricket. (Bott later became a director of Sheffield United FC in the 1890s.) Wharton was being trained to run by George Wallace of Sheffield in 1887. It is possible that Wallace and Bott were acquainted and that the former may even have recommended Arthur to the latter.

NOTES

1. Simon Turnbull, 'Wharton the Evens Favourite' *Northern Echo*, 14 July 1993.
2. Jenkins Papers. Herbert Burgin, private correspondence with Dr Ray Jenkins, 13 January 1988.
3. *Darlington and Stockton Times*, 17 April 1886.
4. *Newcastle Weekly Chronicle*, 24 April 1886.
5. *Darlington and Stockton Times*, 20 March 1886.
6. *Newcastle Weekly Chronicle*, 1 May 1886.
7. *Darlington and Stockton Times*, 10 April 1886.
8. Ibid., 25 December 1886.
9. 12 February 1887.
10. *Northern Echo*, 21 February 1887.
11. Ibid., 26 February 1887.
12. *Athletic News*, 29 March 1887.
13. *Northern Echo*, 4 April 1887.
14. Ibid., 4 April 1887.
15. Ibid., 3 & 10 September 1887.
16. *Northern Echo*, 3 March 1888.
17. Ibid., 10 and 12 March 1888.
18. Ibid., 25 October 1887.
19. *Sheffield and Rotherham Independent*, 28 February 1888.

2 *The burning Black star of amateur sprinting 1885–87*

Even by today's standards in sprint competition, Wharton's record time of 10 seconds dead in both the heat and final of the 100 yards (91.4 metres) at the AAA Championships at Stamford Bridge in July 1886 is remarkable. He managed to achieve 'even time' – the holy grail of sprinters – at a major meeting just one season after first participating in athletics events in the North of England. While Arthur had rivals for the title 'fastest runner of his generation' – most notably Harry Hutchens – his time at Stamford Bridge is now recognised as the first official achievement of 'evens' at a national championship anywhere in the world. It has been formally recognised as the first world record for the distance. Furthermore, he was the first runner from outside the London Athletic club to win the AAA sprint title. One prominent member of the AAA establishment, Montague Shearman (1887), lamented that the 1886 Championships marked the demise of the southern 'gentleman' athlete and the rise to pre-eminence of the working-class runner from the North. To deepen further Shearman's nostalgic melancholia, another northerner, F.T. Ritchie from Bradford, was third to Wharton.

Fine tuning the engine: 1884 and 1885

In an interview given to the *Athletic Journal*, 21 June 1887, Arthur says, 'The first sports that I ran in were at Darlington in May 1885'. He won the 120 yards and quarter mile handicaps at the Darlington Cricket and Football Club athletics meet. However, over the shorter distance, had it not been for the generous spirit of second placed runner Tom Mountford the young novice may not have recorded his first victory at his new club.

> Wharton's prowess as a sprinter was then virtually unknown, and he was given a few yards start [a 'handicap']. The brown shoes he wore, and which incidentally, he retained for many years later, blended so closely with the colour of his skin that spectators had the impression that he was running in bare feet. Wharton kept the lead all the way. It was a surprising performance, for the newcomer was competing against athletes who had gained conspicuous success in many a fast and thrilling race ... An innocence of the rules of the running track ... nearly transformed success into defeat. When he reached the tape – a comparatively easy winner – he ducked underneath instead of breaking it.[1]

He repeated these victories with a reduced handicap at the same meeting a week later, winning prizes to the value of £6.6s.0d (£6.30p) in the 120 yards and £5.5s.0d (£5.25p) in the 300 yards, equivalent in total to over three months' pay for the average industrial worker (though Arthur would not have been able to cash-in his prizes for their paper value). The lure of obtainable, lucrative prizes and sense of camaraderie as articulated through the action of Mountford, may have appealed to – and met in part the emotional needs of – the young student a long way from home. The athletics coach at Darlington, Manny Harbron, had other runners of note at the club including professional sprinter Bill Johnson. Training with other proven and respected athletes, with ready access to skilled and knowledgeable coaching, would have speeded the development and refinement of Wharton's unorthodox technique, most noticeably his upright stance, slow start and flat-footed running.

As the 1885 athletics season progressed so did Arthur's reputation. Having established himself as faster than most local runners he ventured further afield to compete with some nationally known stars such as James Cowie and American runner Lawrence Myers who won the 440 yards at the AAA Championship that year. At Stoke, Arthur beat the American in the 440 by 9 yards, having been given a start – handicap – of 24 yards. (Myers won the 880 yards title at the AAA Championship the following year.)

Handicap races have an integral relationship to betting. They came about in order to prevent races becoming foregone conclusions. Promoters of – usually professional 'pedestrian' – races felt that scratch races – everybody starting from the same mark – would be too easy to predict. Simply, they would run to form. This reduction in chance would have a depressing effect on betting odds. As betting was such a fundamental feature of pedestrianism, handicapping was used to ensure a degree of unpredictability by equalising each competitor's chance of winning. This made the outcome of races less predetermined by form, thus increasing betting odds and the attraction of betting. This in turn, it was hoped, would increase both numbers and punters attending meetings.

Handicapping became known as the 'Sheffield System' because of its common usage at professional events, the most prestigious of which were held in Sheffield. It worked on the principle of the handicapper giving each event a standard time. The starting position of each competitor would be determined by the relationship of their best times to the standard time. As a result contestants would start at different points along the track. The runner with the fastest recent times would have to run the greatest proportion of the advertised length of the race. Distances of the sprints at the unofficial Professional Championships at Sheffield could, therefore, vary from 165 to 215 yards. A runner with a handicap, say of 79 yards, meant that length being deducted from the formal distance. Thus in a 215 yard race such a handicap would involve the participant covering only 136 yards. Consequently this made the calculation and ratification of records difficult. This system carried on in club athletics until the 1940s. It was to put Wharton off running in some meets, if he felt his allotted handicap destroyed any reasonable chance of winning. Handicapping therefore created the conditions where various strategies would be employed by runners, trainers and backers to outwit both the handicapper and the bookies. One such activity was called 'roping', that is, running to lose.

Arthur's success and the confidence it brought soon encouraged the proud, eccentric features of his personality to surface: at a meeting in Middlesbrough in June he felt he had won his race 'fairly by three yards'.[2] Wharton's supporters thought he had won without question. The reporter of the *Darlington and Stockton Times* felt the race had been fixed. On being awarded the second prize of a salad bowl he smashed it in front of the organising committee and told them to make a new one out of the bits. To compound his anger and frustration he came third in the quarter mile. A week earlier at Sunderland Arthur had been indirectly involved in another controversy. The winner of the 120 yards handicap had been exposed as a professional. Arthur, who came second, was awarded first place after the fact became known. Despite winning a 15 guinea watch (£15.15s.0d/£15.75p) in one competition at a meeting at Crewe, he also claimed first and second prize in the throwing the cricket ball contest. After the other competitors had completed their throws and failed to beat Arthur's mark, he threw again. His second throw beat his first. After argument he eventually accepted just the first prize!

It takes a combination of confidence, courage and pride – as well as pig-headedness – to smash a prize in front of the givers. Apart from these characteristics it is a commonplace that, aside from ability, the other important ingredients of success are a determination to improve and the tenacity to ride through periods of loss of form. Wharton had these qualities in abundance particularly self-belief; an acute sense of his own worth.

'His colonial exhibition is very fine': 1886

At the beginning of the season, in May, the correspondent of the *Newcastle Weekly Chronicle* was predicting Arthur's entry for the quarter mile – 440 yards – at the seventh AAA Championship at Stamford Bridge on the first weekend in July. But after watching the 'Durham County goalkeeper' win the 120 and 220 yards handicap races in front of his home crowd at the Darlington Cricket and Football Club sports at the end of May, the reporter revised his forecast. On present showing he thought the young student would also have a good chance of bringing the sprint title to the North East. Another local journalist commented: 'He has neither system nor style, but he runs like an express engine with full steam on from first to last, with a result that makes both system and style unnecessary.'[3]

The defeat of James Cowie in the 100 yards scratch race at Widnes at the beginning of June confirmed to all that the new sprint prodigy was good enough to enter the National Championship. Cowie, a member of Oxford University Athletic Club and London Athletic Club, had won the 100 yards title in 1885. He had also set a world record of 22.2 seconds in the 220 yards. The Widnes meet was considered an important event on the calendar of the northern circuit. The 20 year old ran out winner by two yards 'in a very decided manner'[4] clocking 10 seconds. Cowie took his revenge in the 220 yards winning by a yard.

(Wharton also ran a third race, the 120 yards handicap, disputing his allotted second place.)

The significance of beating Cowie was twofold. It reaffirmed his status, newly acquired the previous season, as one of the best sprinters around; and delivered a warning to those preparing to compete in his division of the AAA Championship. Whether Manny Harbron, his trainer, chose an early run against Cowie to test his young protégé, or as part of his ascent to peak form, or for gate purposes – unlikely given the meet was not at Feethams – we will never know. Whatever the reason, it is unlikely to have been an unscheduled coincidence. What we can be sure of is that it set the scene for London by establishing Arthur as 'a contender' (to quote Marlon Brando). As a northern club runner southern audiences and the metropolitan-based athletics establishment were keen to eye his runs. His participation at Stamford Bridge was eagerly awaited. Montague Shearman, founder member of the AAA executive and president between 1916–30, noted the anticipation of the cognoscenti when he recalled the event a year later. 'The public ... [were] looking forward to seeing Wharton, of Darlington, who is a coloured *gentleman* (my emphasis).'[5]

His last competition before the Championship provided confidence-sustaining wins in the 120 and 220 yards handicaps at the Sunderland Sports, back 'home' in the North East. However, this fresh injection of assurance may have been a little diluted by his failure to be placed in two other races, the 100 yards and quarter mile; though given the nature of Victorian athletics we can never be sure that Arthur – or any athlete – was always running to win. There was now just two weeks of preparation and training in readiness for the high point of the amateur season.

A brown skinned 'gentleman' represented an embodiment of ethnicity and class rare in athletics in Britain. Brown skinned runners were not unique. A star of the 1860s was First American, Deerfoot Hagasadoni, also known as Louis Bennett. The man credited by some to have popularised the crouching start for sprinters was Scotland-based Maori runner, Bobby MacDonald, who introduced the style in 1884. Billy Isaac was a Sheffield-based Black runner and trainer against whom Wharton would have competed later in his professional career in the Handicaps in that city. None, however, were considered 'gentlemen'.

Cowie, despite his proven excellence, was not the main opponent in the 100 yards that Saturday – he was injured – but Frank Ritchie, another all-year-round sportsman. Charles Wood, a renowned 220 yards and quarter-miler was also fancied. Ritchie played rugby football as a three-quarter back for the Bradford and Yorkshire County team. For a time the careers of the West African and the West Yorkshireman ran parallel. They became bitter rivals, to the extent where it seemed the opportunity to ridicule and demean the other became more important than the running.

Competing under the banner of Darlington Cricket Club, Wharton won his heat by six yards and increasing on the next placed runner, Basset. Half an hour later, in front of two thousand people, he lined up for the final. A contemporary report helps us capture what was seen as an exotic and fantastic occasion on account of Arthur's participation. While self-consciously respecting Wharton's 'otherness' it at the same time illustrates the growing habit of assuming different physiological attributes in people of colour.

> Wharton is a gentleman from very sunny climes, and by no means a representative Englishman in appearance. If not a champion to look at, he is an extremely good one to go, and his colonial exhibition is very fine … he has a long, low stride, he does not seem to get on his toes in the style to which we are accustomed. I make some allowance for optical illusion, because on Saturday he wore untanned or unblacked [shoes] … of a brown some shades lighter than his complexion. These arrangements in colour caused the observer who was not very sharp to believe that the man was running barefoot, whereas he had merely fitted himself with nearly flesh-coloured pumps … His style of running is associated with men of colour, who as a rule have a good deal of heel. Wharton is a brunette of pronounced complexion …[6]

He won by a yard from Wood who was half a yard in front of Ritchie. By reaching the tape first the young West African secured the Prince Hassan Cup worth £50, first presented in 1871. Wharton's time of 10 seconds made him the talking point of the day. That it had been achieved in both heat and final – on the same afternoon – added further stature to this speed phenomenon compared, as we have seen, to the fastest machine on earth. At once Arthur became exotic and excellent. (But not infallible. Charles Wood took his revenge in the 440 yards final where the first two placings in the 100 yards was reversed.)

This was not the first occasion in athletics that 10 seconds for 100 yards had been recorded. That honour had gone to C.A. Absalom in 1868; but it was the first occasion even time had been recorded at a national championship in Britain. The previous best was 10.2 seconds achieved by a number of runners, including Cowie, the previous year. A sub-committee of the AAA later ratified a series of times for events, including Wharton's 100 yards, which became generally accepted as a world record list.

Some observers questioned whether 10 seconds had been equalled. But unfairly, and often with ulterior motives, according to 'Pendragon' in the *Darlington and Stockton Times*. Defending the 'coloured Colonial amateur' he argued that the runner had actually clocked the fastest time ever.

> Wharton may be able to do all that has been put to his credit … I have seen him run the hundred in a shade under 10 sec., but that feat was accomplished under most favourable conditions. Since then official clockers have from time to time startled the athletic, that is to say, the non-professing (*amateur* – my insertion) foot-racing world, with wonderful figures for the dusky flyer. [Professional runners] … laughed at the records … Of my own knowledge I can speak of one only, and that is the Hundred Yards Championship spin, in which I am satisfied that even time was honestly done.[7]

The irony – hidden agenda? – of this debate emerges when examined alongside Arthur's reputation as slow off his mark. T. Wilkinson, official starter at the Sheffield Handicaps, believed Arthur the worst of all amateurs in this respect. Indeed, bad starts were often a feature of the reports of his racing. Arthur acknowledged this weakness in his 1887 *Athletic Journal* interview. 'I was an awful bad starter; indeed I am not a good hand at it yet, and often in my early races I was left at the post.' Indeed, the 1887 season was noticeably bad in this respect. However, this initial slowness was obviously not an insurmountable problem. Arthur did not get fully into his stride until the closing half: he was an extremely fast finisher. 'I start with a seven foot stride, but I soon make it eight feet, and in the last few yards I try and put in strides of nine feet' he counters in the same interview.

Discussion of Wharton's record should acknowledge the general nature of clocking in athletics during this period. Victorian competitions were beset by scandal and accusations of scandalous practice even more so than today. At present the taking of performance enhancing drugs is one of the issues at the top of the agenda of problems-to-be-dealt-with. During the last quarter of the nineteenth century the veracity of recorded times was a major issue, especially with professionals eager to guard their livelihood from audacious newcomers and former amateurs with spectacular personal bests attributed to them. The outstanding Scottish sprinter of the 1890s, Jamaican-born Alf Downer, discussed the issue of starts in his autobiography *Running Recollections and How to Train* (1908) – the front cover describes him as 'The Champion … of the World'. It was common, he argued, for competitors to go before the gun. 'No one who is "on the job", ever dreams of waiting for the report of the pistol, or whatever the signal may be, but is generally running some five yards (and this is no exaggeration) when the signal is given.'[8] A frequent accusation thrown at Ritchie was that he got 'fliers'. This was one of the causes of ill-feeling between Arthur and the Bradford man. 'Ritchie is a grand starter but he gets flying starts on more occasions than even starts. I don't think he can get up his speed as he says, after going two yards. I have to be on my journey 10 yards before I feel I am going.'[9] Charles Wood also thought Ritchie twitched and bolted early in anticipation of the gun's crack. At a meeting at Wordsley Cricket Club sports, Stourbridge, in which Wharton, Ritchie and he were competing – just over two weeks after Stamford Bridge – Wood pulled up after a yard adamant that the Yorkshireman had cheated. Angered and irritated Ritchie was forthright in his denial: he got good, fair starts.

The AAA drew up rules for its inaugural Championship in 1880. Number 2 stated: 'Any competitor starting before the signal to be put back at the discretion of the starter.'[10] A second false start and the runner could be disqualified. The objective of these Championships was to attract the best athletes, thus increasing the possibility of breaking records, elevating the status of the Championship and its organisers and making the sport more popular. The Championships were the showcase for the sport. To be seen to be shoddy about starting and timekeeping would be self-defeating for the authority of the AAA and would undermine the legitimacy of the records and status of athletics generally. When all was said and done, however, money taken at the gate was of primary importance. It gave everyone – athletes, officials and administrators – a role. Without it there would not have been the sport in its existing form. Club athletics did not operate within the same framework of considerations and it would be dangerous to make the same assumptions in respect of local events.

After Stamford Bridge, Wharton was immediately challenged by Cowie. As he had already beaten Cowie that season he did not feel the need to prove his worthiness as champion by doing the same again. He devoted his time instead to Birchfield Harriers Athletics Club, based at Aston Lower Grounds, Birmingham. Their acting secretary was W.W. Alexander, an official of the Cyclists Union and noted timekeeper. The track was famous and notorious in almost equal measure for the number of record-breaking runs timed there.

The earlier discussion of Arthur's football career at Darlington noted his decision to leave the club in the summer of 1886 – the time of his greatest success to date – created hostile feeling between himself and his former colleagues. This decision was influenced by the priorities of his running career. He embodied a valuable, viable and scarce commodity – the status of AAA 100 yards champion: he was prime box-office attraction and his participation at meetings was publicised well in advance. It is possible that he thought it a good time to maximise this earning potential through appearance money, betting and prizes, even though he was officially an amateur. The prestige, status, connections and location of Birchfield Harriers in the more central and less geographically isolated Midlands would have improved his chances of earning. A prominent official of the club was Dr Gray. Arthur and he were friends. Dr Gray may have persuaded Arthur to join his outfit; and not merely because they were happy in each other's company.

It is no coincidence, then, that a fortnight after Wharton had beaten Ritchie in London, they met at the Lower Aston track. On top form the latter took his revenge by winning the 25 guinea (£26.25p) Challenge Cup. On the following Monday Ritchie again beat the champion at the Wordsley Cricket Club sports at Stourbridge, but in controversial circumstances already outlined above. Nonetheless, from Arthur's point of view beating Ritchie at the AAA Championships surely outweighed these subsequent defeats in less important races. It meant also that he had peaked at the right time. 'Olympian' of the *Sporting Life*, 24 July, put a different gloss on the event. He felt Wharton had not tried, possibly for a bribe. This public innuendo led to a literary joust between 'Olympian' and the Midlands correspondent of the *Sporting Chronicle*, 28 July. The latter felt Arthur had integrity but simply was not as good as Ritchie. But he did put in a mitigating plea, complaining that the starter's mistake with his pistol at the Wordsley meeting allowed Ritchie a four-yard flier.

At the Cowen Challenge Cup meeting at Gateshead, 7 August, Arthur was thought to have broken his record and ran under evens. However, the mass of spectators crowding the finish prevented an accurate timing. The champion had returned to form. At Aston on 4 September, he is said to have broken the record for 150 yards at least twice if not three times (depending on which newspaper report is used as source). However, 'Pendragon' of the *Darlington and Stockton Times*, 18 September, was unimpressed. He felt that the club, in particular one of its officials, put economic considerations before principle.

> The 14 and two fifths [seconds] advanced on the authority of W.W. Alexander [of] Birchfield Harriers, who are running a series of gate money speculations called sports, held and to be held in the Midlands … [as promoter and] the person most interested in procuring sensational performances [he] is the very last to set up as time-taker. Wharton's beating record meant a big advertisement for the next gate-money show at Coventry.

This was not a grave charge nor surprising given what we know of athletics at this time; although it was bluntly revealing of the commercial values at its core. (A modern analogy would be the accusation levelled at the 1996 Atlanta Olympics organisers that they laid a hard track specifically for the benefit of sprinters, an event at which the USA has traditionally been very strong. Distance runners, among whom are few North Americans, would have preferred a more shock-absorbent surface.)

During the week 11–18 September, Arthur ran around the Midlands with Birchfield Harriers in their 'gate money speculations' referred to by 'Pendragon'. The tour had been organised to 'assist in liquidating debts owing by the Midland Counties Cross Country Championship Association and the Birchfield Harriers'.[11] It was a hectic, startling end to the season. He attended six meetings, won eight races and competed in many more. At the first fixture, at Aston Lower Grounds, he clocked 14.4 seconds in the 150 yards scratch; at Burton-on-Trent Cricket Ground he ran 120 yards in 12 seconds. He also won the 220 yards handicap in 23⅖ seconds. These times were remarkably fast. The first two representing 'evens' or under. Arthur's 'express' really did have the 'steam' full on.

Wharton, Ritchie and the 'Big Boom': 1887

Wharton took the Prince Hassan Cup back to his rooms at Cleveland College – under whose vest he competed – when he won the AAA sprint title for the second year in succession at Stourbridge Cricket Ground on 2 July. His winning time was 10.2 or a yard outside evens. Although slower than the previous year it was nevertheless thought good because the track was new and the weather hot. Untypically the Darlington student got a good start. Charles Wood narrowed the gap in the closing stages but was frustrated into second place yet again. Pre-race speculation had favoured Wood whose form suggested he would have the edge over the champion. But Arthur had peaked on time once more and broke the tape three-quarters of a yard in front.

He had run at two meetings only before Stourbridge. The first of these was on home turf at Darlington, 4 June, where he won the Members 120 yards Handicap from a scratch mark, making up over six and a half yards on the second placed runner, J.H. Browick. Starting from scratch again in the Open Handicap he could not make up the eleven and a half yards start given to T.D. Davidson and came second. A week later – three weeks before Stourbridge – Arthur competed at the prestigious Widnes meeting. He won the 100 yards scratch, beating Salford runner Billy Rayner by two yards, although the Lancastrian was past his best times. Wharton had another success in the 440 yards scratch with a moderate time of 55 seconds. He came second to Fred Staveacre in a heat of the 120 yards Handicap and did not make the final. It had proven to be a day of mixed fortunes. After arriving late and missing his scheduled heat of the 120 yards Handicap, he had to change quickly and run against Staveacre within ten minutes of entering the arena. For his pains he left Widnes with a thigh strain. However, with just three weeks' sprint training his accumulation of 15 guineas in prizes at Widnes meant the day had more ups than downs.

Although he had intended to, Ritchie had not run at the Championship. He pulled out after being bitten by a rat, going out of his way to make this plain to all who cared to listen. His *bête noire*, Arthur, was not convinced by the explanation. When the two finally met on the track at the Northern Counties Athletic Association Championship in Manchester Arthur could not help provoking his adversary.

Ritchie: 'Don't you see it?'

Wharton: 'No, I don't.'

Ritchie: 'It's a bad light. It was a case of blood poisoning but I'm all right now.'[12]

Dr Gray accompanied Arthur to the line. The only other runner was Billy Rayner. Ritchie's ire was no doubt fired by Arthur's teasing. The Bradford three-quarter back got his typical good start. He had short – in contrast to Wharton's long – strides, and according to Lawrence Myers, scrambled along the track. The different styles added further interest to the duel. Consequentially Ritchie's strengths were in the first part of the race, Arthur's in the latter. In fact it was Rayner who took an early lead. But for a few seconds only. Ritchie was the first to pass him, followed immediately by his rival. At 50 yards the new leader had a couple of yards in hand but Arthur was now increasing his stride to nine feet and gaining. At the line it looked a dead heat. The judges had a parley and gave the race to the rugby footballer by six inches, an extravagant margin in the circumstances. The same reporter who recounted the rat dialogue above thought the Manchester sprint 'one of the grandest 100 yards races ever witnessed'. Wharton disputed the result. He felt he had caught his competitor at the line. The *Athletic News* man agreed that it was extremely close. 'No one but those stationed at the tape could tell which had won.'

Frank T. Ritchie was now the Northern Sprint Champion, the Cock o' the North. A title to rival any other, thought many of those runners, officials and spectators on the northern circuit. It meant a lot to him. Oddly – given his solid middle-class background as a grammar school boy and son of a doctor – Ritchie felt the southern-based AAA did not play fair; that his northernness counted against him. 'I never got credited with a record, for, as soon as I ever did a record it was said that there was a slope, wind or else I got a flying start. It is a pity I was not a cockney as then I would have a record before this.'[13]

Unsurprisingly, promoters of athletic events saw the rivalry between the West African and the West Yorkshireman as great box-office. The few meetings they did have were billed the 'Big Boom'. Their undisguised antagonism, while it conspired to keep them apart, added a crowd-attracting combustible element to the contests which did take place. Their pre-match encounter and the controversial finish to the race at Manchester was every promoter's dream. Two weeks later a crowd of 15,000 turned out at Bradford to see them compete for the Hawcridge Challenge Cup, worth 40 guineas. The cup had been donated by Joe Hawcridge (and his brother), a playing colleague of Ritchie at Bradford Rugby Club. Though a native of nearby Otley the latter was treated as one of their own by Bradfordians. The vast majority of the 'enormous' gathering at the Bradford Cricket and Athletic Club Sports at Park Avenue on 23 July, were locals anticipating Wharton-the-AAA-Sprint-Double-Champion falling again to their hero in a *live* replay of Manchester. And this is what he would have done – literally – had he competed.

Those that had paid their entrance in the hope of witnessing something extra had their expectations met. But not in the way they had envisaged. Wharton did not make the gun. At the start of the race he was nowhere to be seen. Making up the numbers was J.T. Priestly of Bradford. His running shoes were a customised pair of boots with the heels removed. His spikes were nails dotted around the sole. He was described as a 'crank'.[14] The entry of poor and unworthy runners into big events was not unknown in either amateur or professional meets. Such practice gave ammunition to those who argued that the sport was rife with corruption. Ritchie probably could have run backwards against the third man and still won easily. However, the boot-boy's entry may not have been solely for comic value. Harry Berry, who has studied Arthur's 1887 career in great detail in *1887 A Sprinting Year* (Private n.d.) suggests Wharton's camp may have felt he was there to disable the foreigner and provide an easy passage for the homeboy. The champion, though, was too cute to fall for it.

Immediately after the event the absentee appeared with his trainer, George Wallace of Sheffield (an outstanding professional of the 1870s, he was described by scribes of his era as a 'model of physical beauty').[15] Arthur played dumb: he had been lying in his bed at the George Hotel – someone had told him the race would be run at 5 o'clock – and had just arrived at the stadium. To 'prove' his innocence he offered to run against Ritchie who refused, but he did run in the 220 yards handicap where he came second to H. Merriken of Hull who had a 12 yard start; and in the quarter-mile flat handicap, giving away 21 yards start to the eventual winner.

Wharton had little or no supporting evidence with which to back his feigned innocence. There was more to damn than clear him. He did not deny having a programme and meeting his main opponent during the morning of the race. Enquiries at the George Hotel found that the Darlington runner had left before noon and had not returned. Soon afterwards a Huddersfield member of the NCAA executive requested an investigation into the affair. On 22 September, at the Crown Hotel, Manchester, 'the dark gentleman'[16] was asked to explain himself before a committee of the NCAA. Again Arthur did not appear. The inquisitors closed the affair by warning him – presumably by letter – as to his future conduct. It was a slap on the wrist and suggests they too smelled a rat – which at Bradford did not have Ritchie in mind as its victim. The whole affair was reported widely in the athletic sports press.

It seems probable that Wharton decided not to run after the situation with Priestly became clear. There was a rumour that Arthur had actually been in the ground during the race. Once Ritchie and Priestly had 'run' the way would have been open for Arthur to challenge Ritchie without Priestly. If Priestly was entered to nobble Arthur on Ritchie's behalf, as Berry argues, the Darlington runner was more sinned against than sinner. This is a plausible interpretation. The Bradford man would not want to lose in front of his home crowd. Furthermore, if he won the following year he could keep the cup. Wharton, in contrast, could only have expected a partisan, hostile response from the assembled masses of West Yorkshire. Also, another defeat by Ritchie that season may have seriously damaged Arthur's legitimacy as the number one 'amateur' sprinter in England. (Yet, paradoxically, it would have lengthened the betting odds on Arthur for his next race, improving his earning potential and that of his punters and backers.) There is no doubt Arthur was willing to race. He had travelled to Bradford and made himself known after the event, offering to compete. Underlying the enmity was suspicion and distrust of the other's actions – the Park Avenue fiasco was the most public dramatisation of the bitter feud.

It was Arthur's first major controversy with the executive administrators of athletics. In mitigation, he could argue he was not the instigator. He would have been justified in turning defence into attack by asking how and why Priestly's entry was allowed. Also as an amateur Wharton was free to choose when and where he would run; and alternatively, when and where he would not. Finally and perhaps significantly it was not a Bradford member of the NCAA that had asked for the enquiry.

As to the conduct of the sell-out crowd, we can only suppose that as the main event did not happen many would have been disappointed and angry. The end of programme races in which Wharton did compete would have been little consolation to the punters in the audience. But his cause in the drama was not without sympathy. Some in the crowd did in fact cheer Wharton when he appeared to face Merriken. The promoter(s) may have felt they got away lightly. A similar non-happening of a scheduled race between Harry Gent and Harry Hutchens at Lillie Bridge in London in September of that year, led to a riot and the destruction of the ground by fire.

Despite and because of the Bradford debacle promoters were keen to match the pair again. A contest had looked possible at the Preston North End sports held three weeks later. Inserted into the programme, specifically for the two, was a 100 yards scratch (leval start) race. This time Wharton, as a footballer with the club, would be on home ground. Two top officials of the northern circuit had been engaged (in order to neutralise any accusations of bias from the Ritchie camp?): Walter Platt as handicapper, timekeeper and referee; Tom Wilkinson as starter. However, William Sudell, the PNE manager, was judge. This time it was Ritchie's turn to play the bad guy. Athletic commentators, aware that both men had complained in the past of the lack of decent scratch races, felt both were missing opportunities to compete that may not come round again.

> The two track sprinters Wharton and Ritchie are playing a foolish game in keeping out of each other's way. There is not the slightest doubt but that the committees put up a scratch race with the hope of these two cracks competing. They don't realise it will be all the worse next year. Scratch races will be cut out of the programmes as they are thus complete farces.[17]

In the scratch, Arthur defeated Billy Rayner for the third time that season.

The early August editions of the *Athletic News* carried a few lines raising and quashing the rumour of Wharton's impending professionalism. There was talk of Arthur being entered for the Sheffield Handicap. Harry Gent, a professional – also of Darlington – had issued another of his public challenges to the young student; and he would

give him two yards start over 120. An initial, unspecified challenge from Gent was reported to have been declared as long ago as 1885. A while had he been after Arthur's scalp. The *Athletic News* did not think the champion would be wise to run openly for money. It followed with the announcement that Wharton had 'not the slightest intention of joining the professional ranks. He is a student of divinity at a college in Darlington … he is designed for the high collar and broad cloth of the cleric'.[18] By the end of the month, in an interview with the *Cannock Advertiser*, 27 August, the runner said he was bound for Africa.

During that busy, rumour-filled August – the last full month of running before the football season opened at the beginning of September – he competed at several meetings including those of the North Durham Cricket Club Sports at Gateshead; the Preston Amateur Athletic Association Sports at Deepdale (mentioned above); the Birchfield Harriers Sports at the Aston Lower Grounds, Birmingham; and the Lichfield Cricket Club Sports where he clocked an unofficial 9.9 seconds in the 100 yards.

The biggest event of that month though was the Cowley Challenge Cup at Cheltenham drawing a crowd of 6,000 attracted by the quality of the field which offered, among other contests, the 'Big Boom'. But, by now absenteeism was becoming a habit. Eleven days after he failed to show at Preston, Ritchie again provided gossip for the onlookers and copy for the journalists. This was the third big event of the season at which one or the other had not appeared. The stage was left for Wharton to provide a cameo performance. He won his first, exciting heat 'narrowly' by six inches. This stuttering start dampened down the emotion of the crowd and their expectation of a spectacular finale. But Arthur, ever the showman, crafted a 'boom' of his own. He set 'an undoubted record for 120 yards on a grass track … In the final he … ran completely away from his opponents. [His time of 12 seconds] equal to if not better than his record … at Stamford Bridge in 1886'.[19] The time keeper was Mr W.W. Alexander and 'may, therefore, be taken as thoroughly accurate'.(!)[20] Eleven runners had entered for the race in advance. Four started. Three finished. 'Swire, seeing the hopelessness of the contest, pulled up.'[21] Wharton's even time startled those with an interest in athletic affairs. Yet again the 'dusky Colonial' had achieved a speed few other sprinters had could even aspire to.

The 1887 athletics season ended with Wharton's reputation for excellence consolidated by renewing his AAA title; enhanced by his performance at Cheltenham; but sprinkled with fallibility by the defeat from Ritchie. His non-performance at Bradford and the subsequent inquiry confirmed both his strength of character and the suitability of the *enfant terrible* tag attached to it. Arthur finished his amateur career (the 1887 season was his last) as *the* master craftsman – Ritchie not withstanding. Few interested in sport would not have heard of him. Those who read the athletic (and football) columns of the national sports papers could not have failed to notice the amount of column inches detailing his exploits. The newspaper speculation during the preceding months of his transition to pedestrianism in April 1888 merely confirmed his public allure. Frustratingly for Arthur, as his reputation grew, so did preoccupation with his colour and ethnicity.

NOTES

1. *Darlington and Stockton Times*, 23 December 1939.
2. *Athletic Journal*, 21 June 1887.
3. *Darlington and Stockton Times*, 5 June 1886.
4. *Newcastle Weekly Chronicle*, 12 June 1886.
5. Montague Shearman, *Athletics and Football* (London 1887) pp. 59–60.
6. *Darlington and Stockton Times*, 17 July 1886.
7. 18 September 1886, p. 2.
8. 'Running Recollections', in Melvyn Watman, *History of British Athletics* (London 1968) p. 20. Downer set an equal world record time of 9.8 in the summer of 1895.
9. *Athletic Journal*, 21 June 1887 (also in Harry Berry, *1887 A Sprinting Year* (private publication n.d) p. 20).
10. Peter Lovesey, *The Official Centenary of the AAA* (London 1979) p. 33.
11. *Cannock Advertiser*, 18 September 1886.
12. *Athletic News*, 12 July 1887.
13. Berry, op. cit., p. 21.
14. Ibid., 26 July 1887.
15. C.R. Bauchope, 'Old Powderhall', in D.A. Jamieson, *Powderhall and Pedestrianism* (Edinburgh 1943) p. 24.
16. Berry, op. cit., p. 27.
17. Ibid., p. 30.
18. 16 August 1887.
19. *Cannock Advertiser*, 27 August 1887.
20. *Cheltenham Press*, 29 August 1887, p. 5.
21. *Cannock Advertiser*, 27 August 1887.

3 *The long and short of Yorkshire and pedestrianism 1888–89*

'Spank', Bott, Billy South and the making of an 'Electric racehorse': 1888

It has been argued by Ray Jenkins (1990) that Wharton was born and grew up in the wrong place at the wrong time for a career in sport. Unfortunately he did not have the benefit of knowing that from 1875 to 1879 Arthur was at school in London. This formative period, between the ages of 10 and 14, was surely important in the development of his athletic, football, cricket and cycling skills. Indeed, his return to Britain in the early 1880s could not have come at a more fortuitous time. If an individual had the necessary physical, mental and social requirements to earn a living from sport, then the North of England was the place to be.

Arthur's decision to move to South Yorkshire in April 1888 marked a brief excursion into professional sprinting and led, eventually, to marriage and a long but interrupted period in South Yorkshire. His failure to post an entry to defend his title at the ninth AAA Championship – to be run in early July at Crewe – signalled his intention to go professional. A list of contestants was printed in the *Athletic Journal* of 26 June. Asking the question 'Who Will Win' (*sic*) it noticed 'in the 100 yards we do not find the name of Mr Wharton, but he may run and win, as he is in his best form at present'. Oddly, in the adjacent column, there was a rare interview with Arthur with no mention of his immediate intentions concerning professionalism or a vocation outside sport. Yet such matters of detail about the athlete's life were being frequently discussed in the pages of the sport and regional press.

Wharton's non-appearance on the list caused some to construct explanations that complicated reality. The *Athletic News* thought Arthur may have disqualified himself by having a benefit match at

Darlington the previous football season, 1887–88. Although no evidence was provided – of when and against whom – the line was that by receiving money in this way he would endanger his amateur status, both as footballer and runner. It was, in effect, a veiled but flawed accusation of shamateurism. According to the rules of the AAA professional footballers could still compete as amateur athletes, unlike professional cricketers who had been banned from AAA competition since 1883. This anomaly regarding footballers was not changed until 1899. Additionally, as an amateur at Darlington Arthur was not formally allowed testimonial matches. (I am not arguing that Arthur received no money over and above his expenses for his services while at Feethams. Just that if he did, it would not have been advertised.) It was not Arthur's shamateurism that led him to the city of steel, but his need and desire to earn a living from and win respect for his talent.

Arthur did run in July but at the Sheffield Handicap, his first professional race. The Sheffield – 'Great All-England' – Handicaps were the major professional events of the season. Promoted by Mr James Bingham they were held five times a year at the Queen's Ground. Wharton's backer – the provider of money for training and living expenses in return for a share of the winnings from bets and prize money – was Mr Tom Bott a well-known Sheffield sports entrepreneur. His trainer was 'Spank' Smith with Billy South, a noted Sheffield pedestrian, employed as the novice's running mate.

The entourage encamped to Nottinghamshire throughout June to prepare thoroughly their protégé for the premier division of sprinting. Arthur had been entered for the earlier 'Whitsuntide Handicap' over 21–22 May and given a handicap of 84½ yards. But as the race approached his minders felt he was unready and he did not toe the line. His development had not been as rapid as had been hoped. While training – their usual base was at Wickersley, outside Sheffield – Billy South, a previous Sheffield winner, gave Arthur 2 yards and beat him. Undeterred, backer Bott, 'Spank' Smith and South himself all felt their man had the potential to win a Handicap, but needed more intense work. Organising a punishing regime 'Spank', Bott and South no doubt reiterated to their young but by now experienced runner that there could be no pleasure in achieving the ecstasy of a Handicap win without the pain of hard exertion. South claimed credit for improving Arthur's running time to 3½ yards inside evens. (Even time equalling 1 yard to 1 second.)

Runners for the July Handicap were publicised in the *Sheffield Daily Telegraph* early that month. To be contested over two days in the middle of the month Wharton was in heat 11 with a handicap of 81¼ yards over 200 yards, 3¼ yards shorter than the May allotment. There were 14 heats with four runners in each; 56 entries in total. The first prize was £80. Among those who had entered were Billy South and another Sheffield personality, H. Simmonite. The last named was trained by Black runner Billy Isaac, also a resident of this sport-mad city. On the eve of the race Arthur, with five 'fifties' (£250) and four 'ponies' (£100) laid on his name (with Bott presumably the largest investor), was equal favourite with H. Thorpe. The odds were 11–2 against. These were very substantial bets. £50 represented just £7 less than the average yearly wage of manual workers in 1886.

In his heat Arthur 'appeared to get badly off, and did not get into his stride until he had run 50 yards, but he finished at a terrific rate, the watch denoting a yard inside 12 seconds'.[1] He won by 2 yards. His second heat two days later matched him against C. Cutting of Brampton – also fancied as a contender – who had a handicap of 82 yards. Forced to give three-quarters of a yard start, the Gold Coaster started slowly. This time he could not produce the blistering finish of his previous heat and Cutting won by a foot. The latter also won the final by 2 yards, quite literally having the edge over the African. (With his name was the Brampton man destined to win in a city famous for its production of knife blades?)

This race provides a case study of both the nature and use of handicapping: Cutting's defeat of Wharton by a foot meant, in effect, that Arthur had made ground on his competitor because Cutting started the race 2 feet 3 inches ahead. By not having level starts punters could never be certain that in-form runners would win, even when they were trying. So much would depend on the level of handicapping. With a severe burden even the runner's own party might decline to back their man. Seen in this context, Wharton's 'defeat' was not so deflating. The next meeting at the Queen's Ground was on 10 September, an athletic curtain raiser to the nearby Doncaster St Leger horse race festival. The Wharton training camp now prepared their man just outside Grimsby, at New Clee Grounds.

In the pedestrian calendar the 'Doncaster' Handicap was seen as the blue-ribbon meeting of the professional circuit. The full distance of the sprint was 201 yards for a first prize of £80. Eighty contestants had returned entry forms, but only 55 accepted the handicap they had been given. Among these were George Wallace, Arthur's trainer at the Bradford fiasco, and G. Grant from Edinburgh, a rival jealous of the West African's success as an amateur. Given a handicap of 77¾ yards, even tougher than his burden in July, to win Arthur had to run 123¼ yards.. The race had caught the imagination of many and by the time of the first heat at 3.30 p.m. 4,000 spectators were inside the ground. The weather was 'of the most approved character' except for 'a nasty cross wind'. The track was 'as level as a billiard table'[2] and the bookmakers chalked Wharton as firm favourite.

Of the 14 heats scheduled, seven 'winners' were produced by walkovers. Wallace and Grant both entered the second day by this route. Wharton, one of those who did have to run, gave 2¼, 2¾ and 5¼ yards start to his rivals through the handicapping system. On this particular day it was not a problem. In his heat the favourite 'left his mark like a racehorse, he had the race well in hand by 50 yards, and going on he won in a canter by 5 yards; 1 yard separated each of the others'.[3] Wharton's margin of victory was the greatest of the heats. Such was the ease with which he completed his task that Tom Bott immediately

> offered to match him to concede either Charley Cuttings (*sic*) or Charley Ransome two yards start in 130, or run anyone in the world 130 yards level in three weeks time for £100 or £200. We believe it is Wharton's intention to shortly return to Africa, where he was born, and it is owing to this that his backers want to run a match within three weeks time.[4]

In other words they wanted to cash-in quickly on their investment with a lucrative race. By the end of the day he was 4–1 on to win the final. Second favourite was C. Ashton of Newton Heath who was 10–1 against. The second round of heats on Monday began at 3 o'clock. The final itself would be soon after 5 p.m. Wharton and Grant were both in the third heat. There was a gale-force wind blowing against the runners which made fast times difficult. Even so, Arthur reached the finishing line 4 yards ahead of the next man with Grant last.

By the start of the final at 5.10 p.m. there was again a large crowd, estimated at around 4,000, eager to evaluate the true worth of the ex-amateur champ that had breezed through his heats. The betting was heavily in his favour, 4–1 on, despite his handicap being the heaviest of the four finalists. Ashton was 5–2 against; Smith and Cutting 100–1. A hush. Then

> Wilkinson fired the pistol to a capital start, Wharton leaving his mark in splendid form ... [Soon] Wharton had given the others the go-by and travelling like a racehorse, he closed with Ashton, whom he had well beaten thirty yards from the tape, and finishing in most resolute fashion Wharton won by fully two yards from Ashton, who was a similar distance in front of Cutting, who beat Smith by two yards for third place.[5]

Between the first and last runner there was a distance of 6 yards, despite the fact that Arthur had given Ashton a start of 3¾ yards and the last two placed a start of six yards. From a level start this equalled a win over Ashton of 5¾ yards over a distance of some 123 yards. Or, put another way, Wharton made up just under 1 yard in every 20 on his main rival who ran a total distance of 119¼ yards. For the third year in succession he had 'astonished' an athletics crowd with his 'electric'[6] performance.

Arthur returned to the scene of his triumph to run in the December Handicap at Christmas. By so doing it was plain to all that he had not returned to the Gold Coast. Perhaps the emphatic victory of that autumn, the financial return and the lament printed in the *Sheffield Daily Telegraph* that 'it is a great pity that Wharton intends leaving England, as there is no telling how fast a runner he might have become'[7] persuaded him to stay. No doubt the 'princely sum raked in by his party'[8] also persuaded them to be more energetic in their efforts to keep his feet pounding the track rather than pacing the deck of a boat. His performance, however, was not as exhilarating as that produced in September. His handicap was a demoralising 76 yards. He came second in his first heat, losing by 3 yards, and failed to make the final.

The end of the track: 1889

Arthur's first race of the New Year was at the Powderhall Ground in Edinburgh, a noted venue for professional Handicaps. E.C. Bredin, a running contemporary, thought the Powderhall track suited to fast times. The New Year event was a special yet mournful occasion being the last such meeting at the old ground. By all accounts, however, the Darlington professional – still running under the town's name – added 'sparkle' to the occasion.

> In the seventh heat … Wharton ran a fast race when clocking 12⅗ sec. for 126 yards from his handicap mark of four yards … A striking contrast to the displays of half-hearted running exhibited by Hutchens and Gent in the immediately preceding year when competing at these grounds.[9]

Billy Isaac also ran in this heat, finishing fourth of five. Unfortunately Arthur failed to steam-up to this remarkable speed in the final, no doubt disappointing some of the estimated 5–6,000 people who may, after his display in his heat, have been expecting a replication of his momentous day in London two and a half years earlier. The 'Complete Record of Results' as listed by D.A. Jamieson (1943, p. 273) in his record of the occasion, cites Arthur running from a scratch mark and finishing unplaced. (He took a similar position in the 300 hundred yards Handicap.) Even so, his earlier performance had 'shocked' the audience with its electric speed.

The breaking of the tape in Arthur's first Powderhall run marked, symbolically, the tearing of his umbilical connection with the elite of running. It was the last time the dust of his athletic toil laid traces that could not be overtaken. For three seasons he had been at the summit looking down, as amateur and professional champion. It had been a magical period that was now at an end. And the descent would be as rapid as the ascent. There was no repeat of the 'electric' performance at Sheffield in September 1888. In fact there were no more supercharged exhibitions. Edinburgh proved a false augury. The 1889 season was not successful. To use a modern idiom it seems Arthur was, from here on in, electrically challenged.

At the first Sheffield Sprint of the season, the Shrovetide Handicap held over 5–6 March, Wharton shared a heavy handicap of 77½ yards with his main rival, Harry Gent of Stockton and Darlington. Both, therefore, ran off a scratch mark. In their preliminary heat victory went to the Gold Coaster by a yard. In his second heat Wharton came third out of four and did not make the final. G. Grant of Edinburgh – whom Arthur had defeated so decisively in the Sheffield September Handicap – won that by 2 yards, and claimed the standard £80.

An analysis of the pre-race betting suggests that the Shrovetide Handicap at Sheffield was a race which Arthur did not intend to win. He did not figure in the ante-post odds probably because his handicap was too great an obstacle to outrun. Yet again, he was positioned behind all but one. His backers had not laid any money on him. Such action could have been strategic, with the aim of reducing his handicap to lengthen the odds with bookmakers for future races. The failure of runners to appear in betting lists, usually in response to an excessive handicap, sometimes signalled a decision to 'rope', rather than a simple reflection of bad form on the track. Such a tactic was designed to cloud the runner's current form in the hope of increasing both the yards taken off his starting mark and the odds for the next race.

Before the event, representatives of Grant, who won the 1888 Powderhall New Year 130 yards Handicap, offered £100 to £60 on their man beating Wharton over 190 yards off a scratch mark. This was quite common in pedestrianism. It harked back to the beginning of the sport, where two runners from rival parties would be matched for a wager. This race, if agreed, would be run the following Saturday. Grant was a member of a noted athletic clan. His brother had won the 1878 Powderhall Handicap under the family name Edwards. The challenge was issued because the backers and supporters of Grant argued their runner was the legitimate professional sprint champion of Britain. Arthur's party jumped at the offer. (Their acceptance of such a large wager throws revealing light onto their reluctance to lay money on their man to win the Shrovetide Handicap, suggesting that they did indeed think the handicap was too heavy.)

This juxtaposition of these two seemingly contradictory, therefore irrational, actions by Arthur's backers should not be taken at face value. Rather, their behaviour should be seen as testimony to the first principle of pedestrianism: it is not the winning of every race that is of value but the calculated, careful and strategic placement of bets. While Wharton's party would not back their man in the Shrovetide Handicap, despite both he and Grant having the same burden, they were prepared, however, to lay-out at least £60 on him to beat Grant less than a week later. (In fact Grant's backers subsequently backed out of a run-off and withdrew their offer. They argued that their representative had misconstrued the details of the proposal in his relay of the terms to Wharton's coterie. In so doing the Edinburgh group forfeited £20.)

Professionals who ran with their wits about them would try their best not to win every race. The penalty for such (unlikely) invincibility was a handicap that would have meant starting on the 'scratch' mark, with odds so short as to make a bet almost worthless. Simply, to be too successful actually devalued the worth of the runner to himself and his backers. It lessened the potential for a financial killing at the expense of the bookies and to the embarrassment of handicappers. This was the case for Harry Hutchens. He had to go to Australia in 1886 in order to find opponents willing to race him, so successful had he been in England. Professional sprinters literally ran a very fine line between success and failure. It was not a line that Arthur trod with dexterity. 'Success' in this context meant being able to control, in some degree, when and where the tape was breasted first; this in turn was measured by the accumulation of prize and betting money. The power to control and accumulate ensured the continued commitment of backers – the speculative capitalists of athletics – to providing the all-round financial security and planning enabling the runner to concentrate on training and performing. That 'security' was conditional upon the athlete providing a decent profit on investment. Very few runners were able to run just for enjoyment: even amateurs. Arthur may have done so in 1885; but by 1889 he was in it for the money. And if the money was not in it, then neither would he nor his backers.

Arthur appeared in other Sheffield Handicaps that season both at Easter and July, winning neither. He was scheduled also to race the September (Doncaster) Handicap but pulled out on the advice of his trainer. It must have been a great disappointment not being able to defend his unofficial title. By now Wharton was consistently carrying one of, if not the, heaviest handicap of all professional sprinters. The betting ploy of Bott and company had not worked. The athletics correspondent of the *Sheffield Daily Telegraph*, 23 April, observed that 'the coloured ex-amateur … was a virtual scratch man' starting from the back mark in most of his races.

Significantly, during August Arthur, 'the well known pedestrian' as he was described in the *Rotherham Advertiser*, 31 August, had run two races at the Greasebro' Sports held in conjunction with the Floral and Horticultural Show. It did not give the results. The significance was in the site of the event. Greasebro' was the home parish of the woman he was to marry a little over one year later.

In an attempt to salvage something from this miserable summer, Arthur's party had challenged the United States sprinter E.R. Donovan, who also ran under the name of S.J. Farrell and who had competed in the July Handicap at Sheffield, to a match at the Failsworth track in Manchester. It seems not to have materialised. He was also entered for the 135 yards handicap at the Nottingham Goose Fair, to be run on consecutive Saturdays, 28 September and 4 October. Along with Harry Gent, Wharton was allotted the toughest handicap. This burden, combined with poor form and the opening games in his new winter profession of football, led him to withdraw. Had he run, there would have been two Black sprinters in the final, for Billy Isaacs had also entered.

After just two seasons as a pedestrian, Arthur retired. The sport that would now pay the rent and buy the food was football, with cricket providing the summer salads. Thus, while from April 1888 he had chosen to chance a living from – in the main – athletics, his decision to sign as a professional footballer with Rotherham Town made him a *waged* sportsman. This was different in nature from his status as a pedestrian. As a professional runner he had a greater individual opportunity to influence the rewards he received. As a professional footballer he was merely one employee among many. To act with industrial power that would have a lasting influence in this *team* game, collective responses were called for. The game, the industry, had had and was to have, an effect upon Arthur's actions that can only be interpreted as political. As a paid employee, in a sport made economically volatile and unstable by transforming itself quickly into a commodity for mass consumption, it moulded his deeds and thoughts fundamentally. While sprinting symbolised the essence of bourgeois individualism as expressed in sport, the industrial relations environment of football was characterised by an Us versus Them culture. Many present-day managers are still called 'boss' – mirroring more sharply the class structure of society.

Before examining Arthur's experiences as a footballer the following chapter attempts to explore the social context of the Victorian running world in an effort to understand the relationship between its administrators, competitors and spectators.

NOTES

1. *Sheffield Daily Telegraph*, 16 July 1888.
2. Ibid., 10 September 1888.

3. Ibid.
4. Ibid.
5. Ibid., 11 September 1888.
6. Ibid., 10 September 1888.
7. Ibid.
8. *Sheffield Sports Special (The Green 'Un)*, 20 December 1930.
9. Jamieson (1943) pp. 68–9.

4 *Running, athletics and the people*

Athletics and the people

The 1880s were years of growth in athletics as a mass spectator sport. Betting was an influential feature in this development. As such, athletics meetings held the twin attraction of excitement and the potential bonus of a few extra pence or shillings in winnings. In this respect betting transformed the sport, for the gate-paying observer, from a passive to an active event. Competitive running had begun as an event organised by aristocratic employers of footmen who had a reputation for speed or endurance, with money being wagered on the outcome. Increasingly during the mid-nineteenth century running fixtures – staged by entrepreneur promoters for profit – drew paying crowds as large as 15,000, many of whom gambled on each race. The age of sport as a mass spectator phenomenon was emerging.

A number of sports and games were undergoing a similar process of regulation and refinement (and, for several, disintegration) during the early to mid-nineteenth century. The motor force behind this change was a combination of the practical and political: there was less freely accessible space for popular games in the city than had been the case in the countryside; and Britain's ruling class saw it as their self-interested duty to discipline, order and morally regulate the unbought hours of the working class. The extension of the vote, the growth of trade unionism and class politics, growing literacy as a result of education reforms – which in turn facilitated wider newspaper readership – were just some of the influences changing leisure patterns. Newly codified forms of – often old – games became commodified: sold as products to an increasing market of consumers. For whatever reason, those games that resisted or were unable to achieve this transformation, remained as local pursuits largely unspoilt by commercial pressure, such as Knurr-and-Spell in Yorkshire and north-east Lancashire, or were largely destroyed, such as cock-fighting in the pit villages of south Northumberland.

The onset of industrialisation in the late-eighteenth and early-nineteenth centuries had the effect of lengthening the working day, despite the technological advances in production methods. (An increase many people would recognise today.) This was followed by a very gradual decline in working hours – for large groups of employees in the manufacturing trades – during the second half of the nineteenth century. A series of Factory Acts, won by pressure from below in the form of numerous 'short-time committees' and Chartist agitation in support of the 10 Hours Bill, legislated reductions in the working day. Factory owners, worried about a drop in both productivity and profit, fought a hard, tenacious battle to resist shorter working hours.

Alongside this rise and fall in the industrial day wages grew during the nineteenth century (falling again at the beginning of the twentieth). An investigation into the wage of manual workers begun by the Board of Trade in 1885, the first of its kind, concentrated upon the staple industries. It did not cover all places of employment, nor domestic servants, casual labourers or follow-up non-returns of its questionnaire, which may have uncovered a further stratum of low-paid workers. What the survey does give us is a rough average of the wage of employed adult males and employed adults. For adult males the average weekly wage in 1886 was 24s.9d (£1.24p) or £57 a year. (The working year was averaged at 46 weeks in order to account for periods of slack, illness, strikes, unemployment and other such disruptions to production.) Within this mean figure great variations are hidden according to trade, occupation and district. For instance, a London artisan – skilled tradesman – in 1897 earned an average weekly wage of 40s (£2); his provincial equivalent some 6s (30p) less. If we look at wage increases over the century, between the years 1807 and 1897 the wage of a London artisan had increased by 25 per cent, while those outside had seen a rise of 60 per cent. Such figures need to be compared with the price of basic foods, and other essential living costs, to give us an accurate picture of the change in working-class living standards. Prices were not rising for most of the 1880s because of the economic depression. Cook and Stevenson (1988) suggest that the cost of living fell until 1889 in contrast with the rise in real wages. It must be remembered also, that these wage rises were won against the backdrop of a shorter working day in some industries. Finally, the figures, for all their inadequacies, provide us with some kind of comparative benchmark by which we can assess the winnings and wages of Wharton the athlete and footballer, with other contemporary workers.

Taken together, the rise in both wages and 'leisure' time of a good proportion of working people was a fertile condition necessary for growth in spectator sport. Additionally, infrastructural developments allowed more people to visit more places more quickly. The expansion of the railway network from 15,537 miles of track in 1870 to 23,387 by 1910, coupled with the improvements in road surfaces which had facilitated speedier horse-powered travel, made possible the hitherto unreachable. Thus, as the nineteenth century progressed, workers were paying to watch various sports in ever increasing numbers at venues near and far.

The spectator sports market – for owners, producers and consumers – was similar to other markets: those with wealth, status and power controlled the means to compete. In amateur athletics, power and control lay with the administrative bodies; the Amateur Athletic Association forming the apex of this pyramid. Below them came the regional associations, such as the NCAA. Running – pedestrianism especially – provided an arena in which the predatory machinations of venture capitalists such as Tom Bott could be given full vent. Individuals who were prepared to invest speculatively in an athlete or a meeting, could rake in large amounts of cash. Their initial outlay could include paying for athletes to train; providing equipment; arranging and promoting meetings; providing stadia and disbursing franchises. Harry Hardwick, one of athletics' first professional promoters, secretary of Salford Harriers (Billy Rayner's club), was also a member of the executive of the NCAA. Embodying these dual roles meant he was involved in creating the conditions – the rules – through which he could speculate to accumulate. And it was lucrative. He earned 6d (2½p) for every entry in events he controlled and £5 appearance money as official timekeeper. Additional earnings could be had from writing reports of his meetings for newspapers and journals.

For the producer – the athlete – the financial return for his labour, in the form of training and competition, was not great. Certainly not as great as the likes of Harry Hardwick. The athletic career was intense and short. Money had to be earned, literally, in as quick a time as possible. And often by covert means or methods that subverted both the moral and regulatory constitution governing competition.

For the consumer – the spectator – a proportion of those waking hours forcibly won back from employers through workplace action and political agitation were now being commodified, packaged and sold to them as a leisure product. Spare time, the 'luxury' of life, was being colonised by, among others, profit-motivated entrepreneurs. Workers could now buy back their leisure time as a sophisticated sports spectacle, over the design and form of which they had little control.

Professional athletes were a part of the working class because they sold their labour power in order to live. Arthur, as a paid producer of a luxury commodity, the Sport Spectacle for the working class of the North of England, was proletarianised by pedestrianism. But he was fortunate in that his acquired and innate abilities on the running track (and football and cricket pitches) were valued, sought-after skills that made his labour power special. And given the level of scarcity of such talent he was able to extract a relatively high price in relation to other skilled workers.

There is a poignant irony here. His proletarianisation was completely at odds with the aims and objectives of his patrons back in the Gold Coast. It was a desire to escape such pressures of downward social mobility that catapulted Arthur to Britain. The paradox of his success was in the inverse relationship between the short-term public adulation for his physical feats and the long-term downward social and economic mobility that ensued. And the more famous he became, the greater was his dependence on the sports industry for a living. This addictive reliance necessitated greater investment in time, effort and money. When he did attempt to fuse his educational and athletic achievements, in application for a career in the Gold Coast Government Service, his past status as 100 yards champion was cited (privately) as evidence of his unsuitability. This will be discussed in Chapter 7.

Yet in the face of all this pressure from above, and in large part because of it, Arthur's deeds had an overwhelming symbolic dimension. Here was an African, at the time of Africa's forced colonisation by the capitalist nations of Europe, beating these 'superior races' at their own sports on their home turf. How much did such victories over the 'White Man' ameliorate the injustice of imperialism? In dissecting this relationship of Wharton the individual – the champion athlete – to Wharton the symbol – the Black Man – we may find clues as to why he was so quickly forgotten. Was his success, in both its real and metaphorical consequence, indigestible to the prevailing institutions of power? This absence of memory of Wharton, the consequence of a racialised history, is sad testament to the degenerative effect such a corrosive poison can have. By concentrating on the colour, culture and ethnicity of an athlete, instead of their unmediated achievement, the gullible are condemned to an understanding that is limited by unnecessary ignorance. So much is missed.

Athletics and Wharton

Like most athletes of his day, especially the increasing numbers that came from working-class backgrounds, Arthur gained an income from his running even when he was formally an amateur. The pejorative label 'shamateurism' was created to describe such practice. In his autobiography 'crack' sprinter of the 1890s, A.R. Downer, explained the secretive deals arranged between athletic club officials, amateur runners and their agents, trainers and backers. If the athlete was a crowd-puller he could expect, and would frequently be offered, appearance money by club secretaries or their representatives. £5 was the commonest figure. On one occasion Downer was successful in bidding up to £8 – worth over £1,000 in 1997 – to appear at a meeting in Yorkshire. Unfortunately clubs would not always deliver the money promised. When this happened, what could the runner do? Cry 'justice' to the authorities?

Downer called his amateur period, 'my amateur-professional days'. He met few 'gentleman' runners. Most, whether amateur or professional, were doing it to supplement their income or provide a wage.

> How many so-called amateurs run for the pure love of the sport? Do not the most, in fact, by far the most, enter and try to win only at those meetings where the best prizes are given, and, in many cases, where there is the most gambling.[1]

Since coming into being in 1880 the AAA had fought hard to prevent professionals competing alongside amateurs as in association football and cricket. Money was set aside in 1882 to finance the prosecution of athletes violating the amateur code. Some professional runners had been tried in court and convicted of impersonation of an amateur and sentenced to six months hard labour. (Compare this treatment to that received by N. Lane Jackson when in court on an assault charge a year earlier. He was then assistant FA secretary and member of Blackheath Harriers, later becoming FA vice-president. Founder of the Corinthians FC, Jackson was a grandee of the Victorian Sports Establishment. The judge, his 'old friend', fined him £20. Afterwards his judicial pal invited him to lunch. It would have been interesting to see the bill and who paid it!)

In 1892 the AAA banned expense payments, a move that was in step with its renewed drive to clear the track of shamateurs. The prohibition applied only to athletes: officials and administrators would still be kept in pocket. Walter Platt, secretary of the NCAA, on a salary of ten guineas a year, was also allowed three guineas expenses to travel to London for AAA meetings.

Four years on Downer and five other top-class athletes were banned for life from amateur athletics for receiving money to compete. Sitting in judgement were some of the club officials who had paid appearance money – or not – to those same athletes. The close of 1897 saw the cull of 'several leading runners in all events from 100 yards to 20 miles'.[2] This cleansing from amateur competition of athletes daring to demean and dirty themselves by dealing in filthy lucre was a form of human-pest control that dovetailed neatly with the late-Victorian obsession with public hygiene. It contrasts vividly with the response to Wharton and Ritchie's theatricals at Bradford ten years earlier where, as we have seen, it seems Ritchie arranged to have Arthur spiked by the only other 'runner' in the race. Then the Gold Coaster did not even bother to turn up to argue his side. For his 'misdemeanour' he received a public ticking-off. While administrative deliberation and resolution of this case was characterised by the bluster of a timid bark, the mood in the kennel in 1897 was choreographed by a closing of the bureaucratic pack: the banning of Downer *et al.* was only possible because club officials, who had been part of the racket, turned 'Queen's evidence' against their former contractual partners. If there was a failure of officials to collude with one another over the Wharton/Ritchie affair in 1887, there was no such disunity ten years later.

Downer was not the only athlete prepared to speak out against this surreal environment. It would have provided an inordinate amount of stimuli and inspiration for writers such as Lewis Carroll had they peeped through the looking glass. The runner E.C. Bredin questioned the ethic of a rule by which amateurs provided the means for the existence of athletics as a sport *and business*, at the real expense of those who were its lifeblood.

> Since amateur athletics have taken a hold on the public, the whole concern has developed into a business which is kept going by the money the public pay to witness the sport. The governing body is to a great extent formed of men who are interested in the accumulation of this money, not for their personal advantage, but for the benefit of the clubs they represent.[3]

The adjectives amateur/professional were used initially as headings for social categories: to separate bourgeois and proletarian in athletic competition. Some athletic clubs would only accept 'gentlemen' as members and competitors. The Amateur Athletic Club, parent of the Amateur Athletic Association, was one such. Their first Sports Day in 1866 was exclusive to all except the 'gentleman amateur'. The constitution of 1867 specifically excluded the 'mechanic, artisan or labourer'. A year later the rules defined an amateur as a 'gentleman who has never competed'.[4] There was also a regional divide: the restrictive clubs tended to be in the South, those open to all in the North of England where most professionals competed. Montague Shearman regretted the overshadowing of the gentleman amateur at the 1886 AAA Championships at Stamford Bridge:

> It became clear that the supremacy of the path had passed for the present from the metropolitan to the provincial runners ... It is a difference of class ... until another development takes place, three-quarters of our amateur champions will be drawn from the masses.[5]

In fact it was not until the formation of the AAA in 1880 that runners other than 'gentlemen' were sanctioned at amateur athletic events. Almost as soon as working-class runners were allowed entry they began to dominate competition. The growing pre-eminence of working-class sportsmen from the North during the 1880s was not confined to athletics either. At association football largely professional – proletarian – teams from Lancashire, such as Blackburn Olympic, Blackburn Rovers and Preston North End, were reaching the final of the FA Cup on a regular basis and usually winning: Blackburn Rovers won the FA

Cup for the third time in succession in 1886. Old Etonians were the last amateur side to win the FA Cup in 1882.

To open up athletic competition to both classes would have been the simplest and most pragmatic answer to the problems faced, and to a large extent caused, by the AAA. But they were unable to reconcile the principle of honest racing, where athletes would be stripped of the necessity to make mathematical calculations relating to handicapping, betting odds and roping, with the need of most runners – amateur and professional – to be paid for their labour. The 'corruption' of an abstract principle – a fair race for all competitors run truly by all competitors – was inevitable when brought face-to-face with the demand upon occupational athletes to make ends meet. Such corruption was the outcome of rules governing athletics that were bourgeois in content, closeting the sport for that rarity, the gentleman amateur of independent means. That the amateur/professional divide was consistently and contemptuously ignored was not a consequence of the sport being chock-full of moral degenerates. An anonymous contributor to the *Athletic News*, calling himself the 'One In The Know' had waited five years in vain to be questioned by a reporter over these issues. In frustration he interviewed himself about the hypocrisy at the heart of his trade! He tells a surreal tale of struggle off the track to compete on it. His role in the drama is that of an actor unwillingly colluding in the moral debasement of his sport, a debasement brought about by the application of class prejudice of its aloof, snob administrators.

> I knocked at my own door, let myself in, lit a cigarette, sat on a chair opposite myself, drew out my notebook, and went right into the interviewing business ... Said I to myself ... *what do you know?*
>
> Been on the path several years, met all the shining lights in athletics, soon tumbled to the ways and means, tried my best to go straight, found that I couldn't afford (*sic*), only had twenty five bob a week at the office, turned up twelve bob a week to the 'old woman' for board and 'grub', three shillings went for washing and barber's account, four shillings I used to put by for my 'togs', another bob went for smoking, and with the balance of my screw I tried my luck as a 'gentleman amateur'. Found I couldn't manage it at first, but I possessed a bit of form, and a pal used to weigh in the fees for me ... But after a bit I got 'in the know'; found it was only a mug's game to be a 'tryer', so I went in for roping.

> Got my expenses by winning an occasional heat; never tried in a final until I knew it was a 'pinch'. Then I used to have a go, and managed to 'get a bit', which paid exe's for me and my pal. Had Platt [of the NCAA] for a Juggins several times; good old Walter thought he had my form to a T, but I waited until I had a bit up my sleeve. Won three of Harry Ellis's handicaps. Harry thought he'd 'found me a mark', but he hadn't. I'd like to have gone straight, but I really could not afford it, as getting to a meeting used to make a hole in ten bob – 5s (25p) fees, railway fare and tea, 5s – and I hadn't got it … I came to the conclusion that to be a gentleman amateur and a trier a fellow must have at least ten bob (50p) a week which he can afford to spend.
>
> What do I think of handicappers? … How the deuce does a handicapper have a chance with chaps like us?
>
> Another cigarette? Thanks, don't mind if I do.
>
> How about the Northern Counties Athletic Association? … I'm not too sweet with the Association, as they tried to get me once, and it *was* a near thing.
>
> I know it will take me a long time to get into the way of going straight, as when a fellow has got used to roping, there seems more pleasure … than coming by it honestly.
>
> Some day when I've reformed, and can say I'm a trier every time (and I really do mean to get into that way, as I have now a decent screw which will just allow me to become a gentleman amateur) but at present I am … [not] anything else but a DEAD WRONG 'UN.[6]

Despite the archaic language the core dilemma is revealed: athletes faced the same economic problems as other sellers in the labour market and should be allowed to earn a living from something they are good at. Primarily, argues the DEAD WRONG 'UN, it was the rules of the sport that corrupted the athlete, not the other way around. In his interview with the *Athletic Journal*, 21 June 1887, Wharton 'recollected once a man offering me £20 to lose a race'.

The social relations of power in sport reflected and expressed the class structure of the British society. In athletics the social division expressed itself in the separate competitions for amateur and professional. This superficial dichotomy continued until the late twentieth century. The very act of becoming a professional restricted the venues of competition. The *Athletic News* was loath to carry reports of professional meetings, giving much greater coverage to amateur events. The AAA by its insistence on sustaining this division – thus preserving a competitive space for gentlemen amateurs – was doing what it saw as its social duty. In cricket and football, while combined amateur/professional teams and leagues had been accepted, class divisions took a different form. In both sports the treatment of professionals – wage earners – was inferior to the treatment of amateurs, or 'gentlemen' as they were known in cricket. In County competition of the latter generally the two groups would change in different rooms and enter and exit the ground by different gates. The Gentlemen would have their initials printed on the scorecard. The Players only their surname. The captain was never a professional.

In association football, the career which Arthur pursued full-time after the summer of 1889, different contracts of employment were offered to amateur and professional. The former were governed by a gentleman's agreement that allowed either party the freedom to terminate their obligations unilaterally. In contrast, the professional was severely restricted in his freedom to move from one club to another. He was contractually tied and bound to the club for which he played, unless it said otherwise. It was next to impossible for a player to leave and play for another team without the full agreement of his employer. The following chapter will examine Arthur's football career during the years 1886–89.

NOTES

1. A.R. Downer, *Running Recollections and How to Train* (London 1908) pp. 27, 29.
2. Jeremy Crump, 'Athletics', in Tony Mason (ed.) *Sport in Britain* (Cambridge 1989) p. 51.
3. E.C. Bredin, *Running and Training* (Northampton 1902) p. 105.
4. Crump in Mason (1989) p. 51.
5. Shearman (1887) p. 67
6. The *Athletic News*, 20 September 1887 p. 3.

5 *'The best team in the world'*

Preston North End

In September 1886 the most professional association football team in England, Preston North End, signed the 21-year-old West African as an amateur for FA Cup matches only. It was Wharton's impressive performance for a Newcastle and District representative team against PNE on 27 April that had prompted William Sudell, chairman of the PNE managing committee, to lure Arthur westwards – if only temporarily.

The label 'amateur' suited both Preston and Wharton. It allowed the club to bypass rules that applied to professional players; and, for the latter, it did not complicate his status as an amateur runner and college student. News that Arthur had signed as a pro – if the option were available – would not have been received with spontaneous displays of joy in West Africa. His family may have even stopped funding his studies. As an amateur he could have the best of all three worlds – or so it may have seemed. Though a punter of the day could have confidently laid a pound to a penny that Arthur was paid lavish 'expenses'. Sudell, the Malcolm Allison or 'Big' Ron Atkinson of his day, was known for his extravagance.

The Lancashire club were not the first to pay players but their name became synonymous with the practice by the early to mid-1880s, so much so that in 1884 they had been disqualified from further competition in the FA Cup after openly admitting playing professional players in a cup-tie against Upton Park. The London club had complained that among their opponents were seven 'imported' Scots. Sudell argued that paying players was a common practice among many northern clubs. It was better, he offered, that the whole debate came out into the open and the practice accommodated by changing FA rules.

And anyway was not the prohibition of payment an unsustainable instrument of elitist hypocrisy? Had not Upton Park recruited four players specifically for the FA Cup? One from Sandhurst and three from Oxbridge. Weren't they also bending the rules, if not in letter, certainly in spirit?

This controversy brought the debate over professionalism to a head. It caused a major cleavage in football for control of the game. The FA was threatened by open rebellion among the northern clubs who paid their men. They formed the Northern Association. A tabulated form sent to all clubs by the FA asking for details of payments to players increased the temperature of the conflict. An honest return of the FA form would have admitted the deception to the London administrators and their regional allies in Birmingham and Sheffield, all faithful to the amateur cause. This in turn would have caused further expulsions if the FA were to remain consistent in their punishment. The northern clubs – now known collectively as the British Football Association – refused to comply. (Clubs would get round the accounting problems of paying players by using some of the money taken at the gate. The remainder would then be entered into the accounts as gate receipts.) The FA, frightened of the formidable strength of northern – free-trade – football, set up a committee of inquiry. Sudell was a member. At a meeting in London on 20 July 1885, the committee uneasily accepted waged footballers. But along with legitimisation came rules of eligibility for professionals in the FA Cup competition proposed by Dr Morley of Blackburn Rovers: contract players would have to be born or have lived within six miles of the ground or headquarters of the club for the past two years; they would have to be registered with the FA; they could only play for one club per season.

Professionalism, then, came at a price to northern clubs and players. The market for buying and selling football-labour was immediately beset by restrictive conditions that suited those who did not need, choose, or want others to benefit by the use of that market.

Wharton, as an amateur, was not affected by these eligibility criteria. His expense-account signing with Preston did not prevent him from playing for Darlington. Agreeing to play for a team in the FA Cup did not debar an amateur from turning out for another club in a separate competition. Professionals could not do the same. It was, in class terms, one set of rules for the (largely southern) bourgeois amateur clubs, another rule for the wholly northern, proletarian-professional teams.

(Woolwich Arsenal were the first southern club to become professional in 1891.) Two football spheres had been created by the rules: that of the work-a-day professional; and that of the gentleman amateur. Though they both kicked the same ball.

Sudell had won the battle over the acceptance of professionals. But the restrictions placed on them involved a further obstacle to be circumvented. He did so by also signing, when necessary, the best amateurs. Football historian Harry Berry has argued that Sudell signed a number of big-name amateur goalkeepers, such as Billy Rose, Wharton, his replacement James Trainer, and Dr Mills-Roberts, to highlight the unfairness of having different rules governing amateur and professional players. The signing of Billy Rose from London club Swifts caused a deal of apoplexy among the gentlemen footballers of the South. It was the first time an amateur of such status had been 'imported' to the professional North.

Sudell felt these rules were conjured partly as a personalised counter-attack by some members of the FA, especially Morley of Blackburn Rovers. His local and arch rival had, initially, been opposed to professionalism. Blackburn did not join the Northern Association. It was Morley who had insisted upon the six mile residency qualification. He described waged players as 'money grabbing get rich loafers'.[1] He was not opposed to broken-time payments which, he argued, would ensure that players who gave up work time to play would not lose out financially; but players should not expect to earn their living from playing football alone.

There was more than a little self-interest in Morley's stance. His own club had three Scots on their books – Suter, McIntyre and Douglas – all accused of being professional. Fergie Suter in particular is held to be one of the earliest 'professors'. (Interestingly, North End played against Rovers on the occasion of Suter's benefit match in February 1887.) However, there is still debate as to the exact status of these players. Berry argues they had other jobs: Suter as stonemason then publican; McIntyre as publican; and Douglas as iron foundry worker. Perhaps of more importance to Rovers was the need to retain possession of their pre-eminent status. Twice winners of the FA Cup – in 1884 and 1885 – they were to win it again in 1886, and the only club ever to win the trophy three years in succession, they were gradually being eclipsed by the scientific passing – or 'combination' – game of North End's professionals. Sudell's view was that the FA, and in particular

Morley, knew the restriction on free, unhindered recruitment of paid players would hinder his ambitions for PNE more than it would any other (less professional) club. The FA had been forced to accept the professional football terrain revealed by Sudell, but all around they spiked it with barbed wire in the form of these rules.

The rivalry of Morley–Sudell/PNE–Blackburn Rovers and the jealousies it generated shaped the initial rules on professionalism. Preston had originally been a rugby stronghold – PNE did not play soccer until 1880. The town did not have the natural resources on offer to association towns like Blackburn and Bolton. To make up the shortfall in local talent Sudell, to induce good 'foreigners' to Preston, would have to pay. For his part Morley – and Darwen FC, the other Lancashire team that refused to join the Northern Association – were not prepared to allow this usurper to get his hands on silverware without a struggle.

Sudell and Wharton held similar views about the relationship between excellence of achievement in sport, and money: in short, that excellence often could not be attained without access to a fair amount of cash. William Sudell, with the honorary title of Major gained as a member of the Volunteers – a forerunner of the Territorial Army – had played cricket and rugby with North End since 1867. From 1874 he had been chairman. He played in the club's first game under association rules as goalkeeper. His other occupation was as manager of a local cotton mill. Sudell's aim had been to make PNE the premier football force in England and Scotland. To attract the best players, often Scots, he would have to promise a 'job' so that they maintained their nominal amateur status. Nick Ross, captain of Hearts of Edinburgh, was enticed south in 1883 with 'employment' as a slater. In 1885, there were 58 Scottish professionals in England, 57 of them in Lancashire, the hotbed of professional football. Sudell had systematically bent the rules prior to legalisation by openly 'importing' Scots for the primary purpose of playing football. His refusal to accept the constitution of the game if it impeded the construction of his 'Invincibles' eventually rebounded on him. In 1895 he was sentenced to three years' imprisonment for the fraudulent use of his firm's money. The total amount in question was £5,326 – an enormous sum. Much of it had gone the way of PNE's players, on expense and hospitality payments. This fact was used in his defence: he had not personally gained from the redirection of the Goodair firm's funds. He later shot himself while in self-imposed exile in South Africa. It was a sad end for the married man with children.

He had paid with his life for the fulfilment of his ambition. Yet he leaves a universal legacy. Without him how long would working-class players have been forced to collude in the sham hypocrisy of football's elite?

To use the language of an erstwhile England manager, Sudell was not averse to giving players a 'bung' to come and play for PNE. This sometimes took the form of a licenseeship of a pub, as was the case with George Wilson. The chairman unashamedly pointed out to the committee investigating professionalism that 'Preston are all professionals'.[2] He managed to assemble a team that were, in fact, unbeatable. In so doing he deserves to be remembered alongside Herbert Chapman, Matt Busby, Jock Stein, Bill Shankly, Bill Nicholson, Alex Ferguson and Arsène Wenger – creators all of unique sides.

Wharton's schooling in the moral ethics of 'amateur' athletic competition probably provided the necessary nous when dealing with charismatic figures such as Sudell. Both men came from, and operated within, sports environments where the exchange of money was the medium through which most transactions took place. If Sudell valued Wharton's skills and wanted to utilise them to PNE's advantage then it seems more than likely that the Lancastrian mill manager would have acknowledged he would have to pay for them. What is beyond doubt is that Sudell would have had no moral or economic problems passing the cash surreptitiously from one Gladstone bag to another. Indeed one of the accusations levelled at Sudell at his trial was the extravagance of the club's expense account. For Sudell football was also a business. A good team, especially in the Blackburn-Bolton-Preston triangle, meant good crowds. Which in turn meant lots of cash, which could be spent – by any means necessary – on the acquisition of a better team. A better team would be more successful, lead to larger crowds and an increase in gate receipts. Formulated thus was the logic of accumulation, which, to some extent, spurred on Sudell. For Wharton football, and sport in general, was beckoning with increasing attraction as a means to a living. It was mutually beneficial for neither to be too fussed about the formal rules governing their relationship. Both were renowned for their unorthodox approach to their sports. Both men, therefore, had something to offer the other, and would have been comfortable with their partner's methods and means of doing business. Jamieson (1943) considered Wharton one of the best professional goalkeepers of the mid-late 1880s. Harry Berry points out that Wharton's name is not included in a list of Lancashire professionals playing in 1887. These inconsistencies in the economic status of Wharton do not matter a great deal. It is the unimportance of the distinction between amateur and professional, *as viewed by some of those who played (and ran) the game*, that shines through in this debate. Sudell elevated pragmatism – doing what was necessary – over the principle of sticking to the rules. Arthur was now enjoying celebrity status and beginning to realise the potential for making a good living from his sports, at least in the short term. If violation of the rules was necessary to reach the different vistas that both he (and Sudell) had imagined, the end justified the means. Each had their own view of what was fair and unfair. And sometimes being fair was not always in harmony with the rules.

Wharton's decision to play for PNE in their FA Cup matches was not popular with his Darlington club mates. There was certainly rumour of ill-feeling between himself and his colleagues at the time of his leaving. The cricket, running and association football teams were all part of Darlington Cricket and Football Club. He had decided to try for greater success elsewhere with two rivals, Birchfield Harriers and PNE, 'the strongest team in the world' according to the *Newcastle Weekly Chronicle* of 18 September 1886. Yet he had not severed his links completely with the North East. He was still a member of Cleveland College. Voluntarily leaving a successful sports club – in Arthur's case, one that had been instrumental in the rapid development of his reputation – and going to another team was not a popular action. To quit three teams of the same club – athletics, cricket and football – and go elsewhere while still living in the town may have been seen by some as trying your luck. The *Northern Echo* thought his move 'bad news for supporters [and] a great loss to Darlington'.[3] The reporter hoped that he would return to play in association football County Cup ties, for there was no one with half his ability at the Darlington club. 'Spectator' in the *Darlington and Stockton Times* echoed the sentiment. 'Personally I have too much admiration for a fellow who has licked creation in the hardest race in existence to allow him to pass away without some word of protest or appeal.'[4] With hindsight the ironic ambiguity of this statement is startling. While 'Spectator' was referring to Arthur's AAA 100 yards triumphs, the modern reader could mistake the sentiment as praise for Arthur's practical refutation – through his athletic achievements and educational background – of the pseudo-Darwinist tenets of Scientific Racism.

However, Arthur was now a nationally known sportsman. Joining PNE was tacit recognition of him as one of the best goalkeepers in the game, a view held by many in the North East. Those at Deepdale – the home of Preston – were not disappointed. He played in all six FA Cup games that season, conceding four goals, three in the last game, a semi-final tie against West Bromwich Albion. The final, official goals tally read: for 17, against 4. Actually there were seven Cup matches. The game against Renton in the third round had to be replayed after a 3–3 draw. The drawn game was expunged form the records. However, it contained incidents characteristic of the modern game. This tie will be discussed shortly.

It was reported in some newspapers that Preston had signed Wharton because the other ’keeper on the club’s books, the (newly) professional Billy Rose, was not eligible to play in the FA Cup until February. This rumour seems to have been space-filling gossip. In fact there were two others goalkeepers at Deepdale, Billy Joy (who later became a director) and Addison, who could have filled in. (A similar rumour circulated the following season in respect of another goalie, James Trainer.) Whatever the case, Arthur’s appearance between the sticks had crowd-drawing potential on four fronts: as a nationally known athletics champion; as a man of colour; as a very good goal-keeper; and as an eccentric performer. Arthur also had his detractors. Some reporters thought his extrovert behaviour unsuited to a team that played the modern, scientific combination style. This inter-passing football harnessed individual flair in service of systematic, co-ordinated teamwork. Perhaps the most recent example is the Liverpool teams of the 1970s and early 1980s. Their strength, their identity was forged through collective expression. What is more, Wharton, this Black footballer with attitude in a White society becoming increasingly colour conscious, had no shortage of combatants willing to knock the Uppity Nigger down.

Are you all Englishmen? The FA Cup 1886–87

The first round of the English FA Challenge Cup was against the self-styled aristocrats of Scottish football, Queen’s Park. Their Hampden Park ground, as now, was used as the national stadium. The club had been remarkably successful, winning the Scottish FA Cup eight times since it began in 1873–74. They were the current holders, having beaten Renton FC 3–1. In that season's competition – 1885–86 – they recorded their greatest ever victory, 16–0 over St Peter's. They had also been English FA Cup finalists in 1884 and 1885, losing both times. They were the last amateur team to appear in an English FA Cup final. Despite their pedigree they were beaten 3–0 in Glasgow by North End. A friendly game a month earlier saw the latter win 6–0. This second successive loss by the pride of Scotland to their 'English' counterparts was aggravated by the presence of half-a-dozen expatriate Scots. It was as if the Lancashire club had come again to revel in their decisive result – with the best players Scotland had to offer. 'Thousands of idiots ... proceeded to hustle and kick and strike and poke the visitors',[5] after Nick Ross – a Scot and ex-Hearts player – of PNE fouled Harrower. Worse was yet to come.

The Lancastrian club again scored six, with no reply, in their second round game at home to Witton of Blackburn. Then it was back to Glasgow for the third round against Scottish Cup finalists Renton. It was a game where the excitement came as much from the supporting drama as from the football.

Sudell was desperate to win the FA Cup. There was no other national football competition; no other contest in which the victors could say they had beaten the best opposition available. The consensus among northern football correspondents, especially those of the *Athletic News*, was that Sudell's men were odds-on to bring the trophy back to Lancashire for the fifth season running. Clubs like Queen's Park, Renton and Glasgow Rangers were equally intent on taking the Cup to Scotland. After all, the Scottish national side had not lost to England since 1879. There had been 15 matches since the first in 1872. England had won one, Scotland nine. To wrap the Cup in thistles would also gratify those within the Scottish FA – in effect the Queen's Park club – who were resentful of the wealthy, new money arrogance of North End. Not only had the mill town players copied and become expert at the passing game that had originated in Scotland, but instrumental in this development were a number of Scottish 'professors'. It was not until May 1893 that professionalism was allowed by the SFA, when the steady flow of good players southwards became unstoppable. Thus, not only had their English FA counterparts sanctioned the corruption of the amateur ideal upon which the association game had been founded, their action was having a direct consequence in Scotland by sucking away its best talent. Seen in this wider context, PNE's result with Renton had meaning beyond determining who should continue in the Cup. It had important symbolic value for the supporters of Renton, the Scottish FA and nationalist Scots.

There were 300 supporters at the railway station to cheer the North End team away to their third round tie with the side from near Dumbarton, north-west of Glasgow. During the journey Wharton slept a while, then played cricket in the corridor with Dewhurst and Ross. They used a footwarmer as a wicket. Arthur was 'cat-like' at short leg. He also had time to play newspaper 'snowball' fights with Ross junior. The Preston party, which included the secretary of the Northumberland Football Association, Mr Phillips, stayed at the Royal Hotel, Glasgow.

The *Athletic News* reporter reflected the confidence Sudell's team had in their goalie: 'Wharton … can still boast that no goal has been scored against him in the English Cup competition. The darkey … can give most goalkeepers a good start and a beating.'[6] As an astute manager, Sudell knew that the spine of the team had to be strong. A sound goalkeeper ensured a solid base. The team had reason to be confident. Up to this point they had played 27 games, winning 24, scoring 172 goals with just 36 against. An average of 6–1 in North End's favour.

After a pitch inspection at the Tontine Park ground, the referee Mr Betts decided it was unfit to play. Curiously a 'friendly' match was begun instead in order to placate the crowd variously estimated at 3,500–6,000. However, this suited the organisers, rather more than it would suit the crowd. The gate money would not have to be paid back and the players would not have had a wasted journey. As important, if not more so, expenses incurred in staging the match could be partly reimbursed, at least, to the relevant parties and maybe even a profit made on the day. (Although, if the lower estimate for the crowd was more accurate, this seems unlikely.)

This agenda, if accurate, did not reckon on spontaneous crowd particiapation in events. An alternative pitch inspection by 'hundreds' of Renton fans massing on the playing surface decided the match *was* playable. They demanded the original status of the match be restored: 'Play the tie or pay us back' was the cry. The ruse of those in control, as the crowd saw it, had been tumbled. The demand of the activists was met. Play recommenced as a cup-tie. Hindsight now allows us to see that this was a pragmatic ploy by officials – most probably the police – primarily concerned with the need to restore public order. Once over, the game became a 'friendly' again.

During the first half Renton piled on the pressure. There was a dispute over the second Renton goal which the Preston players claimed was 'handled'. In return, Renton felt unjustly treated when Wharton appeared to 'scoop the ball out' of the net without a goal being awarded. While the emotional gauge of the crowd, early on, had been up and down more times than a spider spinning its web, the level of excitement grew steadily as the potential of a thrashing for the full-time professionals from England awakened. To the delight of the home crowd the score at half-time of this official/unofficial/official/unofficial cup-tie was 3–1. Their proud anticipation of an upset soon evaporated. The second half saw the trained, fitter and better prepared 'professors' match the first-half goal tally of their opponents. Wharton was 'called upon frequently, but he was always at home and made no mistake'.[7] Though permissible, no extra time was played.

There was uninhibited bad feeling between the two sides. To many Renton supporters the effervescent self-confidence of North End was yet another characteristic manifestation of English arrogance. The Preston team, as away sides did in nearly any competitive game, received verbal abuse from the crowd, much of it anti-English in character. The England/Scotland dimension to the contest added extra spice. Nick Ross and his compatriots were singled out for special treatment. A year earlier the Scottish FA had told all Scottish journeyman footballers such as Ross, who plied their trade in England, that they would not be allowed to play again for Scottish clubs without SFA permission. The migrants to England were seen as unpatriotic.

A banner fixed to the roof of the seating stand proclaimed 'The Queen and the People'. The 'People' indeed made their presence felt, and forcefully, against those in authority, though not in the way the banner had intended, with its subliminal text of 'Sovereign Mistress and [subservient, passive] Subjects'. The contradiction between this narrative of loyalty and obedience to authority and the reality of fan-power was glaring. When the Anglo-phobic element of the occasion is considered the banner's message becomes farcical and confused. The Scottish 'People' quite clearly had not stuck to the script. The message of the Renton supporters' rallying slogan was simple and clear: do not take us for granted. Looked at in this way the hierarchical culture of

Scottish football had been turned upside down for a short while, despite the unlikely occasion and venue for such a revolt.

The replay/original match was a week later. The Preston club were unhappy with their treatment at Tontine Park and wanted a change of venue – it has to be assumed Renton did not – and Hampden Park was suggested. The Queen's Park club agreed on the condition that the admission fee be raised to 1 shilling (5p) to 'keep out the rougher section of the masses'. They did not want those Tontine Park hooligans dirtying the carpet at Scottish football's HQ. To ensure more orderly proceedings the ruling class of association football in England and Scotland took greater control of the game. Major Sir Arthur Francis Marindin KCMG, president of the FA, refereed, while Mr Phillips of the Northumberland Association and Mr Lawrie of Queen's Park and president of the Glasgow FA, were umpires. Until 1891 the two umpires were usually officials, one from each club, exercising direct control of affairs on their allotted half of the pitch. The referee would be on the sidelines. He would assume his role only if there was an incident the umpires could not agree on and arbitration was needed.

'The dusky goalkeeper' led his team out to 'faint cheers' from the crowd of between 6,782 (the official estimate) and '8–10,000' (the *Athletic News* estimate). Marindin had inspected the boots of both sides before the game. On the pitch he gave them a two-minute lecture on the rules of the game and the nature of fair play. The contest was played in a better spirit. The tough, physical Renton team were beaten 2–0 through a polished display by the ball-passing artisans. Arthur in particular had a good game. This eulogy was written by 'Jonathan Oldbuck' the unashamedly partisan *Athletic News* Scottish football correspondent not known for his willingness to shower compliments on English team players.

> Wharton is, indeed, a born goalkeeper; he never loses his head, and his hands are always in readiness. His was one of the best exhibitions of goalkeeping I have seen for a long time. Whether considered individually or collectively the team is a magnificent one, and their excellent play is not only the result of hard training.

Oldbuck chastised the 'nobs' of Queen's Park FC who

> were in front of the pavilion on Saturday, and their bearing would have disgraced a Billingsgate fishwoman. They did not disguise

> their chagrin at the Renton boys being snuffed out. The shots they levelled at Mr Sudell, who was in close proximity, were in shocking bad taste, but fortunately they hurt nobody.[8]

Some of those of the Queen's Park hierarchy who had insisted upon the shilling entry had certainly made up for the absence of the 'rough masses'. The amateurs of Queen's Park had been given a second, unexpected and unorthodox chance to take revenge of sorts upon their victors of the first round. Although their mastery of the ball had not matched Preston's, their mastery of the direct, incisive insult was, it seems, excellent. While not wanting to mix with the rough trade, they certainly showed a great ability to ape their supposed atavistic mannerisms.

PNE's fifth round match – they had been given a bye in an earlier round – was a week later against the Old Foresters. An amateur club, they played at Leyton in east London. Before the game referee Charles Crump, vice-president of the FA, inspected the players' boots as was customary. However, he did not feel the need to inspect Old Foresters' boots. This undisguised bias did not auger well. While at Tontine Park and Hampden they had received anti-English abuse. At Leyton they were now subject to class prejudice. On both occasions administrators were involved, if not instrumental. Crump's action conveyed clearly his contempt of (working-class) professionals (from the North). The Manchester *Athletic News* replied to this executive arrogance by laying the facts bare. 'Though a man is an amateur, and speaks with a horrible London accent, it is no guarantee that he will not break the rules whenever he gets the chance.'[9] The oiks from the North had the last kick, winning comfortably 3–0.

Sudell may well have enjoyed, in retrospect, passing the image across his mind of Crump examining the boots that were to stamp out the pretensions of his precious southern gentlemen. Both had served on the FA committee investigating professionalism, with Crump, a chief clerk on the Great Western Railway and president of the Birmingham FA, a firm opponent. He had done his best to continue prohibition by tabling a counter-motion to the one that was eventually accepted: 'The introduction of professionalism will be the ruin of the pastime and it is most unwise to permit it.'[10]

Just four days later – Wednesday 2 March – North End played their fifth round opponents, Old Carthusians, at Kennington Oval, also the venue for the final. The Lancashire club had offered the amateurs £100 to play at Deepdale stadium, unsuccessfully. Carthusians, old boys of Charterhouse school and one of the founder members of the FA, had won in the Challenge Cup in 1881 and were the last southern amateur team left in the competition.

Marindin was again referee. By most accounts the game was a good spectacle. North End won 2–1 after extra time in front of 8,000 people. Arthur's explanation for their success, in an interview with the *Athletic Journal* three months later, argued that the superior fitness of his team had enabled them to cope better with the extra half an hour of play. One assessment argues Preston got through by the 'skin of their teeth'.[11] Most observers thought the game was close. The correspondent of the *Northern Echo*, 3 March 1887, thought Arthur had 'played well', despite conceding his first goal in the competition which was 'unstoppable', 'brilliant' and 'out of his reach'. By any account it was a test of endurance and not the best preparation for the semi-final, three days later.

This penultimate tie of the competition was played at Trent Bridge, Nottingham, the following Saturday, 5 March. Their opponents, West Bromwich Albion, had a formidable FA Cup record. They had been quarter finalists in 1885; and finalists in 1886 losing to Blackburn Rovers 2–0 after a replay. For the third time in two weeks the president of the FA, Marindin, was referee. Thus he had yet another opportunity to evaluate the goalkeeping abilities of Wharton. This should be remembered when we come to assess the claims for an England cap put forward on Arthur's behalf.

In front of a large crowd – gate receipts were £478 – fellow professionals West Bromwich defeated the favourites 3–1. Arthur's display in goal was 'blameless': two of the goals were 'irresistible'.[12] West Bromwich's excellent FA Cup record continued. (In fact they won the Cup in 1888 and 1892. In 1887 and 1895 they were losing finalists.)

The result upset the predictions of the football cognoscenti, though it pleased the referee

> … a staunch disbeliever in Scottish imports. After the game, Marindin entered the Albion dressing room and asked if the team were all Englishmen. Upon receiving the answer 'yes', Marindin presented Albion with the match ball and expressed his hope that Albion would go on to win the Cup.[13]

So ended North End and Sudell's hopes of emulating their arch-rivals Blackburn Rovers in capturing football's most prestigious piece of silver. The *Athletic News*, 8 March 1887, thought that PNE were 'still ... the best team in the world'. The draw had not been kind to them. They had played in Glasgow three times, London twice and Nottingham. Only one tie out of six had been at Deepdale. Their railway mileage must have set a record in itself: while Sudell's hurt pride and deflated ego would have been consoled with the knowledge that at least Blackburn Rovers were not going to get their hands on the trophy – again.

Wharton's journey with PNE was also nearing the end of the track. He would play just two more games. Quite why will be speculated upon: his goalkeeping record had been up to the standard expected of him; and he had performed well even in those games where he had conceded goals.

A talent in demand: Other matches

To celebrate 50 years of Queen Victoria as monarch a 'Festival of Football' was arranged at Kennington Oval, the playing heart of the football establishment, for 12 March 1887. Two exhibition games were scheduled and under the association code North End would play the Corinthians. This gave it a North/Lancashire v. South/London, professional v. amateur, patricians v. plebeians flavour. The match ended 1–1, with Wharton having only two real shots to save, despite facing ten internationals and one international reserve. It was North End's third game in ten days. An earlier game in December 1886 against the same opponents had resulted in a 2–0 win for the paid labourers. It was becoming clear to all who wanted to see that the most accomplished exponents of the game were now those who honed their skills day-in, day-out for a living.

Four thousand tickets, which started at 1/6d, had been sold in advance. Total attendance for the day was 10,700 despite a heavy snow-fall the previous evening. Gate receipts totalled a massive £800. The Prince of Wales was guest of honour despite having refused, five years earlier, to be a patron of the FA. Though the FA, rebuffed but still determined to court royal favour decided, with royal approval, that all the proceeds would go to the Imperial Institute. (The Prince of Wales accepted the offer to patronise the FA in 1902, a year after his accession to the throne as Edward VII.) The destination of the profits did not please the *Northern Echo*, 12 March. Why is not the money going to charitable causes, as was the case with the inaugural Charity Festival held the previous year? 'Can toadyism grovel further?'.

Arthur's eccentric and imaginative interpretation of the role of goalkeeper was expressed to wonderful effect in a New Year's Day/Hogmanay game against Third Lanark of Scotland, at Deepdale. One of the visitors, 'Auld from half-back gave him a hot 'un, [shot] … [Wharton] having to pull the bar down to put the ball over.' In this game 'Wharton did some good things, once fisting the ball away nearly half the field.'[14] Such actions were, by now, Wharton's trademarks.

However it seems his supreme confidence was also beginning to distort his perception of the real power and reach of his sporting talents, admittedly exceptional by any standards. Sometime while PNE were strolling to victory against Glasgow Rangers Wharton and Ross swapped positions.

> Wharton the champion sprinter is not a success as full-back, and is not likely to try that position again … after making several fruitless attempts to stop Fraser and Peacock of the Rangers, he kicked a goal for the Scotchmen (*sic*). This was more than Jack Ross could stand, and Wharton had to go back between the sticks.[15]

Some thought he should not have been playing at Deepdale at all: the Northumberland County FA were expecting him to play for the Newcastle and District representative team against the Corinthians. His non-appearance in Newcastle spurred more than one newspaper hack to pen-prick the young man's conscience. The *Athletic News* stated Arthur had 'promised' to play and that he had written on the Friday preceding the Monday game confirming this intention. Why, when he wrote the following day to cancel his appearance, had he not given a reason? Compounding the wrong, the Newcastle and District secretary had not received the letter until the day of the game, leaving just a few hours to find a replacement. 'Did he [Wharton] not even think it necessary to telegraph?' The tone of admonition continued. 'Considering that Wharton is mainly indebted to Northumberland for his present position in the football world, his conduct requires some explanation.'[16]

The 'debt' referred to was Arthur's selection for Newcastle and District against PNE the previous season, his goalkeeping catching the eye of Sudell. Additionally, Mr Phillips, the Northumberland secretary and presumably the recipient of Arthur's belated letter of Monday morning, had taken a keen interest in Wharton's career. It was he who had travelled up to Glasgow for PNE's first Cup-tie with Renton. Phillips may even have facilitated Wharton's move to North End by acting as an intermediary. Wharton's snub was taken very badly. In light of this, it's reasonable to assume that Phillips ignited the fire of press disapproval by going public with the episode.

As it happened, his replacement, Foster of Rendel FC, played a good game and was more than adequate. The crowd was the best to date for an association match in the city. A week later the 'North' representative team to play the 'South' was announced. Unsurprisingly, Arthur's name was not included. The position of first choice goalkeeper went to R. Roberts of West Bromwich Albion. The reserve goalkeeper was H.J. Arthur of Blackburn Rovers and England. It is worth reminding ourselves at this point that nine months earlier – 20 March 1886 – 'Rambler' of the *Darlington and Stockton Times*, had argued that 'by general agreement' Arthur was the 'best goalkeeper in the North'.[17]

The green stage 'Othello': 1887–88

Wharton played just two games, during the early part of the season, against Burnley and Halliwell. In the 7–2 win over Burnley Arthur was blamed for one of the two. He was 20 yards out of his goal when the ball crossed the goal-line. His mistake in the game against Halliwell, in which he fisted the ball downwards onto a defending team-mate causing an own goal, provoked a hostile response from reporters. The *Athletic News* was 'irritated' by his detached nonchalance – self-control? – bordering on arrogance.

> I have heard Wharton, the 100 yards champion say that he does not know what it is to be nervous. I can quite believe it, for he is the coolest customer that has ever stood between the goal posts. He was positively irritating at Halliwell on Saturday, standing with his arms akimbo, when the ball was almost under his nose. His coolness, however, does not make him a king by any means.

Blood now racing in his expanded vessels, the correspondent concluded, without any sense of irony, that Arthur had put in 'a very amateurish performance'.[18]

The patience of 'Whispers', who authored a gossip column in the *Football News and Athletic Journal*, had also snapped. He went further in the scope of his comment, making a connection between Arthur's intellectual ability and his colour.

> Good judges say that if Wharton keeps goal for the North End in their English Cup tie the odds will be considerably lengthened against them. I am of the same opinion ... Is the darkie's pate too thick for it to dawn upon him that between the posts is no place for a skylark? By some it's called coolness – bosh![19]

Had Arthur bothered to read the piece he might have replied 'tosh!'. A person with the agility of a skylark would be an ideal sticksman. Whatever doubts Wharton's play may have raised about his intellectual abilities – and it was not made clear by 'Whispers' how theatricals that livened play through the use of suspense, imagination and feline athleticism did so – his goalkeeping record of four clean sheets in FA Cup games the previous season stood testimony to his ability. And to that of his defenders and team has a whole.

However there are always those who like their footballers to be without frills. For these, to borrow the refrain from a popular song of the 1950s, it was not what he did but the way that he did it that drew their fire. His style pleased a good proportion of the crowds but did not please the purists. It was his method, not the result it achieved, which got up the nose of scribes such as 'Whispers'. In much the same way as the apparently lethargic insouciance of players such as Matt Le Tissier or Faustino Asprilla today, the crowd-pleasing cheek of Stan Bowles in the late 1960s and 1970s, and Len Shackleton and Garrincha of Brazil in the 1950s, attracted – and still attracts – a similar distrust by contemporary apologists of Charles Hughes type orthodoxy. While the *Athletic News* hack had been mild, initially, in his criticism, he too soon joined the anti-Wharton camp.

> Wharton has been invited to assist the North End in their English Cup tie against either the Wanderers or Everton. An old hand who saw the dusky champion at Stoke on Saturday [playing for

> Durham against Staffordshire] thinks Mr Sudell is making a great mistake in trusting so important a task to so fickle a performer. He did some of the simplest schoolboy tricks, and proved that he is altogether unreliable. Addison, despite want of inches, can give points to 'Othello'.[20]

For nearly three months, up until the third round of the FA Cup on 28 November, there was press speculation that Arthur would turn out again for PNE. He had in fact faced Sudell's side while playing for a North East District's XI on 1 September. Despite retrieving the ball from his goal on six occasions, the Preston boss saw enough positive elements in Arthur's play to select the Darlington student-cum-tutor for the game against Burnley two days later. However, Arthur was not picked for the first round tie against fellow Lancastrians Hyde. The Preston boss thought the game would be easy and it was. But this omission deprived Arthur of adding another honour to his list. PNE won 26–0, setting a record for an FA Cup win that has stood unbroken. Yet Sudell still insisted that for the next two months Arthur 'keep himself in practice for future competitions' [of the FA Cup].[21] If such an instruction was meant to hold out hope of a brighter future it was misleading. Arthur never played for the 'Invincibles' again.

There may have been a number of reasons why. Sudell had made his point to the football establishment with his signing of Wharton: that he could still bring excellent players to the club who were able to play *immediately*. They would just be called amateurs. As well, Arthur may have outlasted his usefulness. At the time of his recall there were reports of a dispute between PNE and the FA over the eligibility for FA Cup ties of the club's other goalkeeper James Trainer. With Addison also on their books it seems North End were considering signing Wharton as a non-playing reserve; an insurance policy against Trainer's ineligibility and the possibility of injury to Addison. In effect this would have prevented Arthur from playing in the FA Cup for any other club. As we have just seen, Addison's case was being endorsed by the *Athletic News* over Arthur's. Sudell, in his own mind, obviously thought Addison good enough cover for Trainer. Additionally, in light of the mill manager's obsession for a 'professional' approach, he may have concluded that Arthur's eccentric, individualist goalkeeping style was increasingly mismatched to the collective pattern of his team's play. As it transpired, neither Addison nor Trainer played in the club's FA Cup final appearance against West Bromwich Albion. The goalkeeping position went to ex-Corinthian and Welsh international Dr Mills-Roberts, another amateur. (Commenting on the latter's form in the final, 'Offside' of the *Northern Echo* thought Sudell would have been better off with Wharton, whom he thought much better in comparison. 'Offside' was to remain a firm proponent of Arthur's virtues as a footballer. It was he who publicised his cause for international recognition.)

From Arthur's perspective his athletics career had reached a plateau of excellence which would have been very hard to maintain had he continued to play football for two clubs. The time demanded by PNE, with their travel up, down and across England and Scotland was exclusive of equal commitment elsewhere, even with technologically advanced 50 miles-per-hour trains. Also, the physical hazards of his position should not be overlooked. Goalkeepers needed to be big, agile, tough and/or stupid. It helped if they had all these characteristics. Arthur was five feet eleven inches tall and weighed 12 stones. He had three of the necessary requirements.

> Besides the courage that has always been required of players in that position, Goalkeepers last Century had to be prepared to withstand a continual physical assault. In fact, assaulting the Goalkeeper was an integral part of attacking play. Prior to 1895, attackers were able to shoulder charge the Goalkeeper whether he had the ball in his possession or not. Obstruction of the Goalkeeper was a standard ploy and used often as away for one attacker to give a colleague a better chance of scoring a Goal.[22]

Of the 11 positions available, that of goalkeeper, with its great risk of injury, was often occupied by those the less brave of us look to when the tables and chairs start flying. The epitome of such a character was William 'Fatty' Foulke. He will land in our discussion later. For Arthur, playing where it hurts, with the undivided attention of numbers of hostile attackers rather than a less exposed position on the wing, meant his football was not compatible with his sprinting. Whether this consideration played a role in his attitude to his custodianship is hard to tell. His sprint trainer was reported to have pressured him not to play football for Rotherham Town, just before a prestigious Sheffield Handicap race in September 1889. (Was Arthur looking for a 'safer' sport with his brief excursion into rugby, which came after his time at PNE?) It seems possible that the risk of physical injury underlay the rationale for many of his eccentricities, such as his habit of standing at the side of the goal, often in a crouched position, out of the way of attackers looking for a shoulder to lean on. When danger threatened his goal he would spring, cat-like, into action. While the reason for such an 'amateurish' approach may seem quite sensible – if histrionic – after scrutiny, it went over the head of observers such as 'Whispers'.

In an interview with the *Cannock Advertiser* on 27 August 1887, immediately after Arthur had set his 120 yards record at the Montpellier track at Cheltenham it was reported that he intended to return to Africa. In two separate interviews, with the *Sheffield Independent*, 11 September 1888, and *Ashton Herald*, 15 February 1896, Arthur cites the latter part of 1887 as the end of his time at Cleveland College. His benefactors would have expected him to have, or be near to, completing his course of studies to pursue the career of teacher or missionary. The *Sheffield* interview states that Arthur opted to run openly for money after his triumph at Cheltenham (at the end of August). Playing again for Preston, though not ideal would have at least kept him aerobically fit during the winter, in preparation for exploits on the track during the summer of 1888. However, PNE played as much football, if not more than nearly any other club. They were always in demand. With a home fixture against the 'Invincibles' a team could almost guarantee a good crowd. The previous season they had played 58 games, starting on 26 August and finishing nearly nine months later on 21 May. (They had played the FA Cup holders, Aston Villa, on 7 May, a month after the Midlanders' win at the Kennington Oval. The Birmingham club fielded the same team but North End beat them 11–1.) It is not surprising that one of Sudell's players told the *Athletic News* correspondent a week earlier that he felt 'overworked'. If Arthur had become a regular member of the side for all competitions, not just FA Cup games and the odd money-spinning friendly, it would have entailed a far greater commitment. Yet if Arthur saw his future outside football – remember he had just won the AAA 100 yards championship for the second year running – it would make more sense to stay and play in Darlington, where exploitation of his body, his skills and his time, would be less exacting and exciting.

NOTES

1. Graham Williams, *The Code War: English Football under the Historical Spotlight* (Middlesex 1994) p. 93.
2. Ibid., p. 91.
3. 24 September 1886.
4. September 1886.
5. *Football Field* (Lancashire) in R.W. Lewis, 'Football Hooliganism in England Before 1914', *International Journal of the History of Sport*, 13, 3 (December 1996).
6. 18 January 1887.
7. Ibid.
8. Ibid., 25 January 1887.
9. 1 February 1887.
10. Williams (1994) p. 91.
11. Geoffrey Green, *The Official History of the FA Cup* (London 1960) p. 40.
12. *Northern Echo*, 7 March 1887.
13. Williams (1994) p. 98.
14. *Athletic News*, 4 January 1887.
15. Ibid., 11 January 1887.
16. Ibid.
17. 20 March 1886.
18. 13 September 1887.
19. 29 October 1887. Quoted by E. Griffiths, director, PNEFC in correspondence with Dr Ray Jenkins, 20 February 1985. Jenkins Papers.
20. 25 October 1887.
21. *Athletic News*, 15 October 1887.
22. Williams (1994) p. 151.

6 *'Wharton for England'*

It was while discussing Darlington's match against Durham College and their Cleveland Cup final against Darlington St Augustine's in February 1887 that 'Offside' reiterated his call, first publicised the previous September, that Wharton should be picked for England. Based solely upon form it was a legitimate plea. Beyond this consideration, according to the meritocratic principle of selection, there should have been few others. Even if we include bureaucratic eligibility criteria such as birthplace precedence would not disqualify Arthur. J.F. Prinsep, an India-born footballer for Clapham, had won a cap in the 1870s. And anyhow, the Gold Coast, like India, was a British colony. Like Prinsep, Arthur too was a 'gentleman'.

'Offside's' timing as Wharton's propagandist was as acute as that of his cause. There had been an England v. Ireland match at Sheffield during the first week of February. The very day Arthur's case was being promoted, England were playing Wales at the Kennington Oval. In both of these matches the 'keeper was H.J. Arthur of Blackburn Rovers. There was still one international to come three weeks hence and it was the most prestigious of the three played at that time, against Scotland at Blackburn. (The venue, H.J. Arthur's home ground, further stacked the odds against Wharton.)

> The English [Football] Association, like many of the smaller county associations, is dominated by a clique who can see no further than their nose. The consequence is that unless the ability of any player is forcibly put before them, there is but little chance of him gaining international honour. Wharton is without doubt one of the most capable goal-custodians in the country, and is undoubtedly deserving of a place in any international team. Therefore it is only just and right that some public expression should be made with reference to his claims.[1]

'Offside' added that he hoped the new North East representative to the FA Council, Mr Reed of Middlesbrough and Cleveland, would voice Arthur's case in a similarly forceful and uncompromising manner. Unfortunately – and as I will argue, shamefully – his plea and that of Reed if he made one, did not penetrate beyond the 'noses' of the FA selection committee. Against Scotland, R. Roberts of WBA, the rival of both Arthurs – H.J. and Wharton – was selected. This was, in reality, Wharton's last chance for an international cap.

The rationale governing selection for an international game was to give good players singular recognition of their talents on a match-by-match basis and not to gather a settled team of component parts that would play co-ordinated football in a complementary fashion over a series of games. Walter Winterbottom, England manager between 1946 and 1962 described this thinking behind the process of choosing that persisted until his time of office.

> We were selecting players for that match, a friendly match against a country, and there was a reward in this: so-and-so has been a great player, it's time we recognized his great ability and let him be in the next England team.[2]

In the seven internationals played prior to 1880, a different goalkeeper was used for each game. Between 1880 and 1887, seven goalkeepers had been used by England in 20 internationals.

In discussion of the merits or otherwise of Wharton's case we encounter incident and evidence that could be interpreted as ambivalent. In support of his cause Francis Marindin – an ex-goalkeeper – and Charles Crump, both senior members of the FA Council, had refereed games in which Arthur had played. In these games for PNE against Renton, Old Foresters, Old Carthusians and West Bromwich Albion there was an abundance of superlatives describing his performances. Further, having played twice at Kennington Oval – against Old Carthusians and the Corinthians – most of the other selectors would have had a chance to look at him. Perhaps they did not feel he was good enough. And/or that his showmanship weakened his strengths. While the evidence does not reveal conclusive proof as to what opinion the selectors had of Arthur's ability, his playing record at this point in his career, as has been detailed, is one of a very effective goalkeeper.

What can be legitimately questioned is the attitude of the selectors to skin-colour. No man of colour played for England until Hong Y. 'Frank' Soo played in unofficial wartime internationals in the 1940s. Wales, by contrast, picked their first Black international in 1931. Obviously the Football Association of Wales had far fewer players to choose from; but they selected Eddie Parris of Bradford nevertheless. In contrast, another Black player of that generation, Jack Leslie of Plymouth Argyle, complained to Brian Woolnough that he had been told by his manager Bob Jack that he had been picked for England only for the offer to be withdrawn because of belated objections to his colour by members of the FA unaware of his ethnicity. 'They must have forgot I was a coloured boy.'[3] It has to be assumed that the nature of the selection process, with each member of the committee arguing the cause of their particular nominee(s), failed to draw attention in this instance to Leslie's complexion. If we accept that Leslie's disappointment was the outcome of a genuine grievance – what would be the point of imagining such controversy? – the attitude of the selectors to the Argyle striker is prejudiced and parochial in the extreme.

'Offside' had not missed the opportunity to link the 'pettifogging parochialism'[4] of his home County FA, Durham, with that of their metropolitan masters. His description was farsighted. 'Parochial' was used subsequently on many occasions to describe the English FA's approach to foreign FAs especially the latter's corporate embodiment, the Federation of International Football Associations (FIFA). Not only could it be small-minded but arrogant and damaging to the well-being and development of the game in Britain. After joining FIFA in 1906 the FA withdrew twice and did not begin to play a full and committed role until 1946. The result of this policy of haughty isolation meant that no England team played in any (FIFA-organised) World Cup until 1950 in Brazil. England's much heralded inaugural appearance – they qualified by winning the British championship – turned humiliatingly sour when centre-forward Joe Gaetjens, a Black Haitian, scored with a header to give the USA their 1–0 and only victory in the finals. Only once have England reached the final itself: at Wembley in 1966. It was nearly 36 years after their first international, against Scotland in 1872, that they played outside the British Isles – versus Bohemia in Prague in June 1908. (Although a group of FA tourists – professional and amateur – did play four games in central Europe in 1899.) The 1950 World Cup finals in Brazil was their first visit ever to South America.

By comparison, professional club sides from England had been visiting the continent since 1904. The FA, judged by the history of their actions in respect of international relations were, it seems, archetypal 'Little Englanders'.

If we accept that 'Offside' was right in his opinion that Arthur deserved an England cap, and cite as supporting evidence: (a) his recruitment by the 'Invincibles'; (b) the fact that it took over 70 years for a person of colour to play for any England representative XI, we are left with the impression that the primary reason Arthur was not selected was antagonism to the pigmentation of his skin and the curliness of his hair. We have seen above why the FA, before the formation of FIFA in 1904 and for a long time after, continued to justify 'Offside's' evaluation of their mindset as 'parochial' with their choice of international opponents. Thus, to the specific charge of blatant class prejudice already levelled by Marindin and Crump in their treatment of PNE must be added one of racism. As in other institutions of establishment power in Britain, such as the Military Chiefs of Staff who also operated a colour bar to officer rank, a Black man did not fit their imagined creation of the racially pure 'Ideal Nation'. Coincidentally, it was another pioneering Black footballer, W.D. Tull, who temporarily broke the bar down in 1917 by becoming the first Black commissioned combat officer in the British Army.

Marindin, a week after 'Offside's' claim on Arthur's behalf, wished WBA success in the 1887 FA Cup final because they were all Anglo-Saxon. This specific remark tells us much about his general attitude regarding the relationship between football, nationhood and ethnicity. As president of the FA his tolerance and acceptance of a Black man playing for the representative XI of England would have been as high as sea level. Unfortunately there is no reason to think this attitude untypical.

The 1886–87 season was the zenith of Wharton's football career. Never again would he play for such an excellent team in such prestigious and high quality matches. No more would his name be suggested for international selection.

'Race', sport and society

For many of the rulers of imperial Britain outdoor-games playing and nation/empire building were complementary activities: to play-the-game conditioned the body and prepared the mind of young men in anticipation of fulfilling their ultimate responsibility and duty as warriors and guardians of 'race', nation and empire. There was ideological harmony between the 'Rules of the Game' as applied to Anglo-Saxon sports, and subjection and governance by the British political elite – home and colonial – of their subjects. Sport had, as one role among many, an overtly political dimension to it. Indeed, the diffusion of Anglo-Saxon, bourgeois values through the playing of sport according to rules, written and unwritten, reflected the values and structure of the UK political system. A large proportion of the British Constitution comprises tradition, custom and convention. Much of the parliamentary system can only be fully understood by the initiated; by those who 'play' within it. According to some constitutional experts the key to real power and success within the political establishment is in that knowledge which can only be acquired from within: gleaned from the secretive workings and nuances of unseen governance.

This structure of formal and informal learning through rules written and rules learned weighs the value of that knowledge heavily in favour of that gained by physical activity. The practical acquisition of (uncodified) moral values – enshrined in the ideal of the 'Gentleman Amateur' – was the quintessential feature of Anglo-Saxon games: the goal was not the back of the net but ascendancy to a higher plane of awareness of one's individual and collective role in life. The real worth of play lay in the symbolism of the event itself: participation for its own sake; the creation of a theatre of honour; to play by the rules; not to seek unfair advantage; collective submission to corporate authority invested in the individual. The *way* the game was played was more important than *why*. Competitive outdoor exercise expressed deeply rooted cultural values that could not be learned simply by reading the rule book. Written rules were only part of the scheme of guidance. Anglo-Saxon cultural values would be transparently expressed in the *nature* of games; and would stand as testament to the cultural superiority of Britain, already the world's economic and political superpower. Such an elevation was, in its turn, a reflection of the superiority of the genetic stock of Anglo-Saxon Britain. Such a view quite easily created a division between those who are acceptable, who fit the ethnic and class profile of this ideology, and the rest, the Outsiders.

Scientific Racism

The confiscation of Africa from Africans in the last quarter of the nineteenth century – 'The Scramble for Africa' – to serve the needs of European capital, coincided, not accidentally, with the beginning of Britain's decline as an economic superpower. Contemporary justifications of colonialism tended to ignore these material causes, proselytising instead a moral agenda. One national broadsheet sought to analogise the activities of the Heroic Sons of Empire with past Great Crusades in the cause of Christianity. One such mission of confiscation was heralded as a new dawn of enlightenment for savage Africa.

> [There] has [been] knit adventurers, traders and missionaries into one band of men under the most illustrious of modern travellers (H.M. Stanley) to carry into the interior of Africa new ideas of law, order, humanity, and protection of the natives.[5]

In this eulogy we find no mention of the overriding preoccupation with competition with other European capitalist nations for profit and new markets. Yet the forced subjection of virtually a whole continent of peoples and the rapacious accumulation and exportation of a considerable proportion of their wealth needed ideological justification. One system of ideas conscripted for this purpose was Scientific Racism, This new body of knowledge, developed during the middle and second half of the nineteenth century in Europe and the United States, attempted to infuse racial theory and discourse – that had categorised the world's populations by distinguishing between 'races' of varying intellectual and cultural maturity – with the irrefutable authority of scientific legitimacy. By applying the methodology of the natural sciences through physiological and philological analysis an objective re-evaluation of the ascribed characteristics of the White, Yellow and Black 'races' would decide their worth to human civilisation once and for all.

The fount of Scientific Racism in Britain was the Anthropological Society of London, organised by James Hunt. The Society, building upon the works of Count de Gobineau, Robert Knox and others, asserted the primacy of 'race', with its human profile of colour and shape and its social profile of class and culture, as a determinant of behaviour. The writings of de Gobineau, Knox and Hunt attempted to revive the theory of polygenesis – that each race of humanity had separate beginnings, there being no common ancestry. In this hierarchical formulation black and brown skinned people were being shoehorned into a vision of distinct human evolutions that devalued non-Whites and their past and elevated the European to the summit of human development. The polygenists asserted that Blacks, and the Yellow 'race' just above them, were unable to reach European levels of civilisation because of their natural inferiority. It was the duty of Whites therefore to act as permanent guardians over their dark, child-like charges. Such views were given credence by contemporary repositories of wisdom like the 1884 edition of the *Encyclopaedia Britannica* which stated authoritatively that

> no full-blooded Negro has ever been distinguished as a man of science, a poet, or an artist, and the fundamental equality claimed for him by ignorant philanthropists is belied by the whole history of the race throughout the historic period.[6]

The validity of this racist discourse – propaganda? – though threatened by Darwin's theory on evolution, archaeological discoveries revealing the pre-history of humanity and evidence of ethnic inter-mixing in Africa and the Americas, continued to influence long after its intellectual legitimacy had withered. In practice, such views were used to reinterpret and reconfigurate histories so that they corresponded to the demands of the contemporary political agendas of powerful social groups and their required visions of the past. This effectively denied any African involvement in the ruins of Great Zimbabwe; lightened the skin and narrowed the noses of the inhabitants of pharaonic Egypt; and encouraged the building of the cultural equivalent of a Berlin Wall between (Arabic) North and (Negroid) Sub-Saharan Africa. South of this Wall, argued the racial supremacists, nothing of important and lasting benefit to humanity had occurred or was ever likely to.

The ethnologists and anthropologists held physical appearance to be a signifier of one's position in the racial hierarchy. The phenomenon of increasing European dominance, influence and hegemony in the affairs of more and more of the world's peoples was explained quite simply as the unstoppable march of history; of the former's natural – therefore cultural – superiority. Twenty-seven years after its 1884 edition had dismissed the possibility of histories of Black peoples the

Encyclopaedia Britannica of 1911 discussed in great detail the (atavistic) characteristics of the 'Negro' (considered the archetype Black). It confounded the uninitiated reader with an array of obscure terms: 'prognathism' (projecting jaw); 'brachycephaly' (short headed); 'platyrrhine' (short, wide nose); 'hypertrophy' (enlargement); 'zygomatic' (facial bone). This was not an editorial oversight. The barrage of unintelligible semantics was designed to underpin the validity of the thesis of Black inferiority by locating the intellectual source of knowledge within the well-spring of *scientific* enquiry. After sharing with the reader its privileged insights it concluded: 'mentally the Negro is inferior to the white ... The mental constitution ... is very similar to that of a child.' And 'after puberty sexual matters take the first place in the Negro's life and thoughts'. However because of their 'dog-like fidelity ... given suitable training, the Negro is capable of becoming a craftsman of considerable skill'.[7]

From being stripped of their histories and their territories, they were now stripped of their status as members of humanity. The practical decivilising of the African that had carried on apace in their continent through the imposition of foreign economic, social and political systems – commodity production, wage labour, private ownership of land, monogamy, centralised autocracy etc. – reached its climax with the animalising of the 'Negro' persona. (This latter development will be discussed at greater length in the final chapter.) With no past, no inalienable territorial rights and their membership of the civilised 'races' of humankind rescinded, no holds were barred in the treatment of the African. While their legal enslavement had ended, the project of economic enslavement of the continent to the needs and wishes of European capital was fully underway during these closing years of the nineteenth century. Britain was a leading player. Its ruling class believed that they were destined, either by divine command or as the most evolved branch of humanity, to recreate and reorder the uncivilised world in their own image. And if this was not possible because of the poor genetic quality of the indigenous people, just to govern.

The practice of colonial government sometimes met the standards it laid down for itself; often times it was a law unto itself. However, with one foul theoretical swoop Scientific Racists were able to square the circle raised by the evident and fundamental contradiction of the practice of imperial conquest with the moral and political codes that directed much commercial, administrative, military and missionary action: the Christian notion of the brotherhood of man and the Liberal concept of human rights, borrowed from Enlightenment thought. A central tenet of Liberalism – an ideology trotted out as the philosophical justification of capitalism *ad nauseam* – stressed the birthright of individuals to do as they please within the law. In respect of economic relations this translated as the right to accumulate unlimited wealth. However, many imperialists – capitalists, officials, soldiers and missionaries – refused to recognise 'natural' rights of any kind in the African. This was the lie at the core of their legitimating ideologies: that the principle of equality, legal or moral, was caste and class specific – applicable exclusively to white-skin males with property. For Scientific Racists this contradiction was explained away with dismissive ease: Africans, as uncivilised, inferior beings are not entitled to claim equality with the Master Race. The development of two separate codes of law for Africans and Europeans in the Gold Coast may be seen as a mediated, legislative manifestation of such a view.

Three lions: Colour, country and the FA

The rapid growth of the British Empire had the effect of thrusting onto the public stage the debate examining the inter-relating concepts of 'race', nation and sport. The FA in London, which increasingly saw itself as a national institution and, as such, a corporate member of the British establishment – we have already noted its courting of royal patronage – identified with the prevailing racialised conception of what 'England' was, what it was about and what it stood for: an Anglo-Saxon nation of teutonic origin propelled – 'burdened' – by its natural pre-eminence to lead the world towards ever greater levels of civilisation. As a consequence, having a brown-skinned goalie for the representative team was just not on, to use a contemporary idiom. The proposition became even more absurd in the minds of the selectors when his eccentricities were included into the discussion. When 'Darkie' swung from the crossbar to prevent a goal, or crouched cat-like in the corner of the goal, he was betraying the animalist behavioural characteristics of a less-evolved sub-species of humanity. In this debate about the racial constitution of the 'Nation' and how this was reflected through sport, the narrative attached to the epithet 'Darkie' explained not only his colour but spoke revealingly of those fixed, less-civilised traits that lay beneath.

During the build-up to the 1996 European Nations championship, held in England, the comedy duo Skinner and Baddiel released a song called 'Three Lions'. It referred to the badge of the England football team. The refrain of the song – 'football's coming home' – echoed the catchphrase used by the hosts of the championship, the FA. The use of African lions to symbolise an English creation – association football – was done without a hint of irony. The original adoption of an animal of Africa as the crest of the FA, to be worn as a badge on the caps and the shirts of the national team was done, probably, without a second thought given to the relevance of the relationship. The association of the lions with the monarchy, the elite of the elite, rather than any symbolic reference to the 'Dark Continent' no doubt influenced the choice. Had Wharton been selected, and worn the three lions on his chest the wearer may, for the first time, have held a legitimate affinity with the emblematic animals.

For the purposes of symmetry the use of the lion could be seen as inappropriate, as yet another feature of Africa and its culture requisitioned, relocated and redefined by 'superior' peoples. Using an animal not found in the wild in Britain as a metaphor for the supposed *intrinsic* heroic qualities of the English character could be seen as stretching the credibility of the emblem's symbolic qualities. It is akin to the landlocked Czech Republic using a haddock as their national badge! Unfortunately an African man sporting African lions on his chest was not possible. The qualities expressed in the animal – strength, courage and pride – were not those that would have been applied to the human inhabitants of that continent, unless they were members of rarefied martial tribes. Thus both the African lion and the African man, in one form or another, were captives through their relocation.

Placing 'Offside's' panegyric in support of Arthur's cause within this colour (in)sensitive social and political context may go some way towards explaining why Arthur was ignored by the FA selectors. Often in such matters the preference of key individuals play an instrumental role. One such was Marindin who, as a former goalkeeper, may not have thought much of Arthur's skills and style of play and presumably made his opinions clear to his colleagues. However, the relationship between ethnicity and selection within the FA can be analysed for a general, corporate trend. It is as a result of this that the accusation of racism is levelled. It could be argued that it would have been difficult for events to have unfolded otherwise. To choose a representative national team must involve an idea of what the 'Nation' is in the minds of the selectors. It has been argued that the type of nation idealised was one that was characterised by ethnic homogeneity. In short, their vision filtered potential candidates through a monochromatic lens: the successful had to be White. An ethnically inclusive, less racialised, more progressive vision of Britain, its histories and cultures would have allowed the selectors a greater breadth of choice and prevented the operation of this colour bar. This more expansive vision would have also helped stifle the incestuous introspection characteristic of football's administocracy. Their rigid, narrow and exclusive sense of the past, their equally restrictive view of their contemporary role and their conservative outlook to the future detrimentally affected not just Wharton, but the culture of football in Britain and proceeding generations of its footballers. While they were men of their time, and as such we should view them in context, there were those – socialists, trade unionists, anti-imperialists, anarchists – who did not limit their vision by prejudices of colour and class.

NOTES

1. *Northern Echo*, 26 February 1887.
2. 'The Selectors', p. 76 in Rogan Taylor and Andrew Ward, *Kicking and Screaming: An Oral History of Football in England* (London 1995).
3. Brian Woolnough, *Black Magic: England's Black Footballers* (London 1983) p. 4.
4. *Northern Echo*, 3 March 1887.
5. *Daily Telegraph*, 22 October 1884, in Thomas Packenham, *The Scramble for Africa* (London 1992) p. 239.
6. 8th edition, p. 318 in Bolt (1971) p. 209.
7. *Encyclopaedia Britannica* (Cambridge 1911), pp. 344–5. Footnote 1 to p. 344 explains how 'Negro' hair is 'unlike true hair and like true wool'. This 'racial' hierarchy didn't preclude sub-types within groups. The Catholic Irish – Celts – were considered to be closer to the Negro than the Anglo-Saxon. See *Nothing But the Same Old Story. The Roots of Anti-Irish Racism*, Information on Ireland (London 1986). For a more positive view of this connection see Ahmed Ali and Ibrahim Ali, *The Black Celts* (Cardiff 1992). There is little doubt that the ideas cited above are highly dangerous when allied with sovereign political power – Apartheid South Africa the most recent example. It's worth noting that such eugenecist hypotheses are again gaining a limited form of academic and political respectability with the publication of *The Bell Curve* by Herrnstein and Murray and the election of openly racist local government administrations in France to name but two worrying examples.

7 *Another field of play: Ethnicity identity and family*

'A brunette of pronounced complexion': Ethnicity and identity

As Wharton became more successful, the focus of increasing public interest, some close to him who saw themselves as promoting his cause claimed him as European. At the annual dinner of the Darlington Cricket and Football Club, 23 December 1886, at which Arthur's colleagues sang his praises, club official Mr T. Watson in a toast to the new AAA sprint champion, reminded the gathering that Arthur was one of their own, 'of north country extraction, his ancestors having sprung from Stockton'[1] (-on-Tees near Middlesbrough). This contrasted with the tone of the majority of the metropolitan press and national sports papers and some local and regional newspapers which frequently referred to Arthur's African inheritance. His public identity as he sought to define it and as others competed to construct it, became a contested area. This was especially noteworthy after his Stamford Bridge triumph. The new sprint champion was 'by no means a representative Englishman in appearance ... [He was] a brunette of pronounced complexion'.

The same report noted the unusual length of Wharton's heel, typical of 'men of colour'.[2] This reference to physiological differences in bone structure was a particular obsession of Scientific Racism, and its preoccupation with anthropometrics – the comparative study of body shape and size. It graphically illustrates the extent to which the detail and ideas of this racial science had floated free from their isolated, academic moorings and permeated the less-rarefied atmosphere of the 'common sense' of society. The *Manchester Guardian*, 5 July 1886, described the new champion as 'South African'; the *Darlington and Stockton Times* was unable to make up its mind. The 10 July issue had Arthur as a 'West Indian student' and 'Darlington youth'. By 18

September the same paper described him as 'a coloured colonial'; the *Sporting Chronicle*, 5 July, thought him 'a gentleman of colour' and 'Darkie'. By autumn 1887 the literary allusions had become a little more imaginative but no less racialised: the 25 October edition of *Athletic News* introduced 'Othello' to the stage.

This readiness to separately categorise Arthur from those around him through frequent allusion to his pigmentation was not accompanied by hard factual detail about his origins, which tended to remain ill-explored and inconclusive. Reporters of the national press, especially those based in London, often referred to Wharton as 'Darkey' or 'Darkie'. Locally there was less inclination to colour-out Arthur in the early stages of his career, though the percolation effect does become apparent during the 1890s when the epithet came to be used more frequently in regional newspapers.

The relationship of Wharton the subject – a Black African sportsman in imperial Britain – to the social and political context in which his actions were situated becomes ever more intense during this last decade of the nineteenth century. The confiscation of Africa and the theft of its natural wealth was accelerating. Real and fictional accounts of the exploits of brave adventurers in the Dark Continent – like Cecil Rhodes and H.M. Stanley – were churned out for domestic readers through the prose and verse of those such as the writers Rider Haggard and Rudyard Kipling. The latter made plain the patriotic duty that befell the Anglo-Saxon young of Britain:

> Take up the White Man's Burden
> Send forth the best ye breed
> Go bind your sons to exile
> To serve your captives needs
> To wait in heavy harness
> On fluttered folk and wild
> Your new caught sullen peoples
> Half devil and half child.[3]

Given the acclaim and popularity of such works as Kipling's jingoistic call, written in celebration of Queen Victoria's 1897 jubilee, it was no accident that the narrative of Arthur's racialisation – media preoccupation with the colour of his skin, the features of his body and his origins – becomes increasingly crude and dehumanising throughout his career. The move to a Lancashire League football club in January 1896 was described locally by allusion to 'new caught' game. 'Stalybridge Rovers have bagged a real nigger as goalkeeper in Wharton, who is none other than the "Darkie" who used to guard the North End citadel.'[4] 'Nigger' Arthur, a short bound and leap up the evolutionary scale from his primate cousins, now captured for the delectation of Stalybridge football folk. (The game hunting analogy was used to positive effect when Arthur left Rovers. The report told how Arthur had been 'lionised'.)[5] However, while the Scientific Racism theorists would have puffed their chests at seeing their ideas flowing freely into popular consciousness, they would not have considered Arthur the genuine article, 'a real nigger'. As a Euro-African he was a racial hybrid. And for these mixed 'race' progeny, argued Edward Long in his *History of Jamaica* (1774) and Hunt and his acolytes at the Anthropological Society 90 years later, the future would dissolve into self-induced oblivion: the biological fusion of Black and White that hybrids represented would cause infertility and eventual extinction. The miscegenous sins of their mothers and fathers would thus be visited upon them with fatal wrath. The proceeding two centuries since this apocalyptic warning to those contemplating bi-tonal union have produced millions upon millions of refutations, one of which is my brother.

A reading of the various newspaper interviews Arthur gave leaves the impression that he was often deliberately ambiguous as to his precise geographical and ethnic origins. Several – in the *Athletic Journal* of 21 June 1887; the *Sheffield Independent* of 11 September 1888, and the *Ashton Herald* of 15 February 1896 – make clear his West African origin, though none refer directly to the Gold Coast by name. He may have thought it preferable to keep this precise detail obscure given the anti-Asante propaganda in the press during the war with that kingdom of 1873–74 and the subsequent war scare of 1881. (There were further uses of military forces in 1896 and 1900, against the Asante.) As well, his formative experiences at school in Britain between 1875 and 1879 – immediately after the war – might have persuaded him to pre-empt any unnecessary prejudice that could follow from coming out with his Gold Coast/Fante identity. That he sometimes emphasised his West Indian and British ancestry becomes understandable. This ambiguity continues. Present historians and sociologists of sport such as M. Watman (1968), P. Lovesey (1979) and E. Cashmore (1982) have persisted with attributing a West Indian nativity – 'Jamaican' or 'Trinidadian' – to Wharton.

This off-track contest fought by Arthur between 1886 and 1902 to be defined primarily by his on-track (field and road) achievements suffered a cruelly ironic twist with his application – dated 16 August 1893 – for a position with the Gold Coast Government Service. The posts for which he had applied – government clerk or inspector – were paid at £250 a year and 'entirely in the hands of natives'.[6] The wages, in amount, would not have been much better than his earnings as a footballer for Rotherham Town, though in real terms such a sum would surely have greater buying power in West Africa than in Britain. Arthur was rejected, in part, because he was a gentleman runner, this despite the fact that the status of 'noted amateur sportsman' was soon to become a prerequisite for entry in the colonial civil service.

The wage of the positions applied for, though probably ensuring a better quantity of life than in South Yorkshire, seems to have been less important than the status, nature and location of the work. Working for the colonial government, like his brother Charles, with its relative, pensionable security would have been considered a respectable occupation among the Fante elders. Though these qualitative gains would be at the expense of Arthur's status – in Britain – as a sports celebrity. This fame went largely unnoticed by the Euro-African population, especially the elite of Accra and Cape Coast, among whom modern sports did not have the cultural significance and worth attributed to them. His mother's brother, newspaper proprietor F.C. Grant, was in a position to publicise Arthur's sporting triumphs through the *Gold Coast Times*. Yet, the Rev. F.C.F. Grant of Kaneshie, Accra, Arthur's nephew and a direct descendant of the newspaper baron, in an interview with Ray Jenkins in September 1985, suggested that his uncle's achievements were unknown or that side of the Atlantic. The startled incredulity and pride with which some African listeners responded to BBC radio's World Service 'Outlook' and 'Sports International' programmes of May 1996 and January 1997 respectively after 'Football Unites – Racism Divides' discussed Arthur's career, support Grant's comments.

Had Arthur asked for a job, his uncle, as a wealthy entrepreneur, owner of an import and export business as well as the *Gold Coast Times*, would surely have been in a position to offer something to his nephew had he a mind to. He may have viewed favourably such a request as part-return on the money he had given for Arthur's education in Britain. Annie, Arthur's mother, was also in business, running a hotel in Cape Coast. She might have been able to find her son employment; and may well have wanted to have all her three surviving children close by. (Was it through working in the hotel that Clara, as a young, beautiful woman, excited the gossiping tongues that damned her brother?) However, what does appear and reappear as a consistent theme throughout Arthur's life is his determination to forge an identity through his own labours without an over-reliance on the patronage of others. Whether he stayed in Yorkshire or returned to the Gold Coast with his wife Emma it would not be with flat cap in hand. If Rotherham FC, who were being difficult, continued to be so, he would go elsewhere. And if going elsewhere meant West Africa he would do it on his own terms, without asking favours from his family. In reality there may have been no favours on offer. His mother and F.C. Grant had been 'strongly opposed'[7] to his becoming a professional runner.

There may have been another, hidden, underlying factor weighing on Arthur's mind at this point in his life: his fathering of one, possibly two daughters by Emma's sister, Martha. The evidence is circumstantial and inconclusive. If true, in part or whole, there may have been pressing personal reasons for Arthur and Emma to leave Rotherham. We will return to this *ménage-à-trois*.

Gold Coast Governor F.M. Hodgson, with the assistance of the Colonial Office in London, rejected Arthur's application. The official explanation, in a letter sent to Arthur dated 28 December 1893, cited his 'ineligibility' through lack of suitable training for the posts available, adding that there would be little chance of any opportunities arising in the future. A classic 'don't call us we'll call you' response. One of the positions mentioned – for which Arthur was listed as inadequate by Hodgson in his reply to Lord Ripon's secretariat at the Colonial Office who were dealing with the application – was 'Schoolmaster Government School'. Yet in an interview given to the *Ashton Herald*, 15 February 1896, Wharton said his last days at Cleveland College were 'in the capacity of teacher'. Unfortunately the PRO have not made available the original application. The document would have provided Arthur's curriculum vitae in his own hand. Unofficially, for the eyes of contemporary civil servants only, three reasons for rejection were circulated: the Colonial Office in London considered his reputation and status as ex-'100 yards amateur champion runner of England' 'inappropriate'; from Hodgson at Government House in Accra the drunkenness of his brother Charles, and the 'life of ill-repute'[8] of his sister Clara. The political executive and colonial bureaucrats wanted it both ways: Arthur was condemned through the alleged actions of his siblings (the shadow of biological determinism casting its spectre!); yet his obvious *difference* from his brother and sister – as 100 yards record holder – was also used to damn him.

To approach an understanding of why Arthur was denied, we have to strip away the righteous moral veneer – what exactly did the alleged behaviour of his brother and sister have to do with a man who was living on another continent? – used by Hodgson and the Colonial Office to gloss over the informal policy of Anglicisation of the Gold Coast civil service that was evolving. After the conclusion of the Anglo-Asante war, the enlarged colonial state demanded an expanded bureaucracy. Within ten years 43 new senior posts had been established, of which the elite were based in Accra. Lesser officials, such as District Commissioners, tax officers, judicial personnel and police, were distributed along the coastal belt. Nine of these were allocated to Euro-Africans. By 1893 there were 80 senior posts yet still only nine were held by Euro-Africans. Most of the latter tended to be concentrated in the lower echelons of the service as menial clerks and manual workers, with salaries ranging from £36 to £200 per year. Posts within this pay scale were held exclusively by 'natives', said the servant who replied to Arthur, '... promoted step by step, and [it would be] *unfair* (my emphasis) to deserving officers any person not already in the service being placed over their heads'.[9]

With his education Arthur would have qualified for any number of positions. Had a low-paid job been offered, it is unclear what he would have done given both its status and the relatively good combined-earnings in England received from football, cricket (and licenseeship of the Plough Inn, Greasebrough from September 1893). Although a return home, even under such conditions may have been attractive, it would have been an embarrassment to himself and his upper-middle class family to return to a menial position given the original reason for his exile. Ironically, while it was the actions of members of his family that had brought him to England, it was also the (perceived) actions of members of his family that prevented Arthur returning on his terms.

Using Arthur's athletic excellence as a reason not to recruit him also flowed against the developing thrust of colonial appointment policy and practice. Odette Keun on her travels in Anglophone Africa in the 1920s noted that the colonial administrators were young and university educated, with 'their athletic record and their physique being taken into consideration [on appointment]. Many of these civil servants were in their time … well known cricketers and football players'.[10] The Warren Fisher Committee on Colonial Service appointments recommended in 1930 that the Colonial Office should look for 'vision, high ideals of service, fearless devotion to duty born of a sense of responsibility, tolerance and above all the team spirit'.[11] This, they thought, would have best been inculcated on the games field, preferably at public school and Oxbridge. The Gold Coast annual confidential report on political officers in the Service in the 1930s contained the specific question: 'Is he fond of games or sports generally?'[12] Participation in sport, the colonial administrators argued, gave a person quality of character that would be needed for a successful career, especially valuable early on when many new appointees would be posted up-country. Between 1930 and 1939, 90 per cent of the recruits to the Gold Coast civil service had achieved distinction at sport. How many would have been world record amateur sprint champions; or professional runners/footballers; or, more revealingly, Black? The attitude of Lord Ripon in London and Hodgson in Accra was consistent in two respects: with the unspoken policy agenda of Anglicisation of the Gold Coast Government Service; and the transparent hypocrisy of colonial theory and practice – in this instance utilising the concept of 'fairness' in public correspondence and acting upon altogether different emotional, arbitrary reasons in private.

Fair and just practice was not a quality of government characteristic of British West Africa. Indeed between 1878 and 1882 the administration had put in place a racist legal system. The new order of wig and gown apartheid reserved local, customary law for Africans and incorporated English law for Europeans. The dual structure not only denied equality before the law for all subjects, but also formally differentiated and categorised the population of the Gold Coast by ethnicity.

British administration had been condemned for its ruthlessness by the Aborigines Protection Society (APS). This was not an anti-imperialist pressure group. They were pro-capitalist, Quaker in origin and based in London. They wanted enlightened, humanitarian government of the colonies, rather than naked economic exploitation. 'Almost the only object for which England holds the Gold Coast and our other

West African possessions is the advancement of trade with the natives for the benefit of English merchants.'[13] Indeed, it would be in the interest of British capitalists, argued the APS, if some semblance of just governing was systematised. Good government was necessary to the efficient development of commerce. It was not the selfish materialism that caused concern but the way in which this was being facilitated.

The Society recorded killings of Africans by government officials and militia: four 'natives' died after 20 in total were given 72 lashes each for the theft of *one* sheep from colonial official Mr C.E. Akers. (A punishment reminiscent of the judicial and corporal punishment regime of eighteenth-century Britain.) Mr Akers was subsequently convicted of assault with intent to do bodily harm. He was fined £5 and bound over to keep the peace for six months. Next to this account of the death of one animal and subsequent retributary sacrifice of four men in the APS journal *Transactions of the Aborigenes Protection Society* is that of the 2,000 inhabitants of the 'deadly' and 'utterly uncared for' ghetto of Moree, four miles to the east of Cape Coast Castle who rebelled against the colonial authorities in February 1899. Over 40 were killed and more injured by the authorities in putting down the revolt. The people of the town had demanded their taxes be used, at least in part, on civic improvement of their destitute lives. Five years earlier, in his closing sentence for the Blue Book – the annual report of each colonial secretary – the Gold Coast governor wrote, 'The people are beginning to feel and appreciate the benefits of civilisation.'[14] In the first decade of the new century Empire Day – a celebration of the progressive influence and achievements of British imperial rule – was instituted in the Gold Coast.

An unsuited sportsman?

If we look at Arthur's life solely from the perspective of his status as a sportsman rather than colonial subject, the relatively few years spent in the Gold Coast may be seen as a fortunate accident of circumstance. Ray Jenkins (1990), who first brought the exploits of Arthur Wharton to public notice, outlined five 'prerequisites' that would be expected to characterise the individual and social profile of a successful sports competitor. First, good health and an untroubled medical history. In the context of the contemporary Gold Coast, those more likely to possess sound physiologies, according to the prevailing views of the time, were the martial Asante of the interior forest zone rather than the coastal Fante and Euro-Africans. However, it could be argued that those such as Arthur who had survived the pestilential climate into adolescence, had durable constitutions well suited to sport. Second, a relatively stable social and political environment in which structured, competitive sport can flourish. This was not true of much of the periods – 1865–75, 1879–82 – when Arthur lived at home. The Asante uprising of 1869–72, the Anglo-Asante war of 1873–74 which led to an influx of refugees into Cape Coast and a disease epidemic, the Asante war scare of 1881 and the uncertainties caused by the colonisation of Africa generally were not conducive to social and political stability. Third, access to sports clubs, teams and coaching. Opportunities for Euro-Africans for playing modern sports existed but were limited. A limitation imposed by both Europeans and Euro-African elders, many of whom discouraged membership and participation, intent instead on maintaining social and ethnic distance and exclusivity. Four, being part of a sporting sub-culture. There was inter-generational conflict over the place and value of British outdoor sports in Euro-African society. The consensus among the elders of the Euro-African elite was that educational achievement not sporting success was the means to personal and collective advancement. F.C. Grant, patriarch of the extended Wharton family, did not encourage sport among the young. (However, given the reputation his sons held as cricketers he appears to have exercised his authority in a benign or inefficient manner.) The fifth and final prerequisite was an empathy with Britain and the value system of its dominant – bourgeois – culture. In particular those values that elevate and cherish the importance of sport. A common interest in British outdoor competitive sports would engender a pan-empire cultural linkage between all sports participants of whatever class, colour or creed. This connection has been labelled by some historians of sport the 'Cultural Bond'. According to this concept sport has primarily an ideological function, its aim to tauten the political chains that captivate subject peoples by diffusing the cultural values of their metropolitan masters, and reinforce economic domination and inequality by instilling a sense of a common identity and unity – an *esprit de corps* – (with their colonisers) that begins on the playing field and translates with ease to the battlefield, workshop and farm.[15]

That many modern British sports, irrespective of their symbolic or political role, have survived and flourished – and in the case of football been nourished by – export is indicative of their inherent strengths. Association football *becomes* 'beautiful' wherever it is played. It is the players which fashion its beauty; who graft their own cultural forms onto its robust stem. This quality of versatility, of transmutation, allows football to appeal to passions the world over because the passionate have been able to remould and redefine the sport – the art? – without destroying its intrinsic vitality. Tony Mason (1995) in his discussion of football in Latin America notes the elevation in that continent of the *malandro*: the rascal (footballer) who brought the wit, nous, spontaneity and unpredictability of the ghetto street into his play. Pelé, Garrincha, Maradona and Asprilla all exemplify the qualities of the *malandro*. The depth of their technical ability and unworried confidence in its creative application are able to wrench out uninhibited flailings of exhilaration and soul-deep despair from even the most reserved of watchers. Such displays are appreciated and encouraged more in South America than Europe. Yet a European lover of football will recognise the beauty of such play and the validity of the player's icon status. The malleability of football, the chameleon-type quality it has to accommodate and reflect the distinctive texture of place and people is also the very reason why ideological hegemony by one particular group – those who hold controlling power in the game – will never be able to influence fully and without resistance the street people who both play and pay. The virility and strength of football are testament to the struggle that continues to this day over those values represented in and through it. Without the potential and ability for football to reflect, through its structure and form – in the way it is organised and played – the conflict and tensions of classes and cultures, it would not be universal.

The history of the relationship between sport and colonialism is dotted with proud moments of both practical and ideological resistance by indigenous participants to the ulterior agendas particular groups of colonialists had in fostering football, cricket, rugby and tennis. In Bulowayo, Rhodesia – now Zimbabwe – for two years between 1947 and 1949, African footballers fought to reclaim control of their affairs after the White-run city council decided to take over the administration of their game. This struggle became symbiotically entwined with that of African workers involved in industrial disputes in the city. The kicking-back by the footballers was 'the first mass popular demonstration by the urban African populace against the [city] Council in

Bulowayo's settler history'.[16] The kicks were hard, strong, numerous, persistent and victorious. The revolt was led by Sipambaniso Manyoba, the organising secretary of the African Federation of Trade Unions, executive member of Football Association and captain of the Bulowayo Red Army team. The defeat of the White councillors heightened tensions in the workplace and shifted the balance of class forces from the European employers towards African employees. This success, argues Stuart (1989), provided the organisational platform for the launch of the general strike of African workers in 1948. Football in late-1940s Bulowayo was the active forum, outside of the workplace, for men to continue their political struggles in another form within an environment of class and inter-tribal solidarity. Success in this realm engendered confidence to fight employers and vice versa.

Immediately before and after the second world war similar struggles over the control of football were occurring, most notably in Nigeria and French Equatorial Africa. They too were about more than who controlled fixture arrangement, access to pitches and the like. In Nigeria, as in Rhodesia, the organisation of the game mirrored the social and ethnic structure of wider society. Despite the overwhelming predominance of African players and teams, British expatriate merchants and civil servants in Lagos ran affairs. When these administrators selected a team to tour Britain in 1949 accusations were made that players were picked for their suitability as acceptable representatives – to the metropolitan elite and British public, in that order of importance – of benign colonialism rather than for their merits as footballers. In other words, the usual principle of meritocratic selection was replaced by the questions: How will he perform off the field? Is he sufficiently Europeanised? This controversy filled the pages of Nnamdi Azikiwe's pan-Africanist *West African Pilot*. Azikiwe – Zik – organised football teams as part of his 'Zik's Athletic Club' – ZAC. Members and participants, hoped Zik, would be attracted to and unified by the club's nationalist, anti-colonialist philosophy. Armed with such unity of purpose members could build communal – African – confidence by defeating colonial teams. And in this way complement workplace industrial action and mass action on the streets.

Azikiwe consistently complained that his best players were poached by the European-led teams. Further, that this was coherent policy – a conspiracy – designed to stunt the political ramifications of nationalist sporting success, and in the process castrate the virility – and in turn, the appeal – of their liberationist rhetoric. Zik's unpopularity with the authorities came to a head during the General Strike of 1945, in which he played a prominent role. He accused the British of a much darker conspiracy – of trying to assassinate him. Specimen evidence of a kind is the 1945 Christmas greeting from Arthur Richards, Governor of Nigeria 1943–47 to his friend Philip Cunliffe-Lister, First Earl of Swinton, with the comment 'it is time to go for Zik'.[17] Unsurprisingly no ZAC players were chosen to visit England in the autumn of 1949.

At the beginning of 1936 during a match held under the auspices of the (European administered) Native Sports Federation (NSF) in Brazzaville, capital of French Congo, an African footballer 'Makossa' broke his leg. He later died from his injury. In response, the NSF decreed that in future all Africans would have to play barefoot. 'Shoes encourage African players to substitute brutality for skill.'[18] A group representing the African footballers of Brazzaville protested about the decision to Governor-General Reste. Not only did they outline the difficulty such a decision would cause practically, they also had the temerity to question the parameters of the jurisdiction of the colonial NSF over indigenous players. The issue (and its outcome) defined in this way, became much more serious. The Governor tongue-lashed the Uppity Blacks: they would just have to accept the decision of the NSF. But the furore over the death of Makossa and the arrogant indifference of the Governor to this tragedy, and to the concerns of African footballers generally, led to a fight at field level which became anti-imperialist in flavour. Congolese players simply refused to affiliate to the NSF. Within two years, by 1938, the controlling body of football that symbolised autocratic colonial rule had died through neglect.

Football – in the colonial and non-colonial world – is a site of struggle: over the values invested in it; about the way it should be played; and, most importantly, about who should control it. This contest can be articulated through the individual in the attitude of mind a player brings to his game. Arthur was considered an eccentric because of his style of play which some saw as unprofessional, and a militant because of his unwillingness to be pushed around by the ruling bodies of his sports and his employees. A modern example might be Robbie Fowler of Liverpool FC who was punished by UEFA in 1996–97 for parading in front of supporters a 'political' slogan on a T-shirt in support of striking Liverpool dockers; and, in the same season – and almost at the same time – applauded by the same body for saying publicly that he should not have been awarded a penalty during a match with Arsenal. UEFA ruled that the T-shirt incident violated the ban on using football to make political statements. (A rationale that defines this as 'political' while reserving and restricting live and electronic access to top level football for the affluent and lucky, while simultaneously impoverishing the majority of professional clubs, as not political, is hard to fathom.) The second incident violated the professional code of silence in such matters. Fowler should not have admitted to the referee that Seaman, the Arsenal goalkeeper, had not touched him. Yet both actions were subversive in that the Liverpool forward broke official rules, upset customary practice and undermined the authority of the referee and instead sought to impose his own interpretation on matters. His behaviour has an organic link with colonial footballers. The scale, context and stakes may be vastly different but the quality and symbolism of Fowler's actions reach back with unconscious empathy to his African fellow practitioners. They too refused to accept the over-arching authority of their (European) masters and sought to refashion the game to reflect and articulate more closely their concerns and aspirations.

In light of this tradition of resistance there is reason to argue that the young Wharton and other rising-generation Gold Coasters, by playing modern British games, did not necessarily internalise the notion of the 'imperial bond'. We can point also to the pan-Africanism and anti-imperialism of many influential Gold Coast Euro-Africans, not least F.C. Grant and his editor Timothy Laing at the *Gold Coast Times*. While they may not have looked with a favourable eye upon the wardrobe of new, alien sports unpacked from the cultural baggage of their young after educational sojourns abroad, they recognised that liberationist ideas of nationhood and sovereignty which they themselves had imbibed and sought to realise, were prominent articles of intellectual clothing also unfolded from the same collection of baggage. Once again it boiled down to utilising for The Cause what was useful or beautiful and discarding that which was neither.

Going pedestrian: The proletarianisation of a gentleman runner

Arthur's decision to run for money – to become a pedestrian – taken in spite of 'his mother and relatives [being] strongly opposed'[19] represented an attempt unique so far in his life to create a professional identity of his own choosing.

The timing – only three years after he vowed not to go professional – could have been due to a number of reasons, the most obvious being the closure of Cleveland College at the end of the 1888–89 academic year. The institution had become unviable as a business. Competition for pupils had intensified with the opening of the new state-assisted Queen Elizabeth Grammar School in 1878. Had Brooks, the principal of Cleveland College, given an early warning of the closure it might have brought forward familial deliberations over Arthur's future. He was 23 years old in October 1888. As a student in England for nearly six years Arthur could have reasonably been expected by his mother and uncle to return to the Gold Coast to assume his predestined role as Professional Euro-African, with all the political, cultural and communal responsibilities this demanded. In so doing, Arthur would have retraced the footsteps of his cousins four years previously, and his and their parents before them. We have already encountered the newspaper report and interview given after his success at Cheltenham in 1887, stating that he was 'about to return to his native land – Africa'.[20] This suggests that his prospects were being given detailed consideration by all interested parties – Arthur, Annie, F.C. Grant, Brooks – as early as 1887.

Had the impending closure of Cleveland College not been announced in the summer of 1888 and Arthur was merely expressing a preference in the Cheltenham interview, becoming a pedestrian – as opposed to earning money from surreptitious betting – might have been the consequence of a determination to act more independently. Up to the spring term of 1888 his education was being paid for by remittances sent from the Gold Coast, despite his own material success on the sports fields and racing tracks, where admittedly the rewards were prizes rather than money. It should be added in qualification that if Arthur was not earning undeclared amounts from betting and inducements – appearance money – from promoters he would have been one of few amateurs not to have done so. Given his entrepreneurial family background – not to mention the other sports in his life – there is a likelihood that reimbursement of his 'expenses' more than covered his actual outlay. While his mother Annie and his uncle, F.C. Grant, may have been quietly impressed and inwardly proud of his achievements the prospect of their investment withering on the vine as Arthur chanced a career as professional athlete/footballer/cricketer would have vexed them, not just because the dramatic change in vocational direction would mean a waste of money so far invested. This may have been acceptable if it provided him with the platform – albeit abroad – to further the interests of Gold Coast Euro-Africans. What may have been harder to live with was Arthur's apparent *de facto* rejection of his familial, ethnic and political obligations by staying in Britain *and* following a sports career. In so doing he would have to make an independent living. The ultimatum, then, from his benefactors may have been relatively simple and straightforward: return home or we stop funding you.

From inside the Gold Coast Euro-African community Arthur's action may have been seen as unpatriotic: turning his back on his duty to 'His People' in pursuit of his own selfish desires. From Arthur's perspective there was internal pressure from his family to complete his studies, pass his exams, qualify for his chosen profession and return home; and external pressure from trainers, promoters, peers to commit himself to athletics. (There may have been similar 'external' pressure in the football dimension of his life.) If he succumbed to the internal agenda of his mother and patriarch uncle he would have to set aside fame, fitness and the potential of his little 'fortune' in prizes being transformed into something greater.

His dual roles of scholar and sportsman did not sit happily together. His achievements on the sports field limited his ability to devote time to his studies, further enlarging the distance between himself and his family in the Gold Coast. While Arthur was setting athletic records for narrowing the relationship between distance and time, these achievements paradoxically lengthened the distance between himself and his family. His – Pyrrhic? – victories, therefore, enforced a dual reliance upon: one, the economic rewards of a sports career that by its nature could only bring short-term success; two, all those associated with it, both in its production and consumption: backers, trainers, promoters, officials, supporters, readers of sports news, bookies and punters.

It is not surprising that Arthur rejected the career path mapped by his family benefactors. His lack of qualifications, while a disappointment after five and a half years at college, was not an insurmountable obstacle to securing a 'respectable' position, given the business interests of his uncle and mother. Pedestrianism was chosen because it empowered Arthur. For the first time in his life he could be his own man, make decisions for himself that relied upon his own actions – his running – which would bring independent money.

Professionalism was to have a lasting effect upon the quality of his life. Initially, it may have been a short-term expedient: to win a relatively large amount of money quickly. (Eventually to take back to the Gold Coast?) A condensed biography in the *Sheffield Daily Telegraph*, 11 September 1888, said the pedestrian had moved to the city the previous April but would leave for 'Africa' soon with running-mate Billy South, although it added both would 'probably return to England'.

Not playing the game? Rotherham and family

Arthur's application to join the Gold Coast Government Service in August 1893 was made before the start of his third season with Rotherham Town FC. The summer had been troublesome and worrying. He was in contractual dispute with the club and had not resigned. As well, his wife's sister, Martha, was just five weeks away from giving birth to Nora. The relevance or otherwise of this will be discussed shortly. He had also applied to become licensee of the Plough Inn public house at 23 Greasebro' Road, Thornhill, Rotherham – which he took over at the end of September – having recently left the Albert Tavern, his first pub, after a year's occupancy. It is clear then, that during the summer of 1893, Arthur was actively considering alternative and secondary ways of earning a living. Why? His dispute with his football employers may throw light on a possible cause. This will be discussed in Chapter 8. As influential, possibly more so, is the nature of his relationship with his wife's sister.

Arthur's first known address in Yorkshire was 21 Greasebro' Road, Rotherham. This is given on his certificate of marriage to Emma Lister, a local girl of 1 Rawmarsh Road, Rotherham. Greasebro' and Rawmarsh Roads meet at a junction at which point Arthur's father-in-law Thomas, a master plumber and glazier, had a shop. Arthur played cricket professionally for Greasebro' in 1889, which suggests he was living in the vicinity of Greasebro' Road, if not in it, a year before his marriage. It is not known how the couple met.

As well as her sister Martha, Emma had a brother, George. Just under eight months after Emma and Arthur's marriage at the parish church of Masbrough on 21 September 1890, Martha – in domestic service at nearby Barnsley – gave birth to her first daughter on 6 May. She was named on the birth certificate as Minnie *Wharton* Proctor. It is not known why she was given Arthur's surname. Indeed the fact was kept secret. Two and a half years later Martha gave birth to another daughter, Nora Proctor. No father was registered. Martha gave her surname as Yates. Nora's daughter, Sheila Leeson, believes a George Yates may have employed Martha as housekeeper, though she has no documented proof. He may even have been the father of Nora. It was not unusual for unmarried female domestic servants to semaphore the consequence of their employer's exploitative sexual gropings in this coded way. It was a hidden, unspoken-of tyranny which was not confined to an unfortunate few.

Martha was already mother to Ben Marsh, born in 1882, from a marriage that did not last. All three children were eventually taken from Martha by her parents, Thomas and Hannah, who assumed the parenting role. Shunned rejection of the errant single-mother by most of her family increased the pain and isolated suffering of Martha's loss. There was no partner for mutual comfort. In his will, Thomas left his grandchildren 'Minnie Proctor Yates' and 'Nora Proctor Yates' £40 in the trust of his son George, towards their maintenance and education. The closest surviving relatives in Britain to Arthur Wharton are the three daughters of Nora of whom Sheila Leeson lives, appropriately, directly opposite Millmoor the stadium of Rotherham United FC.

The mystery as to: why Minnie was given Wharton as her middle name; why this was subsequently erased so as not to feature in Thomas Lister's will; the identity of Nora's father, opens up the possibility of Arthur being the father of Minnie, and Nora even. Minnie was described by her niece Sheila Leeson as 'swarthy skinned'. Further, the complex web of relationships within the extended family seems to support this view and draws sharply Arthur's profile into the frame as 'likely suspect'. On Emma's death – 21 April 1944 – Minnie bought the burial plot and gravestone at Masbro' cemetery and was later interred alongside her aunt. Emma, it has to be assumed, did not want to be buried with Arthur at Edlington; nor did she make any provision for a headstone to be placed at her husband's grave in the 13 years between their deaths. Was this bond of loyalty between Minnie and her aunt Emma premised upon the notion of a shared understanding of being wronged by the same man? In contrast, Minnie's sister Nora 'had no time for Aunt Emma'.[21] Because Emma refused to confirm with Nora the identity of the latter's father (so preventing a (loving) relationship?) Nora refused to talk to any of her children about who their grandfather may have been.

One of the causes of Arthur's death was epithelioma, a form of cancer. The second contributory illness recorded on his death certificate was syphilis, a sexually transmitted disease. (Had he been putting 'it' about as a young man?) Before the effects of epithelioma began to show – an enlarged nose and tumerous growth on one side of his face and neck – he was physically attractive, had confidence, was self-possessed and travelled. His status would also have made him attractive to some women. He would have needed a great deal of self-restraint not to have been sexually active.

For whatever reason Emma had no children. In contrast, Arthur's parents had ten. Did the outward appearance – embarrassment – of infertility affect his sexual behaviour? Did he feel his identity as a (virile) man undermined by the absence of young Whartons? Was he determined to have children come what may? It is not possible to answer with confidence any of these questions; to know conclusively why he and Emma never produced. If he was the father of Martha's daughters, the biological 'problem' – for want of a better word – of procreation lay with Emma. In the Gold Coast, with its numerous cultural influences – indigenous, Islamic and Christian – being sexually active outside marriage would not have been considered as grave a cultural violation of morality as in Britain, dominated as it was by a bourgeois moral code obsessed with repressing and inhibiting sexual behaviour. Not everybody felt bound by the rules; especially the employers of domestic servants, one of the largest group of workers in late Victorian Britain. Having children, whether in Britain or the Gold Coast, as well as an investment in the future survival of the species, bestowed a badge of fertility on the progenitors that elevated their social standing in comparison to those married couples without. Could it have been the case that Arthur's 'field of play' was not confined to competitive outdoor sports; that when it came to private, indoor activities Arthur was as expressive of his emotions, and as captivating a personality as he was in his more public pursuits? Or was he simply exploiting both women for his own ends?

A number of possible strands of evidence have been exhibited linking Arthur to Martha and her daughters. The firmest is that suggested by the middle name of Wharton on Minnie's birth certificate. It is also the most intangible. Further, it seems to be corroborated by the oral history of the family which has passed the intrigue down through successive generations of the Lister-Proctor-Leesons. The latter did not know until 1996 that Minnie had the name Wharton; or that Nora had no father entered on her birth certificate. Only in the course of recent research into their family history, by various members of the family, were these skeletons in the closet revealed. Nora's attitude to Emma leaves the feeling that some have taken their secrets to the grave. It is up to you, as reader and brief excursionist into this subterranean world, whether you want to name these skeletons. Sheila Leeson feels confident that 'swarthy skinned' Minnie was the daughter of Arthur. She is less certain, though still persuaded, that her mother too was Arthur's daughter. While I write – January 1997 – Sheila's grandson Liam is the South Yorkshire schools under-13 cross-country champion!

NOTES

1. *Darlington and Stockton Times*, 25 December 1886.
2. 'The Referee', as reprinted in the *Darlington and Stockton Times*, 17 July 1886.
3. In Tony Bogues *et al.*, *Black Nationalism and Socialism* (London 1979) p. 65.
4. *Northern Daily Telegraph*, 18 January 1896 in Berry (n.d.) p. 48.
5. *Ashton Herald*, 29 December 1900.
6. PRO, CO 96/238/2044, 2 November 1892.
7. *Sheffield and Rotherham Independent*, 11 September 1888.
8. PRO, CO 96/238/2044. Also in Jenkins, 'Salvation for the Fittest? A West African Sportsman in Britain in the Age of New Imperialism', *International Journal of the History of Sport*, 7, 1 (May 1990) p. 50.
9. Ibid., Jenkins.
10. Odette Keun, 'A Foreigner Looks at British Sudan' (1930) in Anthony Kirk-Greene, 'Imperial Administration and the Athletic Imperative: The Case of the District Officer in Africa', in W.J. Baker and James A. Mangan (eds), *Sport in Africa* (London 1987).
11. 'Committee on the System of Appointment in the Civil Service' Cmnd. 3554, 23, in Kirk-Greene, op. cit., p. 92.
12. Kirk-Greene, op. cit., p. 93. See also Henrika Kuklick, 'The Imperial Bureaucrat: The Colonial Administrative Service in the Gold Coast 1920–1939' (1979), in Kirk-Greene, op. cit.
13. *Transactions of the Aborigenes Protection Society* 1890–96, 4, 1, p. 79.
14. See J.A. Mangan, *The Cultural Bond: Sport, Empire, Society*. Mangan is careful to offer a balanced view of sport in its role as cultural bond of empire – negative and positive. This balance is maintained in a fuller discussion of the 'Cultural Bond' in *The Games Ethic and Imperialism: Aspects of the Diffusion of an Ideal* (Harmondsworth 1986).

15. Ibid., pp. 79–82, 592–3. A deputy commissioner, McMunn, was sacked from his post in 1890 by governor Sir Brandford Griffiths, for his over-zealous prosecution of slave holders and traders. The governor returned Nyamie Domah, an enslaved 7-year-old girl, to her owner, Fanny Hagan, after the latter had been convicted of breaking Ordnance No 1 (1874) forbidding slavery, in a prosecution initiated by McMunn. *Transactions*, pp.115–16.
16. Osmond Wesley Stuart, *'Good Boys', Footballers and Strikes: African Social Change in Bulowayo, 1933–53* (unpublished PhD. School of African and Oriental Studies, University of London 1989) p. 109.
17. Swinton Papers, Churchill College, Cambridge. Swin II/6/1.
18. Phyllis M. Martin, 'Colonialism, Youth and Football in French Equatorial Africa', *International Journal of the History of Sport*, 8, 3 (May 1991) pp. 67–8.
19. *Sheffield and Rotherham Independent,* 11 September 1888.
20. *Cannock Advertiser*, 28 August 1887.
21. Much of this information about Wharton's extended family history comes from Sheila Leeson, interview with the author, Rotherham, 24 April 1996.

8 *Professional footballer: Rotherham Town and Sheffield United 1889–95*

Arthur signed for Rotherham Town as a forward in August 1889. One of four players to join the Clifton Lane club at the beginning of their first season in the newly formed Midland League, he was described as 'fast … safe and tricky on the ball'.[1] One of the other newcomers, De Ville, was signed as a goalkeeper. Rotherham also had another custodian, Watson. (Assuming it was Arthur's decision to join the club as an attacker, his choice would have been determined by the need, as a professional runner, to lessen the chance of injury.) In fact, Arthur's sprint trainer did not want him to play football at all. He was still preparing his man for the September Handicap at the Queen's Ground, Sheffield. However, Arthur may have seen things from a longer perspective. His second job, as professional footballer, would provide a steady income over at least eight months while pedestrianism was pay-by-performance. This may help explain why he was willing to play a contact sport and put up with a few knocks now and again. The compromise with his trainer was over the position he would play; as an attacker Arthur may have felt there was less chance of injury.

The creation in 1888 of the Football League and its immediate success in both disciplining teams to fulfil fixtures and attracting crowds on a regular basis led to the formation of regional leagues. The Midland League, formed a year later, was one such. It included clubs from Lincolnshire, Nottinghamshire, Staffordshire, Derbyshire, South Yorkshire and Warwickshire. It saw itself as a regional feeder to the Football League rather than a rival. The 1889–90 season was momentous for professional football in England because of the creation of numerous leagues catering for the growing numbers of clubs. Almost every professional and amateur club that wanted to play regularly in a league against other clubs could now do so. While the Football League on its inception had admitted only 12 members, the establishment of regional leagues absorbed the disappointed bystanders. Through this development football was rapidly being commodified: the labour of players sold by entrepreneurs as a leisure package to consumers. The 1890s, a decade in which both the playing and spectating of sport became a fixed part of the cultural life of working-class people saw a cascade of clubs into regional leagues.

Violence and strikers: Rotherham Town 1889–90

For Rotherham's opening game of the season against Burton Wanderers on 7 September, Arthur played at centre forward but ended up in goal after injury to De Ville. He soon became first choice custodian, although he did play at right wing in a fixture against Derby Junction at the end of that month. The end of his professional running career at the close of the athletics season in 1889 may have influenced his return to the most dangerous position on the field. With the dubious quality of Arthur's past outfield performances, the Rotherham management may have left him little choice.

The highlight of the 1989–90 season was the visit of Preston North End in November as part of the club's contribution to the town's 'Statutes Festival', a social occasion of fairs, music and celebration that also included the hiring of 'hands' or labour. (The last festival was in October 1978.) The 'Invincibles' were both FA Cup holders and the champions of the Football League in its first season of competition. They had won the former without conceding a goal and went unbeaten in the latter. They were the benchmark of excellence against which other teams measured themselves. A large crowd of 7,000, including a sizeable contingent from Sheffield, saw North End win 4–3. Wharton excelled and laid the ghost of his dreadful performance in his previous game against his former club in Billy Mosforth's benefit 20 months earlier. The *Sheffield and Rotherham Independent* of 4 November, in its description of Preston's fourth goal refers to the role of the 'rusher' – the forward whose job is to take out the goalie while his colleague shoots – and to the hazard of Arthur's position. 'Russell, with a long shot, secured another goal, Ross senior taking care of Wharton meanwhile.'

In the FA Cup Rotherham reached the fourth qualifying round. It was a landmark Arthur would not forget quickly. Their third round tie in November involved a contest with arch rivals Rotherham Swifts for which Town trained full-time for three days. The crowd was the largest to date for a football match in the town. Typical of so many local derbies it was a rough house of a match, at the end of which Arthur finished in hospital after twice being kicked – during the game and by a spectator on leaving the pitch. Rab Howell, a Swifts player, was hit about the head with an umbrella, and his team had mud thrown at them by Town supporters. Rotherham won the replay the following Monday without their injured keeper. Violence at football matches, between rival fans, by fans against players and officials, and by players against players was common in the 1890s. Much of the last form of violence was within the rules; vigorous shoulder charging was a common feature of the British game. It was not until 1895 that charging a goalkeeper when he was not in possession of the ball was outlawed.

Arthur's team were knocked out of the FA Cup, after a replay, by their other, grander local rivals Sheffield United. However, they took revenge by beating them 1–0 in the final of the Sheffield and Hallamshire Senior Cup for a second successive season. Fittingly victory came after a replay. This was the most prestigious local competition. The status of regional champions was one of importance and pride in the intense sporting environment of South Yorkshire. There was no love lost between these two teams and contests were usually physical to the point of excess. United – the 'Cutlers' as they were then nicknamed – had been formed in March 1889. Four players from the Swifts left to join the new club which, with their larger and more densely populated catchment area, held out greater prospects for the aspiring professional. Soon after the exodus Town were the only professional side in Rotherham. (The logical outcome here should have been that Town were eternally grateful to big city neighbours!) In their first drawn FA Cup match with Sheffield Wharton was at the sharp end of some very rough treatment. Saving a shot on the line, he was 'charged down as he did so, and hurt, and even as he lay writhing upon the ground'[2] a goal was scored. Coming so soon after the battering at the Swifts match, it illustrates both the frequency of violence goalkeepers were subject to and how much it was an accepted – and integral – part of the game.

In return, Wharton's attempt to give the forwards some of their own medicine did not meet with such passing indifference. Against

Gainsbrough Trinity he 'somewhat roughly ... charged down [Gainsbrough forward Spikesley causing] unpleasantness'.[3] At the end of the match Arthur was surrounded by home supporters, but managed to remain unharmed. Spikesley was five feet six inches and slightly built, which may explain the anger of the crowd. (Later during the 1890s the diminutive forward became a great favourite with Sheffield Wednesday and played for England.)

The enmity between Town and United became hot again at Rotherham's Festival of Football, a schedule of four games over Easter designed to rake in as much money as possible during this short holiday. Sheffield United were the warm-up act. Their fifth meeting in four months, before a crowd of 5,000, repeated the violence of the FA Cup ties. The home team had two players badly injured, while United complained that they had been attacked by Rotherham supporters at the close. 'Echo' of the *Rotherham Advertiser*, 12 April 1890, accepted that rival supporters may have 'brawled', but denied that any players had been harmed by spectators. Rotherham were later cautioned by the FA, who supported Sheffield's version of events.

Banging the kettle drum: The economy, the community and football

The largest group of workers in Rotherham – known locally as 'Stove Grate Town' because of the numbers employed in the iron foundries making kitchen and fireplace fittings and accoutrements – went on strike during mid-March 1890, towards the end of the football season. The men were asking for a 10 per cent rise in pay. Feeling between employers and those withholding their labour, who numbered in their hundreds if not thousands, was bitter. The owners of capital were adamant that they would not pay the rise. The foundry workers were firm in the justice of their cause. Two effects were felt by the football club: first, lower attendances. 'Echo' from the beginning of the shutdown had voiced his prophetic fear that the conflict would lower attendances as strikers and their families simply had less money; second, the apparent rise in the frequency of violence by supporters at games.

The strike lasted nine weeks, although the bitter feeling had been fomenting much longer. Coursing throughout the history of Rotherham

Town between 1889 and 1896 is the class conflict between workers and employers in the town, and its dramatic effect upon the club.

The hardship brought by the conflict pounded many working families throughout the town. The hard-nosed, dispassionate attitude of the employers was illustrated by a civil court case that, coincidentally, involved Rotherham footballer George Medley. He was being sued by his employers, Wheathill Foundry, for taking six days off work as a moulder. They were demanding 30s (£1.50p) compensation for his labour that had been lost to them. Medley in his defence argued he had given seven days' notice of his absence. He had gone to Derbyshire with the rest of his team, to prepare for their Sheffield and Hallamshire Cup final against Sheffield United. And, anyway, he couldn't understand the amount of the claim as his wages were only 16s per week. The court decided in favour of the employers. It is not known whether Rotherham paid the damages on behalf of Medley.

The football club, too, as employers were no slouches when it came to litigation in pursuit of their own cause. Two weeks earlier they had sued William Bennett for £5 in damages for allegedly breaking a contract to play. Instead, Bennett had gone to Sheffield Wednesday. (Known more popularly as 'Mick' he won an FA Cup winners medal with his chosen club that season.) Once again the action had gone against the player.

The violence arising out of workplace struggles between the two classes may well have found a displaced outlet at football. The 1890s was a decade of rising union membership, especially among semi-skilled and unskilled workers, a consequence of the victorious match-girls, gasworkers and dockers strikes of the late 1880s. By 1900 there were over two million workers paying weekly subs. The growth in union membership, known as 'New Unionism' – some of whom would have been football supporters – was a sign of rising working-class confidence. The gas workers' strike of 1889 for an eight hour day had a particular impact in the industrial North. Not only had they physically resisted attempts by employers to use blackleg labour, their success led to other groups of workers, such as those employed in the wool trade in west Yorkshire, becoming unionised. The Rotherham men and their families held out for nine weeks and won their pay demand. Their battle enlarged and tightened working-class solidarity in the community. Blacklegs were confronted by hundreds, the most vociferous often being the women who would rattle and bang kettles, pots and pans to signify their disgust of those still working. Even the Town management, somewhat hostile witnesses to the unity forged by the conflict, had been forced to give in to public pressure and organise two charity matches for the strikers.

The community and football

This environment of open conflict between two of the most powerful social groups in Rotherham, the foundry workers and their employers, gave an extra charge to the emotion of those at matches most vociferous in their local patriotism. For some football writers, especially those on the left, the nature of the game with its emphasis on geographical rivalries, village v. village, district v. district, town v. town, city v. city contests, has the effect of inculcating a local or regional identity in place of (a more progressive and unifying) class consciousness and solidarity. The self-image 'I am a Rotherham Town supporter' would overlay the alternative 'I am a foundry worker'. While the football-based identity may have provided both an emotional escape from hard, unremitting, unfulfilling and exploitative toil and a sense of pride and belonging, it did not instigate a generalised awakening to the common cause of that drudgery or its elimination through collective action, as espoused by labour leaders of the time. As such it could only bring a limited respite from everyday hardship.

The admittedly tenuous explanation – of growing working-class confidence through greater work-place organisation – for a proportion of crowd violence at matches in the 1890s has parallels with some interpretations of football-related violence during the 1960s and 1970s. These decades, like the late 1880s and early 1890s, witnessed a heightened level of trade disputes, a growth in working-class living standards and the greatest amount of workers ever enrolled in trade unions. While this relationship between class confidence and violence at football is speculative it should not be ignored.

Class solidarity, of both workers and bosses, is usually heightened at times of industrial disputes. And while the stove grate dispute may have had the effect of clarifying bread and butter issues for many workers, one supporter of Rotherham Town seemed confused by the sharpened Us/Them dichotomy. His ire had been raised by the increasing number of 'imports' playing for the Town side, the most high profile of whom was Wharton. His letter to the *Rotherham Advertiser* asked, 'Is Wharton as good as Watson?' (a local). These 'foreigners' from outside the district of Rotherham who now formed a majority of the Town team were driving away interest. Replies were in favour of Arthur. One supporter thought him 'vastly superior' to Watson, who was, according to another writer entitling himself 'Rotherham Committee Member' 'nervous, timid and wanting of vigour in fisting out'. The charge of declining interest was countered by the fact of a rise in gates. This was the litmus test. 'Our first team is a purely professional team, and that the object is to make money.' This in turn will attract more crowds, more money and better players creating a virtuous cycle. 'Echo' weighed in: Rotherham had gone further in the FA Cup, played better against Preston, and had beaten the Swifts on their own ground for the first time. The club were 'very fortunate' to have got Wharton.[4]

This debate about the merits of locals versus imports was an example of the ideological differences that existed in all dimensions of the game. In the discussion of Arthur's non-appearance in an England shirt we found lurking the ideologies of 'Race' and Nationalism. In the exchanges recounted above, Arthur faced hostility from a minority because he was not native born or bred. He was an 'outsider'. An interesting feature of the affair was the support he inspired through his excellence as a goalkeeper. This was noticeable in the majority of letters published by the *Advertiser*, which criticised the irrational prejudice of the original letter. Arthur's ability on the field of play – his actions – was a greater influence upon their thinking, than the appeal of scapegoating and isolating an individual for the problems of the team. Arthur, then, finished the season with a sizeable coterie of loyal supporters and a lesser band of detractors.

Good team and bad management? Football success and economic failure

The realities that Arthur faced during this first season – financial difficulty, violence, regional rivalry, class struggle – were those that dominated his career at Rotherham. And to a lesser extent at some of his other clubs. Accordingly, any evaluation of Town's successes and failures on the field of play should acknowledge their uneven influence.

What follows, then, is an attempt to deal with both the economic and football dimensions to the relationship between Rotherham Town Football Club and its community, and Arthur and his wife Emma.

By concentrating upon particular issues, rather than seasons, as the focus for this episode of Arthur's life, from now on the narrative will move backwards and forwards in years. Season will not follow season. In so doing I hope it will be easier to dissect the overarching theme of 'football success – economic failure' which characterises Arthur's Rotherham years.

For much of the time during his first four seasons the club thrived on the field. They won the Midlands League twice in succession. Their first championship in 1891–92 was gained in large part by closing the season with a winning sequence of seven games, during which they scored 43 and conceded six. Of the goals scored, 29 were accumulated in four matches played over the Easter period. This was a great ending to a season that had not begun well. Town's first game at their new ground in Clifton Lane saw them trounced 11–0 by Bury. (They managed to unburden their shame by defeating Leicester Fosse by the same score seven months later.) And, after Gainsbrough Trinity knocked them out of the FA Cup, Rotherham responded by out-distancing them to the Midlands League championship with Trinity as runners-up. Not surprisingly, contests over the season between these two rivals were fierce affairs. One particularly violent match was characterised by fouls, fighting and an early exit for Jarvis of Gainsbrough. This was followed by an inquiry by the Lincolnshire FA. (Earlier we recalled how Arthur had downed Spikesley of Gainsborough with a charge that incensed the home support, during the 1889–90 season.)

Arthur's contribution to Town's success had been fairly consistent, though he was dropped after the massacre by Bury and again in January. After both omissions he returned quickly. In recognition of his key role in providing the club with its first league title, the committee granted Arthur a benefit match at the end of the season. Doncaster Rovers were invited as opposition. Scheduled to begin at 5 o'clock, it eventually kicked off at 5.50 and even by then Rovers had just ten men. Perhaps it was fortunate that there was a small crowd to witness the fiasco, although the numbers of spectators did increase as the game 'progressed'. Overall, the occasion was a pathetic affair 'considering the services Wharton has rendered to local football'.[5] It must have been a disappointment to Arthur also as a resident, married member of the community that so few turned up. The supporters of Rotherham seemed to have made little effort to show appreciation of their eccentric celebrity, though in fairness the allure of friendly matches to most supporters was akin to a cold bath in an unheated room.

The second championship the following season was achieved with accomplished football. 'Echo' described the team as the 'best ever'[6] to wear the chocolate and blue of Rotherham. They began 1892–93 with an invitation from Liverpool to play in the club's inaugural game at their Anfield ground. Despite losing 7–1 this honour – as Midland League Champions – provided the elevated platform from which Town could continue what they began last season. The defeat had the same effect on their self-satisfied complacency. They went on to head the league table for much of the season, remaining unbeaten until mid-December. Quite what degree of the team's excellence 'Echo' attributed to Arthur is confused by the signing of Hugh McKay, the former Heart of Midlothian goalkeeper. He replaced Arthur at the turn of the year and played in most of the following games. Meanwhile, the former regular played the second half of the season for Rotherham United, Town's reserves, in the Sheffield and Hallamshire Football League Alliance. The confidence-deflating experience of being dropped from a successful team, who won the Midland League title again, was compounded by the refusal of the chairman and directors to recognise Arthur's contribution with a championship medal. Fourteen gold medallions were struck, one each for the 11 members of the first team, plus three for reserves. Despite playing at least 29 games, over half the season's total of 53 (these figures include non-league matches), Arthur was snubbed.

The second successive title helped Rotherham win election to an enlarged second division, from 12 to 16 clubs, of the Football League for 1893–94. While the club were moving forward in their relationship with the wider football world, the decision of the directors not to give Arthur a medal caused a stagnant hiatus between themselves and their disaffected employee. At the dawn of that season there was still no agreement over a renewed contract of employment. On 8 August, 'Echo' voiced anxiety over the stalemate. 'Who will be the mediator' to ensure the re-engagement of a man 'who has played so brilliantly for the team?' With cringing, coincidental bad timing the club held a dinner at the Crown Hotel at the end of that month at which the medals were presented. Or not. The directors, for their part, may have felt Arthur played the second half of the season as a reserve and therefore did not deserve recognition.

However, from the fragmentary evidence available it seems that it was a dispute over wages that had much to do with Arthur being denied his Midlands League medal. The team's success inspired the directors to apply for entry to the second division of the Football League, which was accepted. They felt, no doubt, that as champions they were good enough to play in a higher standard of football; and by playing against better opposition they would attract bigger crowds, thereby increasing income. Yet, as a personal reward – not least, for his part in enhancing the market potential of the club – he was being asked to take a cut in wages.

To make sense of the dispute we have to understand the economic context in which it took place. The club, as a limited liability company owned by its shareholders, exposed itself to the ebb and flow of market forces. As a business, its main objective, theoretically, was to maximise the return in dividend payments to these shareholders of which, ironically, Arthur was one. (The Football Association had prescribed a maximum dividend payment of 5 per cent.) In effect, in Rotherham's case, this meant throwing good money after bad. Economic success had to be bought. The club had no choice but to seek out the best players around with lucrative offers of wages that caused the directors sleepless nights in competition with other like-minded and similarly constituted clubs. As we have already seen in the discussion over the introduction of professionalism, some directors disliked the idea of paying any wage, let alone one that created labour aristocrats out of work-a-day footballers.

The Rotherham players, by contrast, should have been able to sleep easy with their conscience. Enough people paid enough money to pay their wages. Home gate receipts usually covered the fortnightly bill; in 1888–89 for example, money taken at the turnstiles had been £585.00s.5d (£585.02p), comfortably meeting wage costs of £346.13s.7d. (£346.68p). But gate money did not, and could not, look after all the expenses run up by the club. This might include substantial outlays, such as new stands, changing rooms and other capital projects that would upgrade the playing and spectating facilities. Yet these improvements gave no lasting financial benefit to present players. The rewards would accrue to the shareholders through the increased value of the company and its enlarged earnings potential. There would also be increased power in the market place in terms of the quality of facilities it could offer to sought-after talent.

At the annual general meeting for 1892–93 the chairman, Councillor G. Gummer, reported a loss of £153.6s.3d (£153.31p). Among the causes cited was players' wages which accounted for £675.6s.8d (£675.33p), almost doubling over the last four years. He promised that this bill would be lowered for next season. While this announcement may have pleased the shareholders, it can have generated little confidence among supporters and a lot of anger among the players. Unfortunately the ambitious directors and shareholders of Rotherham Football Company were an inept bunch, consistently miscalculating the balance between expenditure and income. They demanded success on the field, but often were not able to meet their financial commitments off it.

The players' wages, usually the highest cost, would be the first to experience the scythe of austerity. It made for difficult industrial relations. The players were being hit in the pocket for being too successful in hitting the back of the net. Wharton was not prepared to accept such attacks without a fight. Twice in his employment with the company they attempted to reduce his pay: during his second season and at the beginning of the 1893–94 campaign. In support of Arthur's case, if directors insisted on using economic criteria to determine wage levels, it could be argued that as long as the gate receipts more than covered the wage bill he (and the other players) should have a wage increase.

As both an employee and shareholder, Arthur's contradictory economic relationship was certainly unique at Rotherham, if not in football as a whole. Mason (1980), in his social profile of football club shareholders in the period 1886–1915 argues that most were middle class, with an abundance from the drink trade. Furthermore, a number of footballers became publicans and therefore had a vested interest in this drink–football industries relationship. For Wharton, publican of the Albert Tavern at Masbro' and Plough Inn, Greasebro' during his career at Rotherham, the working (publican), playing (footballer) and investing (shareholder) dimensions of his relationship with the club were not mutually beneficial. Being a celebrity publican cannot have harmed his trade, especially after the collapse of the Swifts in 1890–91. With only one professional club Arthur's drinkers would not suffer any potential conflict of loyalties, though both pubs were outside the vicinity of Clifton Lane. However, his economic interests as paid employee and investor/shareholder were incompatible. While being pressured to take a drop in wages, he was being asked to invest more of his money as a shareholder. Those who own and run companies usually recognise the direct relationship between labour costs, quantity of production, time and profits. If the producers can work longer, harder and for less pay a growth in profits is often realised. The Rotherham Town players had been 'asked' to fulfil their side of this equation – to play more matches for less money – yet the shareholders had not received their dividends as a consequence of this fulfilment by the players. Thus for Arthur, his dual persona of player and shareholder was hit by a double jeopardy: he was increasingly exploited as a player and losing money on his investment as a shareholder. The apparently spiteful – in Arthur's eyes – refusal of the directors to give Arthur a championship medal was a further kick at his vulnerability.

Economic failure and football failure 1890–91

Arthur's second season was not a happy one. The team spent much of the season in the last third of the League. Gates were below expectations, reflecting the team's unspectacular results. The 4d (2p) admission fee demanded by the Midland League and a harsh winter were also cited by Town watchers as causes of low attendance. The club's desperate financial condition acted as a drag upon the players. Letter writers to the *Rotherham Advertiser* at the beginning of December questioned also the routine for away matches of train and horse-brake travel with the players arriving shortly before kick-off without having had a proper lunch. Was this the best preparation for winning matches? This sparked off a debate-by-letters of causes of the team's poor results. 'Echo' confirmed that a 'prominent' Town player had complained that no meals were provided for the team on away journeys. This belief in the maxim that an army marches on its stomach touched a sympathetic nerve with a good many contributors. One suggested travelling on Friday if the opposition were distant.

To add to their troubles, Woolwich Arsenal and Kidderminster failed to turn up for matches over Christmas, a period during which most clubs looked for large crowds and bankable cash. Sheffield United

Reserves also failed to show in January. This further depleted what little money was left in the kitty. (It was the frequency of late cancellations and non-arrivals that led William McGregor of Aston Villa, founder of the Football League, to suggest putting fixtures on a more organised basis, similar to the County Cricket Championship.) By the middle of January the club announced they were in arrears and set up a committee of five guarantors to the debt. They immediately slashed wages – the reserve team were told to play for nothing – and to show they really meant business extra games were arranged. For the players, these actions impacted in two ways: an increase in production – more football matches – and less pay.

For a sports celebrity of Arthur's status, whose name on the team sheet would alone be an attraction for many spectators, a drop in wage for more effort and commitment was not welcome or seen as fair. The balance sheet which was presented at the end of season AGM – but not at the time – showed that gate receipts were £118 over wages of players. The directors used the age-old tactic of divide and rule. Not one 'of the local players', they argued, had objected to a reduction in wages. The inference being that the 'imports', or at least some of them, had. While the Rotherham directors were making thinly veiled accusations about the loyalty of team members such as Wharton, in private they knew the financial return received through the signing of such players to the club would probably be greater than the expenditure for their services. In fact the previous season they had paid Middlesbrough £2.15s.6d (£2.77p) in order to release Arthur from a contractual obligation he had made to play for the Teesside club. It is interesting to note that after the state of the finances was made public Town lost their next three matches, against Bootle, Burton Wanderers and Long Eaton Rangers, by 6–0, 6–0 and 1–0 respectively. Of the next five games after these three defeats, they won one and lost four. The results of the eight games preceding the directors' decrees were four wins, three defeats and a draw.

The black dust of the Coal War: 1893–94

Rotherham's first season in the second division of the Football League in 1893–94 was dwarfed in its importance to the cultural life of the community by another violent and bitter economic struggle between capital and labour. The dispute, known as the Great Coal War, between owners of coal mines and the hewers of coal involved thousands of pitmen and their families and affected many more. The capitalists wanted to reduce wages by 15 per cent. Organised by the Miners Federation of Great Britain whose power base was in Yorkshire, the colliers refused to labour for 16 weeks. They returned underground only after a conciliation board had been established to mediate between the two classes. Though not as prolonged as the Great Coal Strike of 1984–85, the violence and intensity of the struggle were as dramatic. The non-production of coal forced the closure of the iron foundries in Rotherham, laying-off between 2,000 and 3,000 workers. It cloaked, and was seen and felt, by all. The scenes of hunger inspired one observer of the London-based *Westminster Gazette* to label Rotherham 'a starvation camp'.

> The sight of the men is sad and bad enough ... there is yet a sadder sight ... women and their children have been forced to the front. The pinch of hunger is getting too sharp ... despair drives them out of their hiding places ... Shivering and haggard they stand about ... The children's faces are terribly pinched, and in most cases their clothes are rags, and of shoes and stockings their seems to be little left at all ... You come across so many scenes of the same kind in this vast starvation camp.[7]

This description of abject hunger and despair leaves no doubt, not least in the eyes and soul of that observer, as to the severe effects of the 'war' felt by working-class people throughout the town.

The football club, for its part, gave free admittance to miners to Clifton Lane during the dispute which overlay the first four months of the season. As a consequence money taken at the gate that season was just over half the figure for 1892–93. However, this was still £150 more than the wage bill. At a special public meeting of the Rotherham Football and Athletic Company, held on 15 November the parlous state of the company's finances was laid out: gates, to date, were £250 down on last season. Outgoings were exceeding income. The atmosphere of financial gloom that overhung the club was overshadowed by the darker cloud of the team's poor results. With such a lamentable playing record hopes for an upturn – in the league or bank – were as sparse as the directors' management skills. The 'remedy' prescribed by Chairman Gummer and the board was a recognisable formula: the players were again asked by the directors to shoulder the financial burdens of the club through another reduction in their wages. This led to an exodus of players, including Hugh McKay. For reserve players there was a termination of contracts and disbandment of the team. Once again those at the bottom of the pile were most affected.

In 1893, 30,440,000 working days were taken up with strike action by workers. Not until 1912, one of the tumultuous years of the Great Unrest prior to the first world war, was this figure surpassed. It does not seem a coincidence, then, that the idea of a Players' Union was first mooted in 1893. Ironically, it was Arthur's predecessor at Preston, Billy Rose who attempted to organise footballers. It was another four years before a union emerged.

However, the environment of widespread labour unrest, locally and nationally, may have awakened a sense of class consciousness and class solidarity in the mind and action of some players. Were not they and the miners fighting for the same objective and against a common enemy: to uphold their standard of living in the face of attacks by employers? It should not be forgotten that Football League clubs held the right to their employees' labour at all times. A player could move to another club only with their permission. If a club wanted to be vindictive, it could retain the services of the player, but not select him. It was a powerful weapon in their armoury of 'persuasion'.

Arthur's personal response to this unwanted hand in his pocket and whip at his back was to withdraw his labour. He did not play in the 8–2 defeat by Lincoln City. He only just made the trip to Middlesbrough Ironopolis for the next game, problems with the club resolved only at the 'last moment'. It did not affect his performance. Despite losing 6–1, he was 'magnificent'.[8] While these two heavy defeats reflected the low morale of the players and threatened a return of the pattern after the last round of wage cuts in 1890–91, a string of successive defeats did not recur.

Arthur's dissatisfaction with his employers was now ingrained. In the first of the Christmas matches, against Doncaster Rovers, he arrived after kick-off and played outfield. In the corresponding match away a week later, he decided not to travel, preferring to play for the reserves at Clifton Lane. At the end of January he did not play for either the first or reserve team. (Was his erratic behaviour also down to supping a great deal of the beer he was selling?) Confirmation that the unilateral decision of the Rotherham board to reduce his wages was the cause of his defiant protests is hinted at by a remark at the AGM at the end of the season. Mr J. Palmer asked the chairman if it was true that Wharton was owed £15. Chairman Gummer replied dismissively that the club did not owe the money. The balance sheet presented at the meeting outlined the amount taken out of the players' pockets. The wage bill had been £330.5s.2d (£330.26p) compared to £675.6s.8d (£675.33p) for the season previous, a cut of over 50 per cent.

The 1893–94 football calendar ended with two applications to the Football League involving Rotherham Town Football Club. One was for re-election to the second division for the following season, a necessary formality after finishing second from bottom. The other was from Wharton, for a transfer to first division Sheffield United. Both, ultimately, were granted. Arthur joined four of his former team-mates at Bramall Lane and Tom Bott, his backer from his professional running days. Bott was a United director and unofficial team manager. He joined his erstwhile patron at a club with frequent crowds of 6–7,000. This would have eased – erased even – Arthur's consistent worry over the last five seasons about the ability of employees to pay his wages.

Arthur and the big man: Sheffield United 1894–95

Arthur may have been tempted to Sheffield by the additional incentive of managing the 'Sportsman Cottage' public house in Button Lane in the city. At United, though still a big fish in competition for the position of goalkeeper, he faced a whale of a man, William 'Fatty' Foulke. The most bulbous athlete ever to have played in the first division, at his biggest Foulke stood six feet two inches and weighed over 28 stones. Arthur could not dislodge him even though at this stage of his career the 19-year-old from Derbyshire was a sprightly 13 stone. (The former miner also fell into the category of a one-cap internationalist, the England selectors picking him for a match against Wales in 1897 on home ground at Bramall Lane.)

While Foulke's most memorable moments were yet to come, it could be argued that Arthur, nearing 30, had no such uplifting vision to inspire him. He played just three first team games, only one in the first division. Fittingly that game was in the North East against Sunderland on 23 February 1895. The 'Cutlers' lost 0–2. (The Wearsiders won the championship that season, each of their players receiving a £10 bonus, worth over £1,000 in 1997.) Of the other two, one opponent was Linfield of Belfast, the other Leicester Fosse. Unable to glimpse a regular space for himself between the posts for the first team, he returned to Rotherham the following season. The (London) *Football Evening News* felt it important enough to merit a paragraph.

> The dusky Wharton, who last year understudied Foulke at Bramall Lane, has returned to Rotherham and will play for the local second division club again. He is undoubtedly a fine goalkeeper, and Sheffield United will be the poorer for a 'bit of colour' which never did them any discredit.[9]

The play upon Arthur's pigmentation typifies the racialisation of sports coverage that had occurred by the mid-1890s. Even with its sympathetic bias, the reporter feels the need to emphasise colour as much as ability.

A short smile of pleasure: Rotherham 1895–96

Arthur's form in his second spell at Clifton Lane was erratic. Initially he played well. Against Billy Meredith's Manchester City, a Mancunian, in a letter to the Yorkshire club's secretary, remarked that the position of 'goal[keeper] could not have been improved'. Away at Arsenal, he 'pleased the cockney crowd by his usual clever tactics'.[10] However, against Burton Swifts some Town supporters invaded the pitch to abuse their team, incensed by the players' dire performance. By the end of November Arthur's hunger seemed to have returned. Against Notts County

> of the players the name of Arthur Wharton stands out conspicuously, that individual giving one of his best displays, and it will be a source of pleasure to many – there were a few early on in the season who thought his hand had lost its cunning – to learn that he has returned to his old form, and that his saving of the last few weeks has been done with all the vigour and accurateness of his former days when he was rightly regarded as prince among goalkeepers. May he still give us further cause for admiration.[11]

Unfortunately Arthur's appetite was soon satisfied and his form lapsed once again.

An anonymous rumour that the club would soon fold because of lack of support was publicised by 'Echo' in the *Rotherham Advertiser*, 26 December. But he eased shareholders', players' and supporters' worries by immediately quashing the scare with a personal reminder that the club had been in this situation before and survived. His optimism seemed vindicated by events over the next few months. The club did not collapse at the turn of the year, though the crisis continued. By mid-January the up-beat tone that sounded out the old year had been smothered by a more dismal 'Echo'. This latest, ominous diagnosis and prognosis of the club's ills was based upon a more incisive investigation of the financial anatomy of the corporate body. Gates had been better, he said, in Midland League days because then the team were winning. Now the standard of football is higher the costs greater but the income lower. The present round of wage reductions is forcing players to leave and this can only worsen the competitive strength of the team and lead to a further fall in crowds. The club cannot survive, he warned, on the present level of support. The future life of Rotherham Town Football Company looks short and fatal.

The prognosis proved correct. Despite benefit performances at the Theatre Royal in the town, a benefit match and a 'Grand Ball' no balls were ever kicked at Clifton Lane after the spring of 1896. By then Arthur had been long gone, playing for Stalybridge Rovers in the Lancashire League from the turn of that year. It was an exasperated exodus across the Pennines, this latest display of financial ineptness by the Rotherham committee finally shattering his fragile tolerance of their pompous muddling.

NOTES

1. *Rotherham Advertiser*, 14 August 1889.
2. *Sheffield Daily Telegraph*, 9 December 1889.
3. *Rotherham Advertiser*, 4 January 1890.
4. *Rotherham Advertiser*, 18 and 25 January 1890.
5. *Sheffield and Rotherham Independent*, 12 April 1892.
6. Ibid., 1 November 1892.
7. Reprinted in *Rotherham Advertiser*, 30 September 1893.
8. Ibid., 16 December 1893.
9. Ibid., 5 October 1895.
10. Ibid., 14 September; 12 October 1895.
11. Ibid., 7 December 1895.

9 *'Lionised' rebel: Lancashire 1896–1902*

Different place, same problems: Stalybridge Rovers

An interview Arthur gave to the *Ashton Herald*, 15 February 1896, shortly after he had joined Rovers, is riddled with inconsistencies and contradictions: he joined Sheffield United before Rotherham; he was at Preston for 'three seasons'; he won the AAA championship in 1886 at 19; he is now 31 years of age. Taken individually a mistake of detail should not distort or mislead. But a consistent flow of such inaccuracies leaves the reader wondering in which ale house the interview took place. Who was responsible for the inaccuracies, the teller or the writer? It acts as a reminder that our biographical reconstruction of moments from the past is not made with materials that have an equality of accuracy and authenticity.

Stalybridge played in the Lancashire League (LL). Being close to many Lancashire Football League clubs that pioneered professionalism, it could consider itself a ripple or two away from the epicentre of association football. Their gates of around 5,000 reflected this. As with his move to Sheffield United, Arthur may have been attracted to Rovers by the financial stability its larger support promised. But there may have been other equally substantial considerations. One of these could have been the desire to get away from Martha and the extended family in Rotherham. There were at least two clubs in the immediate South Yorkshire area, within commuting distance of his home, that Arthur could have approached: Barnsley St Peter's and Doncaster Rovers. There were also numerous lesser clubs in the vicinity of Sheffield who, had he signed for them, paid wages and would not have forced the Wharton's to move. However, the couple chose to transport themselves and their possessions across the Pennines rather than change the furniture in South Yorkshire. What they would find there would not be terribly different. Eight and a half miles from the Cottonopolis of Manchester the industrial landscape of the Cheshire town was dominated by numerous mills. It was, like Rotherham, a working-class town with a population in 1891 of 28,783 the working majority of whom were factory hands. And it too had a proud tradition of class struggle that held a uniquely significant place in the history of labour. In August 1842 textile workers in Stalybridge and its sister town of Ashton-Under-Lyne downed tools in protest at wage cuts attempted by their employers. The action spread quickly to Manchester and beyond, feeding into widespread discontent that had been gathering momentum in over 23 English, Scottish and Welsh counties in support of the six points of the Charter. Within a week, over 500,000 workers had joined in what became the first General Strike.

Signing for Rovers half-way though the club's first season in the Lancashire League was a mixed football blessing for Arthur, who would now be playing in the blue and gold of a better team but against lesser opponents. Created at the same time as its Midland counterpart, the LL acted as an unofficial conduit to the Football League second division for ambitious clubs based in Lancashire and Cheshire. Liverpool and Bury were both former members. The majority, however, were 'reserve sides of Football League clubs and small town sides made up of amateurs and part-time professionals'.[1] Arthur soon confirmed his reputation to the paying faithful of Crookbottom – Rovers' ground adjacent to Riverside Mills, off Northend Road – keeping two clean sheets in his first three games in which his team went unbeaten. Eulogies followed. He was

> a masterhand in his position … [it is] a source of satisfaction to know that such a difficult position has been filled … by one who is recognised by all footballers as an ideal goalkeeper … to Wharton [we] extend a cordial welcome to the town, feeling assured that in him we have a genuine footballer, and one who is incapable of resorting to any suspicious tactics [!].[2]

We can only guess what the writer had in mind when he penned 'suspicious tactics'. (Arthur getting his retaliation in first against rushers and other hostile forwards?) A week later the same paper was criticising as 'dangerous' [the] 'gallery play' the 'ideal goalkeeper' was indulging in. Such antics may be good for the crowd but, added the reporter, the benefit to the team was dubious.

Whatever doubts some football scribblers may have entertained about Arthur's ability to apply his talents consistently for 90 minutes, according to the *Ashton Herald*, 29 September 1900, he was 'lionised' by the majority of Rovers' supporters. Between early February and the first week in April they did not lose. Arthur's influence since his arrival had been to galvanise and transform a mediocre eleven into good *team*. By the latter part of the season they were known as 'Wharton's Brigade',[3] eventually finishing sixth in the table. The Brigade leader was selected for the Rest of the League XI versus Nelson, the LL champions. The following season, in an effort to transfuse the guru's power's into the veins of the club he was employed as player/coach. Arthur's footballing life, in the first half of 1896, was milk and honey.

In contrast, and almost predictably, the patrons of Rovers had a bitter tasting fare before them. At the end of February, less than two months after Wharton's arrival, there was a public meeting in the Town Hall to discuss the club debt of £450. Figures presented showed weekly average income from gate receipts at £19 – a minimum entrance-fee of 4d (2p) was fixed by the League – while outgoing on players' wages was £18. Once again, the solution proffered was to register formally as a business. It was proposed the club become a public liability company and 1,000 £1 shares be issued.

This ambition to become a football business was facilitated – and to a lesser extent engendered – by the formation of the numerous regional leagues. This had created the conditions for clubs to compete against each other within a more organised environment. In turn many committees became more ambitious in attempting to realise the economic dividend from this reorganisation. They employed a greater number of professionals as a sure-fire policy to bring success. Grand-stands and enclosures were mooted, planned and sometimes built in order to maximise gate revenue. Unfortunately, and sometimes disastrously, this competitive environment had its losers as Arthur's experience at Rotherham testifies. The committee men there were certainly not good at limiting the scope of their ambition to the club's income.

Becoming a business also changed the political economy of the club. It reallocated virtually all power, held and exercised formerly by members who paid an annual subscription, to shareholders. And within this category it was usually a small group with large holdings that had the greatest influence. From being nominally democratic – power allocated equally among fee-paying members – clubs who opted for limited liability became plutocracies, in that influence and control would be dependent upon the amount of money invested and shares held. Some recognised quickly the political ramifications of economic change. When the idea of incorporation was first mooted at Woolwich Arsenal in 1891, the year in which the club officially became professional, committee member John Humble argued against. Until now affairs 'had been worked by working men and his ambition was to see it carried on by them'. He did not want to see WA corrupt itself 'into a proprietary or capitalist club'.[4] The humble social origins of the team should continue to be reflected in those who ran it.

Ironically Arthur may well have been instrumental in the cause of Rovers' money worries. His wages as a senior professional would have been disproportionately high compared to those in front of him. He was not given to underselling himself. Yet it could be argued, given the turn-around in the team's fortunes, he was worth every undisclosed penny sealed into his weekly pay packet. Also, in terms of gate-income and wages paid out the players, collectively, were in the black. During the close-season Mr Thorpe, the secretary, presented figures showing total income to have been £1,208.2s.6d (£1,208.13p). Outgoings on players' wages had been £664.16s.9d (£664.84p – very similar to Rotherham's wage of £675 in 1892–93). These figures did not cause the alarm of those presented in February. However, there were still 'startling' debts of over £353, which may well have hardened the club's resolve to continue with its incorporation (as eventually did Woolwich Arsenal). Stalybridge Rovers Football Club Company Ltd held their first AGM in August with 400 shareholders. The share capital raised immediately wiped out the debt.

Departure of the 'Brigade' leader: 1896–97

Wharton the trainer and 'without exception the cleverest goalkeeper in the Lancashire League'[5] – well, the writer was the local reporter – got them together for training two weeks before the start of the season. The first game, away against Cheshire rivals Stockport County, was a rough house of a match that Rovers won by the only goal. The crowd was 5,000 plus, with an estimated 1,500 travelling from Stalybridge.

'Wharton's Brigade' went from good to better, reflected by the steady increase in crowds. At the beginning of December 'support at Stalybridge Rovers [was] stronger than ever'.[6] They remained undefeated at home until Christmas, and against arch-rivals Ashton North End at Crookbottom 8,000 paid 4d (2p) and up to see Rovers win 2–0. And they reached the first round proper of the FA Cup – the equivalent today of a team from outside the Football League making it to the third round – by beating Chorley 3–2 away. The ascent into more rarefied air slowed the momentum. The 'Pets' away form declined in a steep gradient of lost confidence, with Arthur apparently taking a devil-may-care attitude. The committee suspended him for a month over the busy Christmas period without either party stating publicly the reason. His return in January was ignominious, many observers blaming his poor goalkeeping for the 0–4 defeat by Southport Central.

> Kirwan gave him a daisy-cutter to negotiate. He made a feeble attempt to save, slipped, and the ball passed into the net … The few shots that Wharton had to deal with seemed to cause him considerable distress … It really was hard lines on the home team's supporters to see the good work their favourites were doing discounted as they were by weak goalkeeping.[7]

The report noted also that the goalmouth was very muddy and slippy. Whatever the difficulty posed by the condition of the pitch, the performance was inexcusable and Arthur was dropped from the team.

Unfortunately his bad form – was he turning up to games drunk? – coincided with a meeting of worried shareholders. The secretary detailed the finances. Reassuringly gate receipts, averaging £52 for league matches, were covering the weekly wage bill of £21 which itself was down on the early season average of nearly £27. Some players must have taken a wage cut or been transferred, or released and not replaced. It was an angry meeting. Some vociferous shareholders felt certain players were not pulling their weight and although none were named there can be little doubt as to the identity of at least one. Should the present form of the team continue to be dragged down by the few, continued the vexed speculators, it would have a damaging effect upon the financial viability of the business. Their vocalised anxiety was not soothed and quietened by the statement that a bonus of £2.10s.0d (£2.50p) had been paid to one unnamed player. Again Arthur was the most likely candidate as captain, trainer and mentor. This thought did little to soothe the knitted brows of the investor lobby.

Yet disinterested reading of match results would have left the impression that they had not been particularly bad, especially at home. The final league table had Rovers ninth of 15. But the principal concern of those who now held power was the economic health of the business and the effect upon this of results. Leaving aside the wisdom of such an ordering of priorities, maladministration by officials was still one of those issues that was not pushed to the top of the agenda. One example of bureaucratic incompetence, which cost the club at least one good gate, was the secretary's failure to register Rovers for the Lancashire Cup. This was their third most prestigious and lucrative competition after the FA Cup and the LL. More importantly, it was the source of at least one local derby which more often than not attracted a large crowd.

To some it must have appeared that indifferent form on the pitch was used as a diversion to gloss over inefficient administration off it. The outcome for Arthur of this rancour was that he joined Ashton North End, the closest rival of Rovers. Whether he was pushed out by the board of directors as a cost-cutting or disciplinary measure, or walked out in exasperation at yet another fine mess the suited ones had made, is unclear. The pressure to cut costs would have unsheathed the directors' sharpened knives with Arthur, as the best paid player/trainer, the prize sacrificial mutton. A single incision to his contractual jugular would have reduced the need for slashings elsewhere. His recent suspension and current bad form would have also provided a more publicly acceptable 'just cause' argument in the face of opposition and recrimination from Wharton loyals at Crookbottom.

'A sorry and amusing exhibition': Ashton North End

Arthur signed as centre-forward in February 1897. The town of Ashton-Under-Lyne, just one mile away in Lancashire, had an expanding population of 40,463 in 1891 (up 25 per cent over the previous 20 years). For the second time in his career, his erratic displays between the posts prompted him to try his luck at another position. Given past experience of this flight of fancy, either ANE were unaware of his shortcomings outfield, or desperate for his signature as a personality.

Had they been on the look-out for a goalscorer they would not have invited Arthur to play. Ironically his debut was at home against Southport Central just three weeks after the lamentable display against them for Rovers. Yet again he had a 'stinker', missing a couple of easy chances. His exertions brought humour to the proceedings, but this time the crowd were laughing at him. He missed the next game, probably dropped, returning as goalkeeper the following Saturday. The weekend off revitalised his self-confidence and he remained as custodian until the season's end, except for one forced appearance at full-back while the usual occupant was injured. Once more his incompetence as an outfield player was cruelly exposed and publicly ridiculed. 'Away from the sticks ... Wharton is a novice. It was a sorry and at the same time amusing exhibition which he recently gave at centre-forward, and on Saturday he was far from being an ideal full-back.'[8] Both attempts to play beyond goal were reminders that though Arthur was skilled at many sports his feet were not as capable of manipulating the ball as they were kicking track dust in the face of trailing sprinters. Overall, then, it was an unremarkable season with the highlight being the beating of Chorley, the league leaders and eventual champions, 2–1. ANE finished ninth of 15, the same as Stalybridge last season.

A brief calm: 1897–98

This was a season of two distinct halves for Wharton. The first was characterised by bad form and a lasting illness. It may have been that the two were connected. (Could the malignant cancer – 'epithelioma' and/or syphilis have already begun their 'long and painful'[9] attrition? Or the pre-match 'scoops' less controlled?) The second featured a prolonged run of good form, both by Arthur and the team. ANE prepared well. They trained every weekday evening for two weeks prior to their first game away against New Brighton Tower which, contrary to expectations, they lost 0–4. Despite this initial upset their pre-season work showed its value and they lost only one of their next five games, and that was to Chorley. This was not the most important game of the quintet. That was home against their fiercest rivals Stalybridge Rovers. North End began disastrously – even before a ball was kicked – taking the field with nine men, R. Yates, the latest of the latecomers, turning up a little before half-time. (This was not the only game when he was behind time or failed to show. Later in the season he let his side down in their prestigious friendly against another of Arthur's old clubs, Preston North End; similarly the following season versus Stockport County.) Though the missing, by their early absence seem to have fortified their team-mates who, having held on while understrength, won by the only goal when full power was restored, each player receiving a £1 win bonus.

Interestingly, given the influential role the management of club finances had played in Arthur's career, there was some dispute over the attendance figure. The club estimated 6,000. The *Herald* gave the much higher calculation of 8,000–9,000 based upon the receipts of £150. Before the turnstiled entrance became a feature of professional club grounds estimates of crowds were just that, and reporters, officials and supporters often disagreed. (The insertion of mechanical gates was usually consequential upon clubs becoming companies, shareholders wanting an accurate recording of attendance figures for accounting purposes. At the first AGM of Stalybridge Rovers a shareholder called for them to be fitted. However, there was pressure not to improve accounting methods too quickly as it was in the economic interest of all clubs to reduce estimates of crowds in order to have undeclared cash at hand.) ANE, unlike their neighbours at Crookbottom, ran a membership scheme, were not a limited liability company and did not have turnstiles. On this count they could argue that in such circumstances there will always be disputes. However, they had given a figure of £150 for money taken at the gate which indicated the actual size of the crowd. The wide discrepancy between the club and *Herald* estimates suggests, therefore, incompetence by Ashton officials rather than an acceptable margin of error. As such it does nothing to detract from the view that the administrators at the majority of clubs at which Arthur played as a professional – with the notable exception of Sheffield United – had the financial acumen of innumerate men with no fingers or toes (or any other physiological protuberances which could be used to add and subtract).

The next two games were disastrous. Arthur let in eight goals, although four of these were against the current league leaders Stockport County. Afterwards, for the third consecutive away game versus Rochdale the goalkeeper was given a 'well earned rest'.[10] His second game back was a 'friendly' against Rovers. What a misnomer this proved to be. There was a hostile atmosphere with the visitors on the receiving end of much verbal abuse. A section of the crowd at Crookbottom – 'young gentlemen' – shouted instructions such as 'bash him' and 'worse expletives' to their players on the pitch. And the Rovers players did not turn a deaf ear. It was a stern test of Arthur's and his team's courage and professionalism. At these times the older players, with their greater experience, are expected to lead by example for the benefit of their younger team mates. Indeed this is what happened, ANE winning 5–0. Arthur was named in one report of the game as joint 'man of the match' with his colleague Saxton. The former had made some 'marvellous' saves and 'performed ... brilliantly'.[11]

After this game, during mid-November events took a turn for the worse. Arthur missed the next match through 'illness'. On his return Glossop North End put seven goals past him. The team then played four times without winning, including a 2–2 draw with their arch-rivals; that they did not get thrashed was largely down to Arthur. 'He alone saved his side from ... a licking.'[12] His inspired performance initiated a brief run of form for the team. They won their two Christmas games scoring seven goals and conceding two. And official gate receipts totalled a comforting £66.

The New Year began ominously with an 0–8 drubbing at Nelson. For the latter part of January and much of February he missed a total of five games through his 'indisposition'. The *Herald*, with a regard for privacy that was rigidly prim, did not provide a clue as to the exact nature. Whatever it was – illness or drink – it did not appear to have a lasting effect on his form. Neither was the Nelson portent realised. North End had a storming finish to the season losing just one of their final 14 games. In five of these Arthur did not let in a goal. They finished a creditable sixth of 14 and, importantly, above Rovers.

Remarkably those in control of the club's money had managed to equal the relative success on the field by announcing a profit of over £80 on the season, after £120 of the club's debt had been paid off. Most of this would have been owed to the club president H. Shaw who, when necessary, had bankrolled the club until his resignation in June 1899. With a balance of £46 in 'spare' cash, the directors prided themselves on their careful husbanding which had bought about this 'eminently satisfactory'[13] position. The sound economic base would provide the foundation to build a strong team for the coming campaign, in practice to lure players with the offer of a better wage; or just a wage.

A tale of the nineties: Third and out, 1898–99

During the summer of 1898 a number of new players were scouted, touted and signed. The squad that began the new season was reputedly the strongest yet seen at the Athletic Grounds, the majority waged professionals. Presumably a good proportion of the £46 had been used up for signing-on fees and other inducements.

Despite drawing once and losing twice in their first three games – including a 2–4 defeat at Rovers – ANE had their best season ever. They reached the third qualifying round of the FA Cup and the semi-final of the Manchester Senior Cup. They defeated Rhyl United 13–1 in the first qualifying round of the national competition. In both cups they were knocked out by rivals Stockport County after a replay.

In the league, for much of the season they occupied second or third place consistently perspiring onto the shoulders of leaders Chorley. During November, December and January ANE went unbeaten. At the end of January they defeated the reigning league champions 1–0. Yet their invincibility had not raised them above second place. The victory, though, could not have been more deceptive. What followed was a rapid decline of form and fortune.

From the beginning of February to the season's close at the end of April they won just ten of the remaining 23 matches. In mitigation it should be said that this period also saw a greater frequency of games. And there is good reason to believe that the congested fixture list and concomitant loss of form were not coincidental. They had played 24 games over the first, more successful, part of the campaign – 3 September–31 January – with its longer timespan: an average of 1.3 a week. Also, one other influential factor should be entered into the equation. Nelson FC and Rock Ferry resigned from the league at the end of January. Indeed, Nelson's last game was their 2–3 defeat by ANE on 14 January. As a consequence of their disappearance, the subsequent recalculation of point totals meant Chorley gained four points over North End. At a meeting at the end of the season G.W. Johnson, ANE secretary, thought this of vital importance in explaining the demise. However, as an administrator, he was hardly likely to consider other reasons closer to home such as an excessive programme, the scheduling of which would have been largely his doing. With the slide in the last

1. Arthur's parents, Henry and Annie Wharton (seated). Gold Coast, *c.*1850s.

2. Henry Wharton, possibly London 1863.

3. Clara, Arthur's only sister. They kept in contact until at least 1901.

4. Charles, Arthur's brother. London, *c*.1863.

5. Alfred, Arthur's brother. London, *c.*1863.

6. Arthur's wider family in the Gold Coast, possibly the sons of F.C. Grant.

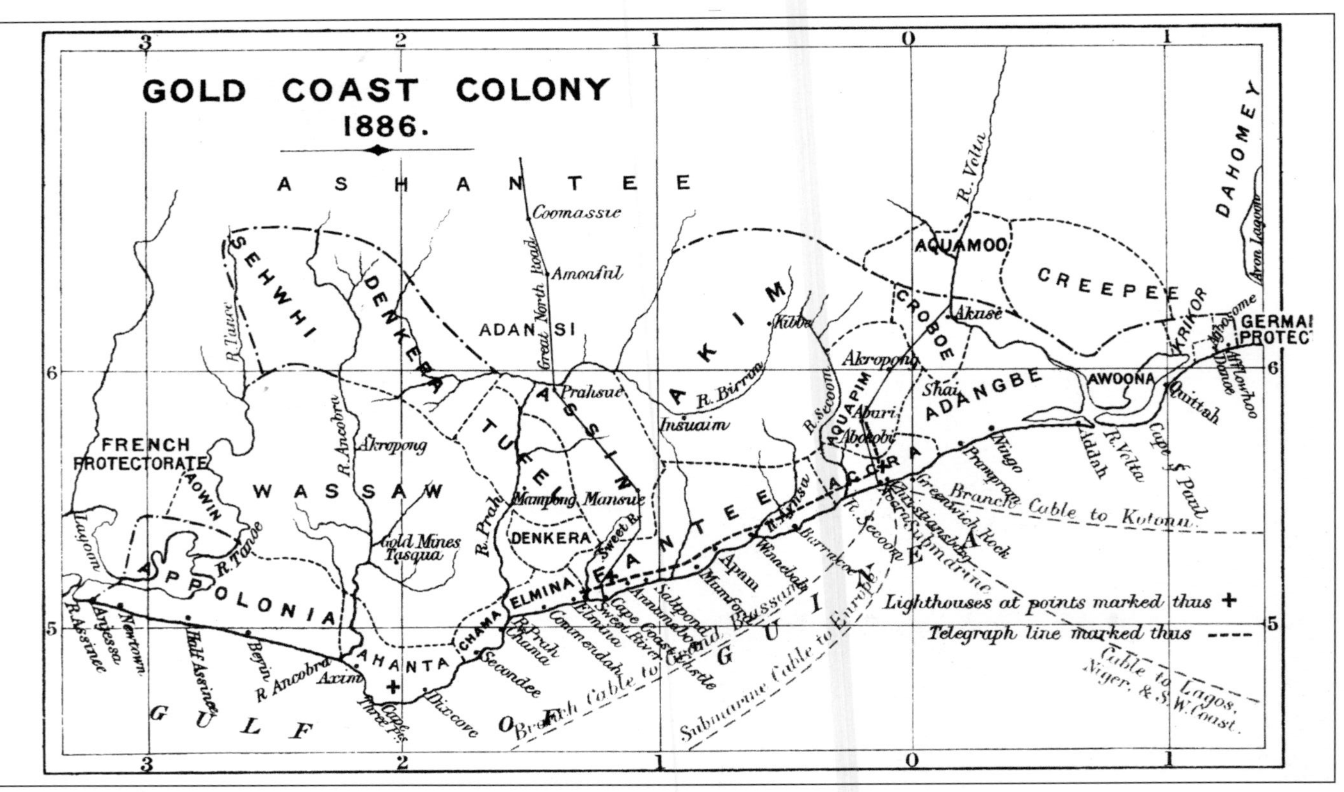

7. Map of the Gold Coast Colony, 1886.

8. The Wesleyan Chapel, James Town, Accra, showing earthquake damage. It was built between 1853 and 1854, while Henry was Resident Missionary at Accra.

9. Cape Coast Castle, a colonial fortress familiar to Arthur.

10. Aerial view of Accra, *c.*1900. The tennis court and chapel (left) represent two cultural institutions essential to the success of the imperial project: sport and Christianity.

11. With the Prince Hassan Cup, presented after winning the 100 yards title at Stamford Bridge

12. Amateur Athletic Association Champions, Stamford Bridge, London, 1886. Arthur set what was later ratified as the first world record for the 100 yard sprint.

13. Arthur (fourth from left) with the 'Invincibles', Preston North End before their game against Corinthian FC at Kensington Oval, 12 March 1887.

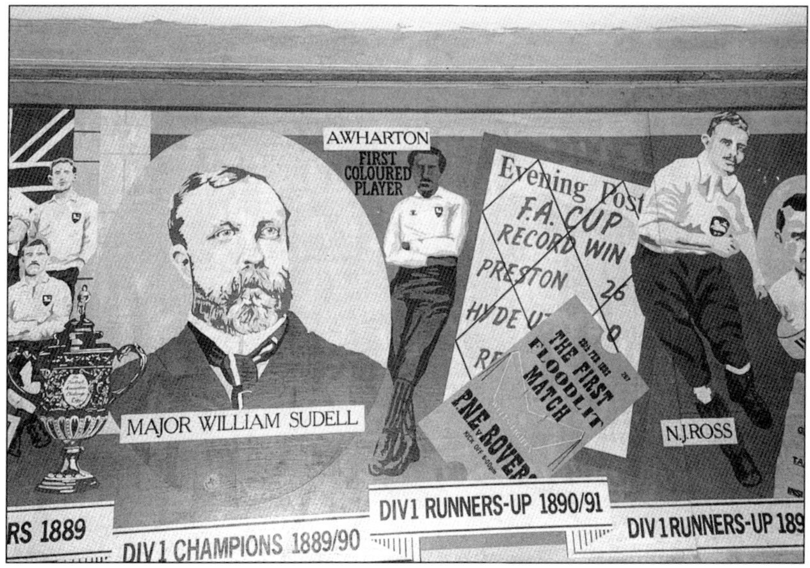

14 and 15. Arthur remembered among the stars of Preston North End's history. This mural runs along the wall of a stand at Deepdale.

16. The following season Rotherham went on to win the Midland League and were elected to the Football League.

17. Stalybridge Rovers, 1896. Arthur also played as a professional for the town's cricket team. He was a very popular member of this mill town community.

18. In football kit, *c*.1890s.

19. Rotherham Town, early 1890s.

20. Arthur's first pub, the Albert Tavern (1892–93), 55 Albert Street, Masbrough, Rotherham.

21. Arthur's third pub (after the Sportsman's Cottage), the Plough Inn (1895), 23 Greasebrough Road, Thornhill, Rotherham.

22. The Champion! Cigar, bowler hat and cane, early 1890s (top). The journeyman footballer and cricketer, mid to late 1890s (bottom).

23. The miner, *c.*1920s.

24. Sheila Leeson, Arthur's closest relative in Britain, by his newly erected gravestone, Edlington, May 1997.

25. Alwyn Tatum (left), Edlington, April 1997. Alwyn remembers Arthur from his childhood.

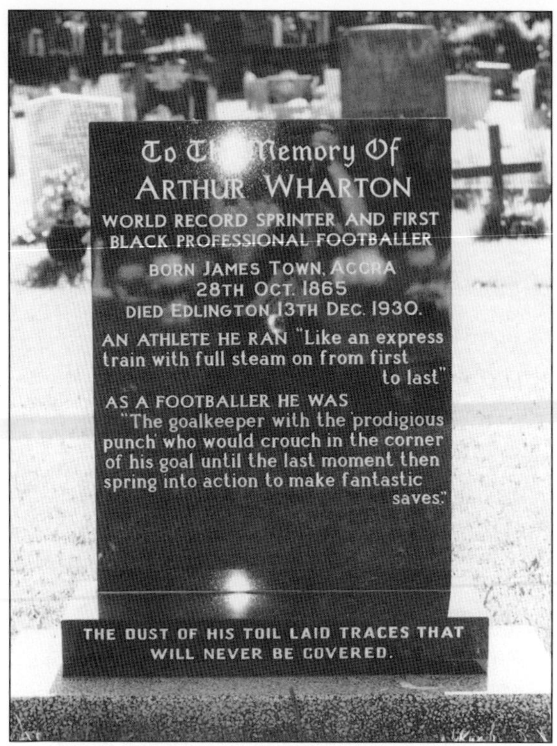

26. Spot the mistake! Arthur died on 12 December, not the 13th.

27. The dedication ceremony, Edlington, 8 May 1997. Sheila Leeson and Howard Holmes of Football Unites – Racism Divides unveil the gravestone. Sheila's grandchildren are in the foreground.

third of the season slipped any hopes of the championship; yet by finishing third it was still the highest position the club had ever achieved. On the back of this they applied to join the second division of the Football League.

Apart from another spell of 'illness' and brief loss of confidence at the start of December Arthur had played consistently well over the season as a whole, and was in excellent form in the defeat of Chorley. 'Some of the saves ... were really miraculous, and had he not been seen in his best "fisting" and "throwing out" form, [his] goal would have been penetrated more than once.' In the 3–0 win over second placed Crewe Alexandra his goalkeeping had been 'exceptionally clever'.[14] As team captain he was one of the bigger cogs in the Ashton machine. His roles as trainer, mentor, guide and inspiration, replicating those he acted out at Rovers, impressed and influenced the younger players in front of him. The quality of Arthur's performances would have been significant, both to individuals and the team as a whole. More, possibly, than any other player given the need by those of his status to act by example. It may also not be coincidental that Arthur's prolonged good form paralleled the greatest success North End ever had.

Off the field, in the counting house the atmosphere was pervaded once more by the tremulous odour of men peering into an empty cash box. At the beginning of May the *Herald* reported that there had been a 'great loss' over the season. Consequently the club may have to be 're-constituted' – made into a limited company. There had been a failed attempt at doing the same as far back as August 1896. A meeting of the club was held on 9 May when the president, H. Shaw, told the assembled that he had used £350 of his own money to keep North End going during the season. He had acted similarly during past campaigns but he was no longer prepared to do so and finished by resigning the presidency. Before departing he added a postscript. Despite an 'excellent' team, the takings at the gate on only one occasion had covered a fortnight's wages. (To do so income from matches would need to be at least £40.) To make up the shortfall he recommended a second attempt at issuing shares. In any case, he reminded the audience, money would have to be raised quickly because the application to the Football League required a £50 deposit. The meeting agreed. Though not everyone present was convinced. Secretary Johnson, interviewed by the *Herald*, thought the club should rein in its ambition, sign local lads and employ 'a few small wage professionals'.[15]

At a meeting of the Football League in Manchester ANE received no votes from other clubs in support of their application. Middlesbrough won the intrigue, gaining the place Ashton coveted and soon afterwards North End folded.

The failure of the share issue was instrumental in the collapse. A successful take-up of shares had hinged upon the club playing in the Football League. Without the promise of elite opposition the following season, investors did not feel another campaign in the Lancashire League would be worth the time and money. Once more Arthur had been a member of a very competent team – the best yet seen at the Athletic Grounds – undermined by intense competition for players and spectators and incompetent administrators. This was the second club for which he had played that had closed. It was little consolation that the formation and disappearance of clubs in the 1890s were a relatively frequent occurrence, Rock Ferry and Nelson being fresh in the mind. Hurst Ramblers, another LL side, collapsed the following season.

Football during this decade, as a sport and commodity, expanded rapidly. Clubs opting to become limited companies in so doing exposed themselves immediately to the potential of being severely buffeted, and in extreme circumstances engulfed and swept away, by the harsh and uncompromising blast of 'market forces'. Hostile conditions, when they do occur, exacerbate the congenital fragility of small-town clubs with unspectacular gates. While Arthur's experiences in this respect were not uncommon, what must have been galling for both players and supporters of Rotherham and Ashton was how so successful teams were *despite* their black-suited figureheads, some of whom were not always competent and circumspect when handling the club's financial affairs. Mason (1980), in a discussion of the relationship between the games directors played in their minds and the accounting procedures used to clear up the subsequent mess, refers us to the *Athletic News Football Annual* (*ANFA*) of the mid-1890s, which took issue with the face value of many club accounts. Creative accounting – 'fiddling the books' – was the method used to hide the administrators' fantasy and incompetence. 'The adroit use of figures in many of the published balance sheets is quite transparent, and must be set down to a strong desire to make the assets remove the big margin of debt on the current income.'[16] It was inevitable, therefore, that wafting across the economic landscape of football outside the big cities would appear with worrying frequency the sight of bursting bubbles filled with the unsatiated ambition of directors and supporters, and the unfinished careers of many a professional footballer.

'The most important match Stalybridge Rovers have ever played in'[17] *1899–1900*

Arthur, the veteran larger-than-life goalkeeper of 33, could not float away to nothingness. Stalybridge Rovers moved quickly to re-sign their former Brigade Leader, his registration completed by the first week in July. The club was equally as sharp in assuring its shareholders and supporters that players' wages will be lower than last season. Although Arthur was not mentioned by name supporters with an interest in the financial side of the club's affairs and memories of the not-too-distant past would have been fully aware of why this pre-emptive statement was made. Those cognisant of his football successes and prepared to see within him talismanic properties (of good and bad fortune) Arthur's return may have been akin to an invitation to team-mates and supporters to party to the end.

After a faltering start to the season in which Rovers lost two of their first three games, they went unbeaten for the next three months. During that spell Arthur was personally unbeaten in eight of the 13 games played. In the 2–1 defeat of Middleton in the Manchester Senior Cup the captain and goalkeeper was described as

> the best man in the Rovers' ranks ... a tower of strength to his side. One of his saves was a lovely piece of work. The ball was sent in with great rapidity, but Wharton pounced upon it, and cleared in brilliant fashion amidst great applause.[18]

We have discussed how Arthur's exuberant confidence sometimes got the better of him – thinking he could do a job outfield, for instance. It was a seminal feature of his career. This latest run of success once more over-inflated his self-belief. In the match against Rochdale in March he spent part of the game 'well over the half-way line encouraging his men'. Three weeks later, in the 8–0 slaughter of South Liverpool, Arthur took the mickey out of the Merseysiders by dribbling the ball and 'shooting in goal from the centre line',[19] much to the amusement of the home support. There were even supporters of the opposing team who were warmed by his eccentricities. However, the problem with these idiosyncratic displays was not the behaviour itself but the context, Arthur sometimes picking the wrong moment – when the scores were level – against Rochdale the score was 0–0 and stayed that way – or the game tight. When he had tried a similar tactic the previous season he had been literally caught out, Rochdale scoring with a long shot towards an unprotected net.

The undefeated run took Rovers into the fourth and last qualifying round of the FA Cup. To reach this stage they had beaten Congleton, South Liverpool and Stockport County – the eventual winners of the Lancashire League that season. Their opponents were now Burslem Port Vale from the Football League second division. Despite having to travel to the Potteries 'Arthur's Brigade' were in confident mood, third in the Lancashire League and unbeaten since mid-September, Wharton having kept three consecutive clean sheets in the games immediately prior to this cup-tie. He may also have felt a great deal of inner satisfaction in the manner of his return to the area where he first played competitive football with Cannock and Cannock White Cross football clubs nearly 18 years previously. In front of a crowd of 2,000 – in contrast the home tie against Stockport County in the third qualifying round drew 6,000, Rovers best attendance to date for the season – 'A. Wharton led the most determined set of players on to the field he has ever had under him.' Winning 1–0 their return to Stalybridge all was music and artificial light. A large crowd carrying burning torchlights, headed by a band, greeted the team at the railway station to celebrate. It was 'one of the most eventful days Rovers had ever had … [The streets] were packed all the way' to the Clarence Hotel, the club's headquarters.[20]

For the first time Stalybridge were in the first round proper of the FA Cup, drawn away to Bristol City. Yet two weeks before this historic match the Board sold Ellis Green, a rising talent at Crookbottom, to Everton for the substantial sum of £120. The *Herald*, 20 January 1900, stated that the player would receive a payment of £10 – his signing-on fee. His wages were to be £4 per week in season and £2.10s.0d (£2.50p) in the summer. This remuneration, if the figures were accurate, compared favourably to that received by other footballers. Steve Bloomer, an exceptional club and international player, started his professional career at Derby County in the 1890s on 7s.6d (37p) per week. However, highly prized performers could usually expect contracts guaranteeing a similar amount to Ellis. Crabtree of Aston Villa was receiving £4 per week all-year round in 1896. (£4 was the maximum wage allowed when a cap was put on players' earnings by the FA in 1901, the figure remaining unchanged for almost a decade.) Although Stalybridge directors had complained of poor crowds during the season – a coded way of saying there was not enough money coming in – selling one of their best players just before one of the most important games in the club's history ranks as an act of strategic incompetence and insensitivity to the needs of the team and its supporters, even by the dismal standards common to football administrators. Had they managed to negotiate with Everton two weeks' grace in the transfer they might have progressed further, which in turn would have brought in much needed income. Ellis was also cup-tied and could not have played for his new team in the competition so there was no clash of interest here. Neither did the two teams play in the same league.

By closeting themselves in the countryside at their grandly named North Britain Farm training camp Rovers hoped their preparation for the historic match against Bristol would be uninterrupted. On the Saturday before Rovers had to play a friendly against Crewe Alexandra. They sent a weakened team – Arthur being one of the absentees – so focused were they on the big event. As captain, trainer and veteran, the one player in the Rovers' team who *had* done it all before, Wharton's experience was no doubt invaluable when deciding how to approach the last Saturday in January. (As well as fulfilling these roles he had also acted as unofficial agent for Rovers and ANE by bringing at least three ex-Rotherham players – Thornton, Nicholls and Norris – for trials.) On Friday 26 the Stalybridge players and their entourage travelled down to their base at the Angel Hotel in the west country. The history of this maritime city, a port integral to the trade of slaves in West Africa, might have added an extra incentive for Arthur to prepare his men thoroughly. Four hundred somnambulant supporters from the mill-town caught the 1.20 a.m. special train on the Saturday, swelling the crowd to 5,000. (Gate receipts were £131.) It was the 'most important match [the club] had ever played in', though Bristol were favourites. Their players were on wages of up to £3 per week. The total wage bill for Stalybridge was £20 per week. Arthur lost the toss and had to play into the wind and sun. They were also irritated and a little concerned that the match officials were all southerners. At half-time they were 2–1 down. Arthur, though, had been 'a host in himself … continually applauded for his clever saves, and in no way to blame for any of the goals'.[21] During the second half neither side added to their score and Rovers were out. Afterwards, in order to revive their spirits and live-to-the-full this memorable occasion the players, supporters and officials held a concert at the Angel Hotel, at which Arthur sang, before catching the 9.20 train home arriving soon after 3 a.m., defeated but not dispirited.

In fact they eventually finished runners-up in the Lancashire League, five points behind Stockport County, whom they had beaten twice and drawn with once that season. Along with the champions Rovers had the least number of goals scored against, 23 in 28 League games, a fitting testament to Arthur's custodial skills. '[He] has given exhibitions in goal which could be excelled by few.'[22] Of the final six games of the season, Arthur had conceded one goal and this was in a friendly against Everton, arranged as part of the Ellis deal.

In recognition of the all-round competence of the team four players, including Arthur, were selected for the Rest of the Lancashire League squad for the customary game against the title holders. However, only Lawton and Johnson of Rovers played because the date clashed with the club's Ashton and District Charity Cup final against Glossop of the Football League first division. In this game the trophy was shared after a 0–0 draw.

'Arthur's Brigade' also played in the Manchester Senior Cup where they were knocked out in the first round by Billy Meredith's Manchester City. Meredith, rebellious and gifted, was to become an equally engaging character of the profession. The imagination and emotions quicken contemplating the dialogue of any meeting he and Wharton may have had off the park. It could be argued that Wharton and Foulke, but Meredith in particular, were the *enfants terribles* of the pre-1915 era. None would touch their forelock to authority, preferring to meet their masters head-on. Meredith was banned from playing for a time, while Foulke had a penchant for eating his team's breakfasts – all of them – and chasing referees naked with a view to putting some questions about decisions made during the game. Certainly all three, in their different ways, were larger than life.

Almost inevitably the success in cup and league created problems the directors did not envisage (this is what was worryingly predictable!) or seem able to cope with. After the Everton game the *Herald* reported the Board 'experiencing much trouble in signing on the men they require for next season'. A week later it noted that only two players had signed: a newcomer and a reserve. In other words none of the first 11 had yet put pen to paper and been re-engaged! The directors, mindful of the need to drum up support for their stance, publicly reassured Rovers fans, who may have been puzzled and annoyed in equal proportion by this potentially catastrophic news, that 'more than 50 players' from other clubs had offered their services. This last piece of information was directed at not only the befuddled fans but also the recalcitrant footballers. To the latter the sub-text of the ultimatum read: accept the terms offered because there are plenty more waiting to take your place. It was a tried and tested tactic of employers of footballers; of the employing class generally.

The players were not being obstinate for the sake of it. They were also playing a strategic game: before agreeing to any wage deal they were waiting to see if Rovers' application to join the second division of the Football League – a move that was the direct consequence of success on the field – would win the required votes. If the club were elected the bargaining power of the players would be improved. Wages in 1899–1900 had been lower than the season before. Yet they had still finished as runners-up. Off the field, also, they had the support of the balance sheet. Gate receipts totalled £813; wages paid £721. Given his pre-eminence in the team and past record in holding out for a contract to his liking, it is not unlikely that Wharton acted as *de facto* shop steward and chief negotiator in all of this. He was no stranger to contractual disputes with employers. So, for the second season in succession Wharton found himself waiting upon the outcome of a meeting of the Football League that would have a great bearing on his future; and yet again he was disappointed by the result.

The 'Remarkably good looking' 'Kaffirs': The first Black tourists

Arthur was not the only African-born Black footballer fans could have watched or read about this century-crossing season. A team of the Basuto tribe from Southern Africa, called the 'Kaffirs', arrived at Southampton at the beginning of September 1899. They were the first Black African team to play outside that continent. They may well have been the first African football tourists – even if we include White South Africans. Their trip to Britain had been organised by the (European)

Orange Free State Football Association (OFSFA) controlled by Anglo-Europeans. (The president was a Mr Hudgson, chairman of the Rangers FC of Bloemfontein. Afrikaners favoured rugby.) The reason for the visit is unclear other than to raise funds for the OFSFA who, it seems, were determined that the team's sojourn in England would pay its way and more: 36 games had been arranged against the best teams of England and Scotland. The White masters of Orange Africa really did expect them to 'work like niggers'. The punishing schedule was due to have begun on 1 September against Aston Villa, the current Football League champions. But the liner *Gaika* on which the 'Kaffirs' had sailed berthed nine days late, eventually arriving on 2 September.

In fact their opening game was against Newcastle United, also of the first division, at St James's Park three days later. The language used in the pre-match publicity to describe the physical characteristics of the visitors hinted at and subtly exploited the myth of the unrepressed sexuality of the African. 'The visitors [are] a fine lot of men … reputed to possess remarkable staying powers. [They are] clever at the game.' A number of the team were over six feet tall and 'proportionately built … Some of them remarkably good looking, and of an intelligent cast of features'.[23] A large crowd of 6,000 assembled with 'a sprinkling of the fair sex'. Some inquisitive and welcoming folk had even gone to Central Station on their arrival in the city. The 'Kaffirs', wearing orange shirts with dark blue collars and shorts, did not match expectations. The Geordies coasted to victory 6–3 as did all but one of the teams they faced. The final statistics read: played 36, won 0, drawn 1, lost 35 with 235 goals conceded.

Other North East opponents were Sunderland – the pre-eminent club of the region having won the first division three times in the 1890s – to whom the 'Kaffirs' lost 5–3, and Middlesbrough, who won 7–3. In all three games the Black footballers were treated patronisingly, as overgrown children: 'They are a very heavy lot and caused a great deal of amusement' (v. Newcastle United); 'The delightful darkey returned to the centre line as proud as the proverbial dog' (v. Sunderland); 'From a corner just on the interval, the Kaffirs amidst loud laughter were permitted to score' (v. Middlesbrough). Without irony it also reported that 'the darkeys played a very gentlemanly game, and it says much for their good temper – which must have been sorely tried – that they did not utilise their obvious strength of body and cranium'.[24]

The various quotes betray a confusion of attitudes towards the

'Kaffirs'. They were big and strong, handsome yet excruciatingly naive and honest. However, while it would have been simple, literally, to portray the 'Kaffirs' as freak-show footballers for the amusement and entertainment of the Master Race, matters became complicated by the unfolding tragedy of the political and military crisis in southern Africa, which descended into the Boer War in October 1899. A feature of the political debate was the allegiance of the Black – or 'Kaffir' and 'Bantu' as they were often disparagingly labelled – populations. Basutoland, the homeland of the 'Kaffir' footballers, was sandwiched between the Orange Free State, which was a Boer Republic, and Natal, an English-speaking colony. With whom the Basutos would side was a live question in British newspapers. Perhaps not unexpectedly but certainly unenviably the Africans found themselves on a tour organised by administrators of British descent in a country at war with the Afrikaans-speaking government and population of the Orange Free State. This political dimension created a dilemma for reporters and editors, some of whom continued to work the tourists as malleable raw material with which to galvanise latent public prejudice. The (Southampton) *Football Echo and Sports Gazette* informed its readers of the 'Kaffirs' arrival via a cartoon situated centrally on its front page: John Bull echoing Kipling's sentiment of the colonies as the 'White Man's Burden'. The *Athletic News* followed in similar vein. Like the cartoon in the *Football Echo and Sports Gazette* it was placed so readers could not miss it. Instead of a group of Africans it had an individual, in football kit, but wearing only one boot. Holding a spear and tomahawk, with a ring through his nose and feathers in his hair, he is kicking a ball. Underneath is the caption: 'Jeeohsmiffikato the crack Kaffir centre forward thirsting for gore and goals.'[25]

Others were more sensitive – to the political needs of imperial Britain. During war-scare September there were fears expressed in the press that 'Boer spies' were inciting the Basutos to rise up against Natal. In light of this should not the tourists be utilised in the anti-Boer propaganda offensive? If so their demeaning image, as portrayed through the press, should be toned down, they and their peoples may well be needed as allies should the emergency escalate.

Much of the ambivalent language used in the reporting of the 'Kaffirs' reflected the environment of naked, competing propaganda that all war scares generate. The zeal with which some scribblers tailored the ideological content of their output to accord with pressing military and political demands and sensitivities sometimes overrode and contradicted 'common-sense' notions previously held. Thus during the war-scare period the Afrikaners became light-skinned savages, a configuration that at one and the same time paved the way for, and justified their imprisonment in, concentration camps, and negated the rhetorical force of arguments which opposed such inhumane treatment by their British captors. In contrast, the anatomy and character of the Zulus and Basutos were scoured for positive representation. Momentarily then, in some newspapers, for some editors and reporters, Boer became Black and Black became something else. This contradictory and confused state of affairs is illustrated by description of other contemporary southern African visitors – human exhibits of the 'Savage South Africa' exhibition at Earls Court – as the 'magnificent men from the Zulu country'. Yet, soon after opening London County Council officials instructed the manager, Mr Edwin Cleary, to section off the 'native kraals' in order to prevent the public from fraternising with the 'heathen warriors' and their 'ebony babies'.[26]

The tourists, bombarded by goals and propaganda, succumbed to the barrage. In their rescheduled fixture with Aston Villa gate receipts went to a Boer War fund. (The fever of patriotism spread to other clubs, including Arthur's. Stalybridge Rovers donated 10 per cent of their gate versus Horwich in January 1900 to the cause.)

The comparison of press responses to the 'Kaffirs', the Zulus and Arthur has shown them susceptible to conditioning by influential political pressures and social events. While Arthur had rarely been the subject of such blatant, humiliating and thoroughly dehumanising racism as the cartoons ridiculing the Basuto footballers – pencilled illustrations of Scientific Racism – the column inches devoted to such poison cannot have left Arthur untouched.

Compounding this 'competition' over the retexturing of Black and White images, the Asante of West Africa were rebelling once more. Their rising against the colonial government led to British military being used at Kumase. The renewed deployment of an imperial killing-force in another part of Africa – with the attendant jingoistic press coverage at home – and its effect upon the treatment Arthur subsequently received can only be guessed at, although we do have a modern parallel to aid this speculation. The unprecedented booing and abuse Argentineans Ricky Villa and Ossie Ardiles received when they ran out, and every time they touched the ball in the Spurs v. Leicester 1982 FA Cup semi-final, was a direct result of the outbreak a few days earlier of the Anglo-Argentine war over the sovereignty of the Falklands/Malvinas. The vilification continued in other games and intensified until it was impossible for them to remain in the team, or in Britain: although Ardiles later returned. (The two were not the first of Spurs' players to be forced out of the team by racist abuse. I have argued elsewhere that W.D. Tull's place in the 1909–10 team was sacrificed by management to pacify racists after just seven appearances.)

Such comparisons are laden with problems – the 1982 conflict was televised and, with reference to Villa and Ardiles, had an immediate effect; the Asante and Boer conflicts were relayed (and delayed) through newspapers, journals, photographs, letters and word of mouth – yet they do provide some sense of how the present can illuminate the past, albeit with varying degrees of relevance and power. Whether public attitudes towards Arthur changed after 1900 (or 1896) cannot be verified. The input an examination of the Villa/Ardiles episode makes to such deliberations is one of quality – it adds to our understanding of the causes of generalised racism but it does not explain or reveal the daily texture and nature of the racism faced by Wharton or the 'Kaffirs' in 1900. However, what is clear is that it cannot have been beneficial to any African in Britain to have the ridiculing and killing of other Africans retold with jingoistic fervour to such a wide and apparently eager audience. For Wharton, the newsworthiness and prominence of incompetent Black South African footballers in the sporting press and troublesome West Africans in the political columns of the national dailies, may have seemed like a pincer movement from which he as a Black man could not escape.

The pieman's augury: 1900–1

The season, which in the preceding summer months had looked as though it were doomed, began with much promise. The contractual problems that retrospectively contaminated the achievements of the previous season had been settled. It seems also that the players were victorious in their pursuit of better wages for in mid-season Rovers were to sell two players for £220, a financial reordering to keep the remaining squad together. The disappointment of not gaining a Football League place was soon forgotten amidst the revived mood of confidence, Rovers sprinting to the top of the table scoring eight goals with none conceded in their first two games. They remained undefeated in the league until 24 November, with seven straight wins. Their only defeats coming in cup competitions: 2–3 away to (re-formed) Nelson in the Lancashire Senior and 0–3 away to Lancashire League champions Crewe Alexandra in the third qualifying round of the FA Challenge.

Nelson, coincidentally, were the first to defeat Rovers in the league, 2–1. The original game had been abandoned 11 minutes from time, the Lancashire FA ordering, not untypically, the clubs to play out the remaining 660 seconds at a later date! The setback at Nelson was quickly exorcised with a 7–1 win over Haydock. The loudest cheer at this match, however, went to the pie-seller who stole the show from Arthur and his men with an unintended forward somersault caused by catching his foot on one of the pegs holding down the goal-net, upsetting his tray of pies and a pot of hot gravy into the mud. Had Arthur been superstitious – pies come before a fall! – he might have read a coded warning in the gymnastics behind his goal. In fact he did not play in a winning Rovers side after this. A draw and two defeats from the Christmas games played after the pieman's mishap redefined the Haydock 'revival' to an aberration. The 7–1 win now represented the only success in the last five games. This sudden, dramatic deterioration of form after such an inspirational opening to the campaign was made worse with a statement by Wharton to the *Herald* that he was 'finished'.[27] The directors meanwhile made it clear through their reaction that they were of the same mind, signing another goalkeeper, Adam Armstrong formerly of Rochdale and Glossop, 12 years younger and of the same height.

Arthur's sudden departure seems to have had more behind it than a loss of form. The directors may have felt that his personality and influence as captain, trainer, scout and agent were overshadowing theirs. And, if Arthur had been the prime mover in the demand for higher wages, which seems very likely, this literal strike at the heart of their power came at the price of Arthur's own security of tenure within the club. Immediately he was not delivering the goods, either individually as goalkeeper or collectively as captain, the opportunity to show him the door would have been too great to resist. For his part, Arthur may have been angered by the sale of two players half-way through the team's campaign effectively breaking up a winning side. His frustration and irritation may have been compounded by seeing their departure as a repeat of the badly timed Ellis Green transfer. From the players' point of view, especially someone as instrumental as the captain – who had more power in the 1890s than their counterparts of the 1990s: to influence the selection of players (made by the directors); devise playing strategy, for instance – the job of directors is to ensure the acquisition and retainment of quality players, underpinned by sound finance. Not to sell such players when the team is doing well. However, such a well-defined division of labour within a football club can never exist when the players, as wage labourers, consistently seek to improve their pay and conditions, while the directors, as employers, with equal consistency attempt to lower costs through holding or lowering wages. Such a clash of class interests inevitably produces the confrontational scenarios that marked Arthur's career in professional football. The directors, as owners and employers, in most instances would have the upper-hand: the power, ultimately, to choose who did or did not play; and how much the active were paid. (This last-named but fundamental economic conflict in the relations between capital and labour in the Football League was decided in the employers' favour with the introduction of the maximum wage in 1901.)

Unity is strength: 1901–2

Arthur joined Stockport County of the Football League second division in August 1901. He had not played senior football since December 1900. The Cheshire club – directly south of Stalybridge, on the south-eastern outskirts of Manchester – was in its second season in the Football League. They finished last but one in their inaugural campaign. The directors felt their lack of success had been primarily a consequence of their players being too small. They had been pushed off the ball with impunity and too easily intimidated. During the summer, in an effort to remedy the brawn deficiency, they had actively cruised for big men. Arthur made his debut alongside seven other newcomers, all 'players of considerable bodily substance'.[28] A 'considerable' amount of 'substance' was shown by all players, not just the big men as we will see, in more ways than was countenanced by the directors.

The game-plan of bulk buying to juggernaut their way through the season, in contrast to applying a strategy that included both muscular agility and thoughtful 'scientific' passing play, did not immediately bring the expected results. The first three league games were lost, with nine goals conceded and none scored. Arthur did not seem to have been more at fault than the rest of his team. In their first win, 1–0 at home to Blackpool:

> Wharton was even more watchful than usual, and on several occasions was 'on the ball' with success when many custodians less marvellously alert would have cut a sorry figure. 'Good Old Wharton' was the general cry of the crowd behind the goal who had the best view of his work.

His agility was sorely tested, literally. 'Wharton was severely bustled with the ball on the goal-line.'[29] However, as the score testifies, he managed to stand his ground and, if past experience of such occasions is any guide, no doubt gave some licks in return.

Arthur played six second division and one Manchester Senior Cup game for the first team. His last Football League appearance was against Newton Heath – now Manchester United – at Bank Street, Clayton. (At the end of a 3–3 draw the referee was escorted off the field by police, home fans angered by his decisions.) Stockport were now fourth from bottom. The veteran sportsman spent the rest of the season in the reserves. The Newton Heath fixture was Arthur's last senior game. It marked the end of his first-team career in professional football.

Stockport finished the season last but one in the second division, five points ahead of Gainsborough Trinity. The finances of the club were as desperate as their league position. At the AGM the troubled state of affairs was examined. The debt of £450 from the previous season had doubled. The weekly wage bill was £40 for the first team, with the average wage being £2, while only twice had the income from a home match covered a fortnight's wages. Senior professionals on more than the average – this would have included Wharton – came in for severe criticism. They were like 'hot house plants' wanting pampering and everything done for them. Some speakers thought the struggle to retain league status, with the attendant necessity of signing these human, footballing equivalent of arboretum exotica, not worth the trouble. The suggestion that County go back into the Lancashire

League with local players, or even the Lancashire Combination League, was met with cries of 'hear, hear'.[30]

The lack of money in the club account had been made public in March. Then the committee, with the Pavlovian response the cynical side of Arthur must have come to expect, attempted to redress the problem by reducing wages. The players steadfastly refused. In fact they went further: not only would they tell the directors to shove their wage cut, for the next game against Leicester Fosse they, the players, would pick the team and take the gate money! It was an unprecedented use of collective strength *off* the field. On it they made two changes to the team originally selected by the committee – and won. Afterwards, they shared out the gate money, taking home 25s.0d (£1.25p) each. The revolt did not last. The following week County were beaten 4–0 by PNE and were not paid their wages.

That such a show of collective muscle took place at a Manchester club represented not only historical continuity with the city's tradition of generalised working-class militancy – it had been the beating political heart of those Chartists who favoured the use of physical force as the means to political ends – but a local rehearsal of what was to come. A few years after the Stockport Rebellion other Manchester-based footballers formed the active hub of attempts to revive the Players' Union. At the core of this struggle to organise, agitate and educate fellow professionals were Billy Meredith of Manchester City and Charlie Roberts of Manchester United. These had no qualms about violating the rules over the maximum wage. Like many others, they felt they were worth more than the £4 maximum wage allowed by employers: how would they, the bosses, react to any similar restriction on their profits/earnings?

While there is no conclusive proof that Arthur had been involved in the dressing-room coup it would be surprising if he had remained a silent onlooker. Despite not being a member of the first team at the time, he was a senior professional who would have had his wages cut if the committee had their way. Given what we know of Wharton's track record in industrial disputes, he would probably have been eager to fist the ball hard and fast into the employers' half of the pitch and be first to deal forcefully with any unwanted return.

In summary, although Wharton played his final games for the reserves in the Lancashire Combination, his last days as a professional footballer were characteristic of themes that played throughout his long career in sport: class conflict and competition, as metaphor. In respect of the former he was at a club where the players had taken part in unprecedented collective action in defence of their economic interests. His period was one of rapid growth and financial insecurity in the sports industry. Where these processes had combined effectively to undermine the welfare of the participants, it is quite obvious that Arthur was not prepared to be passive. With regard to the latter, his last game was against a club that has, in the second half of the twentieth century, become a giant in English football and provided the initial platform for the writer of the introduction to this book to launch his career. Arthur achieved national fame as goalkeeper with the 'Invincibles' of Preston North End, the 'best team in the world' and departed the Football League bowing out against a club that were to become pretenders to that title over half a century later. The trajectory of his football career, a rapid rise followed by a slow but inexorable decline, had a curious symmetry with his life outside the game. He came to England as a 'gentleman' and finished as a working man in poverty. A sport that Arthur Hopcraft (1971), in attempting to explain its overwhelming attraction to working-class people, described as an escape route from routinised drudgery acted for Wharton as a route *into* the 'ghetto'.

Arthur's playing career in senior football – 1885–1902 – spans the years between the Conference of Berlin, at which rules for the continuing looting of Africa were decided by the political representatives of the grabbing parties, and the end of the Boer War – a conflict that exposed the relationship between technological advance and the scope and depravity of imperial military brutality. The symbolic relationship this geo-political context has to Arthur's attempts to beat his European competitors at their own game, on their own ground, has been discussed, is transparent and is a subject to which we will return.

Sport, and football in particular, is an industry in which contributions are all too quickly forgotten; in which there is a void, an absence, of memory. A pertinent example of this historiographic amnesia is the lack of *any* mention of Wharton in Maurice Golesworthy's *Encyclopaedia of Association Football* (1973 edition). (There were 11 editions between 1956 and 1973.) Under the heading 'Coloured Players' we find: 'Before World War II probably no more than three coloured players had made Football League appearances.' Even a brief survey of contemporary newspapers between 1888 and 1939 would have thrown up at least six 'coloured' FL players. And there were others who played in the Southern League, such as the Cother brothers of Watford. The section that deals with 'Foreign Players in [the] Football League' again fails to note Arthur's achievements. Similarly the material on 'Goalkeepers'.[31] The most astonishing feature of Golesworthy's omission is the relative prominence of Wharton as a Victorian sports celebrity in comparison to less publicised careers of other Black players who are included. Golesworthy, it appears, had assumed the outlook of the school of monochrome British history, that implies Black settlement of any note is a phenomenon of the second half of the twentieth century. A fuller discussion of the causes of this erasure from the collective memory of the history of football is continued in the final chapter.

NOTES

1. T. Mason, *Association Football and English Society 1863–1915* (Brighton 1980) p. 171, n. 60.
2. *Ashton Herald*, 11 January 1896.
3. Ibid., 11 April 1896.
4. PRO Board of Trade 31/5563, 38703 in Tony Mason, op. cit., p. 34.
5. *Ashton Herald*, 28 August 1896.
6. Ibid., 5 December 1896.
7. *Ashton Herald*, 30 January 1897.
8. Ibid., 20 March 1897.
9. *Sheffield Daily Telegraph*, 16 December 1930.
10. *Ashton Herald*, 6 November 1897.
11. Ibid., 20 November 1897.
12. Ibid., 18 December 1897.
13. Ibid., 6 and 20 August 1898.
14. Ibid., 4 and 25 February 1899.
15. Ibid., 6 and13 June 1899.
16. 'Rob Roy' *ANFA* (1895 edition) in Mason (1980) p. 58, n. 125.
17. *Ashton Herald*, 3 February 1900.
18. Ibid., 7 October 1899.
19. Ibid., 17 March and 7 April 1900.
20. Ibid., 16 December 1899.
21. Ibid., 3 February 1900.
22. Ibid., 21 April 1900.
23. *Newcastle Evening Chronicle*, 2 September 1899; *Sporting Man* (Newcastle) 5, 6 September 1899.
24. *African Review*, 9 September, xx, 355; *Sporting Man* (Newcastle) 7 September 1899; ibid., 8 September respectively.
25. 18 September 1899.
26. *Illustrated Sporting and Dramatic News*, 9 December 1899, pp. 573–4.

27. 29 December 1900.
28. *Cheshire Daily Echo*, 17 August 1901.
29. Ibid., 23 and 28 September 1901.
30. *Cheshire Daily Echo*, 7 May 1902.
31. Golesworthy, pp. 44, 83 and 89–90.

10 *The all-rounder: Cricket, rugby and cycling*

Cricket

From 1889 Arthur played cricket professionally during the football close season. It was the team sport that he was active in longest – until his fifties at least. It may well have been the first game he encountered as a boy in the Gold Coast; and at Burlington Road School in London. We know for sure that the game was established in the Cape Coast–Accra coastal belt during Arthur's time in the colony. He also played cricket at Cannock and Darlington. Many of his athletic triumphs while a student in the North East were under the vest of the Darlington Cricket Club. But it was the local Yorkshire and Lancashire leagues from which he earned a summer living. He was described by the secretary of Rotherham Cricket Club as 'a magnificent fielder, a safe catch, and his well known running abilities enable him to make a lot of clever performances ... a good all-round cricketer'.[1] Greasebro', the home parish of Emma, hired his services for six seasons from 1889 to 1895, with an interruption for one season – 1891 – at Rawmarsh (playing alongside a Lister, the family name of his wife). He finished sixth in that season's averages. In 1895 he turned out for both Rawmarsh and Greasebro'; and in 1891 and 1894 for Rotherham Borough Police. (Arthur as publican ensuring his licence?)

He signed as a professional for Stalybridge Cricket Club in 1896. A 'large crowd' turned out for his debut on 2 May. Within weeks he was their star attraction, encouraging many of his newly won football acolytes at Crookbottom to take an interest. 'On Wharton issuing from the pavilion there was perfect hurricane of applause, and amidst whistling and shouting and cries of "play-up, Rovers" he walked leisurely to the wicket.'[2] At the end of his first season he was allowed a benefit, over two evenings against Dukinfield. Yet, despite his overwhelming popularity, Arthur did not play cricket for Stalybridge after 1896. There seems little doubt that his departure was caused by his leaving the football club in 1897. He did turn out for Ashton Cricket Club on one occasion in August 1897. During the rest of his time in Lancashire he appears to have played little or no cricket.

On leaving professional football in 1902 and Lancashire at some unspecified time shortly after, returning to Yorkshire this more – superficially – genteel attraction took pride of place in Arthur's affections. Playing for Rotherham Town in 1907 he was still, at the age of 41, forcing reporters to scribble superlatives. Under the heading 'a bit of colour in the game' the correspondent of the *Rotherham Advertiser*, 10 August, eulogised Arthur's attacking power in scoring 86 not out in a total of 168.

> If one could be sure of seeing such cricket as was played by Arthur Wharton, the 'coloured gentleman' at Clifton Lane on Monday in the match with Denaby pretty regularly, one would have no hesitation in predicting big attendances at the home matches of the town club. Wharton played a wonderful innings of forceful cricket against his old club, which was quite the feature of the match … Wharton scored at a Jessop-like pace … He put on 16 runs in one over, and he hit two successive balls out of the ground, for six each … I never thought Arthur could hit so hard, and play such sound and merry cricket.

It is not known whether Arthur was being paid to smack balls onto the roofs and into the road beyond, but his reputation was such that he was offered the chance to coach a cricket team in Burnopfield, Co Durham in 1914.[3] He eventually turned it down because the promise of employment alongside his coaching duties was not fulfilled.

It was at Edlington, playing for his works team, Yorkshire Main colliery, that Arthur faced his last balls. With 1,400 men mining the newly sunk shaft, the pit was one of the largest in the South Yorkshire coalfield. The sports and social club thrived. To this day the Miners' Welfare Club backs onto a cinder running track, cricket and football pitch. There is even a purpose-built hall for cricket training in the winter months. Alwyn Tatum, a lifelong resident of Edlington, as a young boy remembers Arthur coming up from hauling coal trucks underground, stripping to shorts, vest and pumps and practising his sprints – well into his fifties. 'He could [still] catch pigeons.'[4]

Rugby

Arthur is listed as having played one game at three-quarter back for Yorkshire club Heckmondwike on Saturday 8 September 1888.[5] Yet the *Sheffield Telegraph*, 11 September, has him running in the heat of the Sheffield Handicap at Queen's Ground in the city. Even a man as fast as Arthur could not have been in two places at once. This was one of the most important weekends of Arthur's professional running career. The following Monday he won the Handicap. He had played rugby while at Shoal Hill, Cannock. Arthur may have played for Heckmondwike sometime during the week prior to his Sheffield competition. They were known to pay their players and this may have persuaded Arthur to give it a try, though he could not get the hang of the three-quarter position. He also played for fellow runner T.H. Mountford's team for the charity match in aid of a Christmas tree at Darlington in December 1887.

Cycling

Arthur set a record time of two hours for riding a tricycle between Blackburn and Preston in August 1887. It seems he suffered more than saddle-soreness. 'A friend of mine who made the journey with him, but who had to be continually returning to hunt him up, says that occasionally he could hear a fearful warwhoop. On looking round he invariably found tricycle and Wharton in a confused heap with the latter always underneath.'[6] Alwyn Tatum has memories of Arthur as a keen cyclist while living in Edlington. He recalls the shed at the bottom of Stavely Street – the Whartons lived at 54 – where the pitman kept his *two-wheeled* machine. And the frequency with which Arthur was out and about.

NOTES

1. *Ashton Herald*, 18 April 1896.
2. Ibid., 9 and 23 May 1896.
3. Jenkins (1990) p. 52 n. 10.
4. Interview, Edlington 10 March 1997. Broadcast on *Black Britain* BBC2 23 April 1997.
5. *Heckmondwike Reporter*, 15 September 1888.
6. *Football News and Athletic Journal*, 3 September 1887. I am grateful to Ian Rigby, historian of Preston North End for bringing this to my attention.

11 *The making of the sportsman*

The Gold Coast and outdoor competitive British sports

Wherever nineteenth-century Britons went so did their sports. In the Gold Coast modern (British) outdoor sports emerged in the 1870s. In May 1874 a rifle club was set up in Cape Coast. Three years later a race course was designed near James Town, Accra. (A gymnasium for the upper echelons of the Gold Coast Police Force was also opened in the 1870s.) At the beginning of the 1880s cricket matches were being played; in the 12 months from December 1881 at least five took place at the Parade Ground of the First West India Regiment, Cape Coast. Among the participants were African-Caribbean soldiers and Euro-Africans, including Charles Wharton and three of his Grant cousins. It would be surprising if the young Arthur had not been included in some way given the level of his extended family's involvement. It was a game in which he later came to excel. Interestingly, from a cultural perspective the description of energetic side-shows by youths entertaining themselves at these cricket matches bares a remarkable similarity to those in the modern Caribbean: 'The ground was enlivened by music consisting of a clarionet (*sic*) and two kettle drums. Young men uninterested in cricket were occupied in dancing and young ladies in watching them.'[1]

The evolution of competitive outdoor sports in the Gold Coast was speeded by the movement, in 1877, of the administrative capital from Cape Coast to the plains and surrounding hills of Accra which provided a more even terrain suitable for sports pitches. Even so, association football took a while to become popular. There was a number of reasons for this: compared to cricket it was a relatively new game; football tended not to be the game of the class of European expatriates working in the colonial service; and, finally, there was the struggle over its value between the rising and declining generations of Euro-Africans.

The Gold Coast was not settled by Europeans to any great extent. It did not have a large settler population, as was the case in South and East Africa. Most incoming European migrants tended to be upper middle-class civil servants, traders, missionaries or short stay soldiers and sailors who would play sports associated with their class background; the bourgeois choosing shooting and game-hunting, tennis, cricket, horse-riding and polo. Most soldiers stationed in the garrisons were indigenous African and African-Caribbean. The latter were more inclined towards cricket, as the quote above illustrates. The practice of temporary postings for rank and file European soldiers meant they were not able or inclined to develop sustainable structures of competition in football, such as leagues, that would outlast their stay. Another consideration was 'the heat of the country' limiting adherents of modern sports to 'a few supporters here'.[2]

In 1882 Arthur's uncle, F.C. Grant, organised as leader of the Gold Coast Temperance Movement, an athletic sports afternoon which included football as part of a package of events, physical and spiritual, designed to steer Euro-African youth away from the allure of alcohol. The promotion of modern sport in this context could be seen as a kind of loss leader in the attempt by Grant and his moralist colleagues to capture an audience of souls-to-be-saved: as the physical means to a spiritual end rather than the legitimation of an imported cultural practice by influential elders. It was not until the closing years of the century, well after Arthur had left, that the growth of British outdoor sports quickened to an aerobic pace that, by then, had its own momentum that was not reliant on expatriate energies.

What seems probable is that Arthur would have been introduced to cricket, athletics and football, as well as other games in the colonial repertoire, as a young boy in Cape Coast and Accra, before his schooling in Britain. In fact, argues Jenkins (1990), it may well have been UK-educated Gold Coast (Euro-)Africans – of which there were over 200 between 1850 and 1900 – bringing back knowledge and experience of cricket and football, that pioneered these games rather than expatriate British. This seems to be the inference in the fears expressed by an indignant reader of the *Gold Coast Times,* alarmed at the prospect of football taking a hold among the indigenous youth:

> I was told afterwards that the intended club for which the circular had been issued [by 'some young gentleman recently from England'] was nothing more than a football club. A football club and nothing else! [It is by] the cultivation of the perceptive faculties only [that] we can affirm those powers of conception which are essential to our future advancement in life … our country's welfare cannot be served by mere football and cricket clubs. The mere dressing gaudily and appearing pompously as is common among our young men, and the only thing which seems to be cared for by them is on the contrary not what makes the man, but the mind when it is well-cultured. [Their time is] only squandered in pursuit of idle sports and vicious pleasures.[3]

There is little doubt that young Euro-Africans – especially those who had been educated in Britain, or in West African schools and colleges imparting a British educational ethos such as the Wesleyan High School Cape Coast or Fourah Bay College, Sierra Leone – faced difficulties in establishing time, space and the facilities for playing modern sports. Athletics, cricket, association and rugby football, while being incorporated into the curriculum British schools, were not encouraged by many influential Euro-African elders. These believed that the muscular dimension to imperial (Christian) culture could not and should not be transplanted to West Africa. Jenkins (1990) identified within them four groups with discernible differences in attitude, varying from hostility to willing participation: (1) the 'Rejectionists', comprising many of the business and intellectual elite who saw modern games as an interference in the traditional concerns of capitalism and Christianity. Working up a sweat on dusty open space would not bring upward social mobility for Euro-Africans; (2) the 'Reformists' included many Masons who encouraged passive indoor games such as chess, draughts and billiards in a mixed environment of Euro-Africans and Europeans. More intellect-engaging pursuits such as lectures, and the reading of periodicals and newspapers would also provide exercise of the mind, an activity of much greater value to the advancement of the community. The composite position of these two groups, sub-divided into four component parts, was that: (a) the wear and tear of repeated physical exertion in the tropical climate would damage the body; (b) the mind could be utilised and conditioned more efficiently in cerebral exercises; (c) the sharpening of intellectual skills, particularly in the ways of commerce, would be more beneficial to the (economic and social) health of the Euro-African community; (d) outdoor sports were in many respects unchristian in that they did not, as a guiding principle, promote civilised ways of thinking and acting. They were opposed by two generally younger groupings that used sport for career advancement or enjoyment, and in rare circumstances, both. These were: (3) the 'Instrumentalists' who saw cultural activity, including sport, as another theatre of struggle in the general advancement of Euro-Africans; and (4) the 'Collaborationists', mostly those young Euro-African graduates of schools and colleges in Britain who, while there, had played and enjoyed competitive sports. To these, sport was more than just a cultural commodity through which economic and social gains could be made. There was a genuine liking for some of the intrinsic qualities such as vigorous exercise, camaraderie and collective endeavour; and the opportunity games like cricket and football provided for breaking down barriers of class and ethnicity, even if only temporarily. However, this is not to argue that modern sports clubs in the Gold Coast (or Britain) were havens of egalitarianism, devoid of social divisions found in society at large. They were not. If there was a moving aside of barriers it was usually symbolic and fleeting. At times, as is the nature of these things, individual or collective effort on the field does momentarily breach class and ethnic divisions. As C.L.R. James (1963, 1994) describes poetically, a Black batsman for Stingo the club of working-class Trinidadians, hitting the White bowler of the elite Queen's Park Club beyond the boundary, excited the emotion and elevated the pride of his community, if only for the time it took to bowl the next ball; as does the victory of a Black football team beating a European XI, as happened in India in 1911 with Mohan Bagan's victory over the East Yorks regiment:

> It fills every Indian with pride and joy to know that rice-eating, malaria-ridden, bare-footed Bengalis have got the better of beef-eating, Herculean, booted John Bull in that peculiarly English sport.[4]

Yet, whatever pretensions sport has to act as an instrument of progressive change in unequal societies, it has never in itself, and by itself, brought about a root and branch subversion of the status quo. It has not proved itself to be the scaffold from which to turn the world right side up; but it can provide a stage for dress rehearsal.

The official British historian of the Asante War, Captain Henry Brackenbury, had other ideas about the predisposition of Gold Coast Euro-African and African young men to strenuous sporting activity.

> … as soon as the boy grows into a man his courage seems to dwindle away, his energy to disappear, and his only remaining idea to be how he can best spare himself all fatigue and danger.[5]

Despite Brackenbury's evaluation increasing numbers of Euro-African and African youth were returning from their education in Britain with a competence in modern sports. To play the game of their desire (Euro-) Africans would have to borrow, beg and share the facilities and resources controlled by Europeans. In respect of cricket the latter would not have the numbers to play without enrolling the (Euro-) Africans yet the situation must have created a confusing paradox of images in the minds of these Gold Coast young. Acculturated into European, usually Anglo-Saxon ways of thinking and acting, they encountered a European elite which would allow ritualised fraternisation at the sports club, while seeking to impose ever more distinct lines of economic and social separation between Whites and people of colour through the legal and economic system. It is not surprising then that as the century came to an end Gold Coast society became increasingly poisoned by inter-communal conflict.

This developing practice of official ethnic segregation – apartheid – carried with it a further irony for Euro-Africans. The Asante War had brought home the cultural differences between themselves and the Africans of the interior, a consequence of 200 years of contact, commerce, colonisation and copulation between coastal Africans and Europeans. However, as college pupils in Britain the Euro-Africans would have found themselves categorised alongside the Asante warriors of the forest zone under the umbrella specification 'Negro', 'Niggers' – cultural and evolutional pygmies of the human 'races'.

The proponents of ideas asserting a hierarchy of 'races', beavering away in the fetid intellectual hot-house environment of the Anthropological Society of London, or writing novels such as those by Rider Haggard, did, however, attempt to distinguish between the racially pure and uncontaminated of the interior, and the miscegenised coastal 'hybrids'. The former were worthy of a modicum of respect. If, further, they were 'noble savages' – considered a warlike tribe and ascribed martial status – the respect was increased by degrees according to their alleged ferocity.

The last goodbye

The death of Henry Wharton in 1873 encouraged Annie to move back to her home town of Cape Coast, accompanied by her three surviving sons Charles, Arthur and William. Clara, her only surviving daughter, was at school in England. The economic impact upon Annie of her husband's death was cushioned by access to the wealth and influence of her extended family, the richest and most influential of whom was her brother F.C. Grant, and her activities as widow hotelier and retailer.

F.C. Grant and Annie became active guardians of Arthur's educational welfare. It seems likely that he attended the Wesleyan Elementary school in James Town before a four-year interval in England between 1875 and 1879 where he was a pupil at Dr Cheyne's Burlington Road School in London. On return in 1879 he probably joined Wesleyan High School, Cape Coast.

Arthur sailed to Britain for the third and final time in August 1882 to study at Shoal Hill College, Cannock. He was accompanied by his patron uncle who already had three sons – George, Justin and Josiah – enrolled at the private Wesleyan Methodist institution. Among the 'very large'[6] crowd waving away Arthur, F.C. Grant and other notables were his mother, civil servant brother Charles and influential Euro-Africans including E.S. Hayford, John Sarbah senior and Timothy Laing, editor of Grant's *Gold Coast Times.* Going to England for an education had become, for the adolescent of wealthy Euro-Africans, a right-of-passage ritual. The object was to undergo the necessary hardships such as relocation, emotional independence and task achievement in an environment of self-reliance, out of which the adult would emerge, returning to enhance the collective status and standing of his or her community. The intended vocation for Arthur was Wesleyan missionary/teacher.

The choice of Shoal Hill College in the Midlands may have been a result of principal S.G. Gwynne having taught elder Whartons and

Grants when a teacher at Wesley College in Taunton. Gwynne placed recruiting advertisements in Grant's *Gold Coast Times*. Its target audience, to use modern advertising jargon, was the Wesleyan and business communities. The prospectus emphasised an orthodox academic curriculum within the framework of an humanitarian Methodist regime. Foreign languages offered were French, German, Spanish, Italian, classical Latin and Greek. English, Science, Drill and the contemporary equivalent of Physical Education (PE), 'Calisthenics' were also available. Its students would be expected to enter university and/or one of the professions such as accountancy, medicine or teaching. A comparison of fees with the Wesleyan High School, Cape Coast, shows the English college to be more expensive. The choice of the latter over the former – or the third alternative of Fourah Bay College, Sierra Leone – can be taken as evidence of the wealth of the Grant/Whartons. It may also have testified to the apparent success of British hegemony – the assertion of power and influence through ideas and social practices that complemented economic domination – after the Anglo-Asante War in 1874. A cultural consequence of this military campaign was the increased status-value of a British education for the children of the aspiring Gold Coast bourgeoisie. This had not escaped the deliberations of elite Euro-Africans considering the schooling of their children.

Dispatching the children to Britain may, paradoxically, also have signalled a commitment by Annie and F.C. to the embryonic pan-Africanist goals. Readers of the *Gold Coast Times* were reminded of the extra-curricula, pan-Africanist objectives of a British education for the 'mulatto' elite and the social responsibilities it bestowed upon each individual consumer:

> If Africa will rise, will be benefited it must be by her own sons and daughters. Let parents who send their children to England, aim not merely at making them good English scholars, or giving them a good … knowledge of the classics, but they must aim at a good practical knowledge as well as theoretical, and endeavour to give them professions.[7]

Also cosmopolitan friends and contacts, first-hand knowledge of metropolitan culture and high status qualifications – cultural capital that could be deployed for economic benefit over the long term – was seen as more important than a bottom-line comparison of school fees; any saving here being short term, financially and culturally. A like education to their European and African counterparts in the competitive economic, social and political pigmentocracy of the Gold Coast was considered by Euro-African elders an essential weapon in the struggle for ethnic and communal survival. And liberation.

Yet the act of survival and the pursuit of liberation often clashed, brought head to head by the process and role of a fluctuating, enigmatic Euro-African identity, the consequence of centuries of triangular trade in slaves and gold and other commodities between various European pirates, sailors and traders such as the Portuguese, Danish, Dutch and British, and West Africans such as the Nzima, Ahanta, Fante, Efutu, Ga-Adangme and Ewe. According to the logic of this historic practice the social status, geo-political security and short-term future of Euro-Africans relied on the continuation of this economic, cultural and biological cross-fertilisation. This was totally at odds with the political strategy suggested by pan-Africanism. Yet those institutions that had been utilised to facilitate this three-legged Bring-and-Buy – slavery, castles, Christian-religion churches, mission stations, trading posts, barracks – were as much part of Euro-African economic and cultural life as they were an integral feature of European power in the Gold Coast. To survive as an ethnic group in what Jenkins has described as a struggle for the survival of the fittest, the 'natives' of the coastal settlements had to participate fully in these institutions. As a consequence, to the interior Africans of the Asante, they were in all but colour 'white men'. To the Europeans, whose ways of acting and thinking were the predominant, hegemonic influences in their lives, they were 'natives'. It was a no-win situation. Euro-Africans were damned by their African kin if they attempted to subvert the regime from the inside; and damned by Europeans as forever inferior whatever their education.

NOTES

1. *Gold Coast Times*, 27 August 1881, in Ray Jenkins, *Salvation for the Fittest?* (unpublished version) p. 22.
2. *Gold Coast Times*, 8 July 1882, in ibid., note 88, p. 39.
3. 9 July 1881 in Ray Jenkins 'Salvation for the Fittest?' *International Journal of the History of Sport*, 7, 1 (May 1990) p. 39.
4. 'Nayak' 30 July 1911, in 'Native Newspaper Reports: Bengal' 5 August 1911, in Brian

Stoddart, 'Sport, Cultural Imperialism and Colonial Responses in the British Empire: A Framework for Analysis' p. 18, in *British Society of Sports History: Proceedings of the Fourth Annual Conference* (July 1986).

5. 'The Ashanti War. A Narrative' II (London 1874) pp. 321, 346, 352, in Ray Jenkins, 'Salvation for the Fittest?' (unpublished version) p. 16. Jenkins Papers.
6. *Gold Coast Times*, 20 July 1882.
7. 5 December 1877.

12 *Methodism, family and community in mid-nineteenth century Gold Coast*

Unlike Britain, the tropical climate of the Gold Coast created a fertility that sustained the needs of the population without demanding overdue toil on the part of the majority that worked the land. However, it also facilitated the production and diffusion of fatal diseases such as smallpox, malaria and sleeping sickness (trypanosomiasis). Of the ten children born to Annie Florence Wharton (née Grant), three survived to adulthood. Life expectancy was 35 years (similar to the present average for (Black) males in the Harlem district of New York, and Bangladesh). Despite the establishment of schools of tropical medicine at several universities in Britain to research into the origin of fatal equatorial diseases, the reputation of the colony as an indiscriminate reaper of fragile and sturdy physiques – demonised as the 'white man's grave' – continued until well into the twentieth century. A founder teacher at Achimota College – the first publicly assisted secondary school for Gold Coast Africans – en route from England in 1924 with his wife and infant son, had the accusation 'murderers'[1] spat at them by a fellow passenger. To take a female and child to the colony was selfish, reckless and, in the mind of the accuser, criminal.

Henry Wharton had immersed himself in the Wesleyan Methodist version of Christianity while a young man in his home island of Grenada in the British West Indies. The progeny of a freeborn African-Grenadian woman and a Scottish merchant and sea captain, he was born in 1819 in the main town and port, St George's. His maternal grandmother had been an African-born slave. Arthur's mother, Annie Florence Grant, was the daughter of another Scottish trader, John C. Grant and Ama Egyiriba, a Fante royal of the Stool family of Ekumfie. The Fante were Akan speakers who lived along the coast of West Africa from the area of Sekondi eastwards towards Accra. As such, the geographical references in the genealogy of the Whartons were those destinations of the triangular slave-trade – Britain, West Africa and the Caribbean.

The Grant family was influential in the Gold Coast, involved in political and religious affairs as well as business. Francis Chapman Grant, Henry's brother-in-law, as well as proprietor of the *Gold Coast Times*, was head of Cape Coast Lodge of the Order of Good Templars and a wealthy Gold Coast 'merchant prince'. In this latter guise he imported manufactured goods and exported palm oil, rubber and gold. His trading network encompassed the Gold Coast, Europe and the Americas. He accrued his spiritual wealth from Wesleyan Methodism.

At the age of eight Henry Wharton left the relatively benign climate of Grenada to be educated in Glasgow. He may have sailed with his father 'who was for some time master of a vessel trading between Europe and the West Indies'.[2] Six years of study and socialisation were spent in this booming work-centre of the industrial revolution in Scotland – rapidly on its way to becoming the second biggest city in the enlarging British Empire. According to his biographer, William Moister, Henry felt the education had been beneficial; and in time Henry sent his own children to Britain to be schooled, a decision that was to have historic importance.

On return, he worked in a store in St George's and pursued those explorative 'pleasures' typical of any adolescent. Around the late 1830s, he explained to Moister, God intervened to save him from further hedonistic indulgences as a good time boy. A period of contemplation reawakened Henry's spiritual yearnings and he began re-attending the Wesleyan chapel of his childhood, gradually taking more of a role in the affairs of the Wesleyan Society. He became a teacher at Sunday School, treasurer and then secretary of the Society.

Soon afterwards William Moister arrived from Trinidad to head the Grenada station of the Wesleyan Missionary Society (WMS). His influence on Henry as spiritual guide, mentor and surrogate father was profound. As his biographer, his ability to shape Henry in the eyes of others has continued long after the death of both he and his subject. Moister describes Arthur's father as 'tall, thin, active; with bronze complexion, dark eyes, black, curly hair; sharp European features, prominent nose, and an intelligent cast of countenance'.[3] Moister's inference here is that it is quality of mind which marks out the hybrid

Euro-African from the African: that Henry had visible African antecedence was indisputable by virtue of his skin colour and other physical attributes. His Celtic – *European* – heritage was, in this respect, hidden within. This lineage would be revealed by his inner-self, through his '*intelligent* cast of countenance'.

Ironically, while Moister the European claimed common origin with the uppermost qualities of brother Wharton, the Asante were willing to go the whole hog and assign him full European heritage. At Dumpoassi village while travelling to his missionary posting at Kumase, the capital of Asante, Henry was greeted with the welcome 'Makio brunie! Makio brunie!' – 'Good morning white man'. It betrayed an altogether different set of criteria that the Asante had formulated to distinguish between Themselves and Others. And the young Grenadian was not slow in discerning this cultural nuance. 'I would just observe here, that it matters not with the people what a man's colour may be, if he is from England, and wears European clothing, though he is as black as your coat, it is quite enough; he is a "white man".'[4] With his cosmopolitan experience and mixed heritage Henry felt an affinity with European, African and Caribbean culture. Yet to those Europeans and Africans who were significant, who had the power to influence and determine events in his life – the London executive of the Wesleyan Missionary Society, the Asantehene and his royal family, ethnic Africans of the coastal zone – he was neither European nor 'native'.

As a child, Arthur's father would have grown up in a Caribbean milieu rigidly structured by pigmentation – skin colour as the primary influence upon an individual's life chances and social status – even more tightly so than West Africa. One life chance, that of access to an elementary education, was often dependent upon colour. In Barbados, for instance, Blacks had been legally prohibited for centuries from instruction in the teachings of the Bible. The Anglican elite – many of whom had dual roles as plantation owners – rationalised that Blacks were not intelligent enough to understand the Christian vision. Perhaps more importantly, in the minds of these slave owners, was terror of their Christianised chattel attempting to practise those principles of personal freedom and choice, fundamental to Protestant doctrine. Consequently, smaller subversive Christian sects – Moravians, Quakers and Methodists – who preached and instructed in the Bible clandestinely attracted many who accepted a cultural trade-off: conversion to

Christianity for literacy in English. This may help explain Methodism's attraction to many nineteenth-century African-Caribbeans.

Henry Wharton's Methodism

Shortly after Moister's arrival on the island as head of the Granada station of the WMS, Henry Wharton came under his influence. The childless missionary began to mould his protégé in mirror image. He placed Henry as Mission School teacher at Constantine, Grenada. Such a duty would train the young man on the job and 'improve his mind'.[5] Within a year, by February 1842, he was being considered by the Annual District Meeting of the WMS in the Caribbean as a candidate for the ministry. Meeting at St Vincent the conclave, after discussion, approved his candidature and recommended him to the British Conference of the WMS. They noted, however, that the location of any future employment would have to be carefully considered 'in view of the prejudices which still existed in reference to colour, most congregations even of Blacks, preferring a European minister to one of African descent'.[6] Moister attempted to assuage these anxieties with an offer to take Wharton as his assistant to his new posting on the Biabou circuit of St Vincent the following year. The WMS in London agreed and approved Henry's application to became 'Assistant Missionary', the first Black man to be ascribed this status in the West Indies.

The duo returned to Kingstown, the capital of St Vincent, in February 1843, just in time to attend that year's Annual District Meeting. It gave other missionaries the chance to meet Wharton – 'a coloured brother who was now invested with equal honour and responsibility [exciting] feelings of the deepest interest'. Henry and William spent two years together at the headquarters of the Biabou circuit, 12 miles from the capital on the windward side of the island, during which time the West Indian Wharton's interest grew in his Africa heritage: 'No part of the globe was so dear to the heart.'[7]

Moister had been a missionary in West Africa. Wharton's interest in his African antecedence and Moister's tales of the continent conspired an eventual passage to the 'Dark Continent'. Though Moister's nurturing of this longing may have had a pragmatic sub-text: the mortality rate among Europeans in tropical West Africa was very high.

In London the opinion was growing that men of colour would be more able to withstand the razor-edged climate. Moister – my 'dear father' as Wharton later called him – also inculcated in his young and eager recruit a sense that amidst 'the spiritual destitution and moral degradation'[8] of Africa there was much useful work to be done. Though his sentiment prefigured Kipling's *White Man's Burden* by a good 50 years the message was essentially similar. In common with merchant adventurers drawn by ambition to exploit Africa's natural wealth, the missionary – a spiritual adventurer – would find a comparable richness of fertile human resources for enlightenment and propagation.

Wharton's interest in Africa was as a Christian and a Grenadian with African lineage. His experiences in Kumase, his first posting into the interior, brought him face to face with a culture and people 'immersed in the grossest ignorance and superstition'.[9] (That may or may not have been so but dispassionate study of the Bible would hardly place rational enquiry and objective reasoning as tools for the excavation of *its* knowledge.)

Class conflict: England 1845

Henry's request to join God's work in Africa was granted just two years after his initial placement at St Vincent. Summoned by the WMS to London for a preparatory briefing, the journey to Southampton was treacherous. The engine failed, a paddle broke, and they were without power, while the wind was against them, for eight days. The calamity left one passenger dead, another with a broken leg. Getting to West Africa was nearly as fatal as its reputation.

In London, Wharton stayed at the home of Dr John Beecham in Pentonville, a leading Methodist and the writer of the letter calling Henry to the city. Most of his time, however, was spent in the company of a fellow African-Grenadian friend and lay preacher James Nibbs Brown, whose visit to the metropolis on business matters chanced to coincide with Henry's.

Wharton attended a number of public meetings. Two were concerned with religious issues. Another, the annual public meeting of the Metropolitan Drapers' Association chaired by Lord John Russell who became prime minister a year later following the resignation of Peel, opposed agitation for a reduction in the working day. It was the success of the shorter working hours movement, part of the wider struggle for improved working conditions, that created the time available for the industrial working classes to take recreation and play, which in turn speeded the growth of modern spectator sport. Henry, therefore, was visitor to a Britain undergoing changes which facilitated the rise of his son to the status of sports celebrity, his presence at the MDA meeting beginning a familial trail that ended with Arthur the professional sportsman. Had the Drapers been successful, this book would possibly not have been written.

The Industrial Revolution transformed the productive capacities and social structure of the United Kingdom. British capital in the 1840s was reaching the height of its power in terms of its share of world manufacturing trade. Exports in the decade 1840–49 were £45,000,000 in surplus over imports. Wealth was being produced for a growing minority, on a scale never before seen or imagined, by a growing majority. The most physically obvious and glaring manifestation of this inequality was the cheek-by-jowl proximity of urban rich and poor. It struck Friedrich Engels when he visited 'Cottonocracy' in 1844.

> I once went into Manchester with … a bourgeois and spoke to him of the bad, unwholesome method of building, the frightful condition of the working people's quarters and asserted that I had never seen so ill-built a city. The man listened quietly to the end, and said at the corner where we parted: 'and yet there is a great deal of money made here. Good morning, Sir!'[10]

The inference – that degradation in daily life was an unfortunate agony many had to suffer in order to create the enormous wealth accumulated by the few, a moral principle of the free-market economics of the 'Manchester School' – tessellated with the Christian parable of the dignity of suffering for the benefit of others. Cotton exports accounted for 45 per cent of the total value of all exports. The commodity was the largest single earner. The relative poverty described above, in a city where two-thirds of its population were factory operatives, would have matched, out-miseried even, that encountered by sun-kissed missionaries and traders. Britain in 1845 – the wealthiest country in the world – was a collection of interlocking societies ill at ease with each other.

Industrial disputes were frequent during the 1840s. As has been noted, Stalybridge and Ashton claim birth of the first general strike. In fact, a bitter four-month strike by miners in the North of England – actively supported by Chartists (and Primitive – but not Wesleyan –

Methodist preachers) – had ended just a year before, in 1844. Chartism in particular and trade unionism in general were working-class movements committed to redesigning a society whereby the producers of wealth had a share in the fruits of their labour. The nationwide Chartist movement wanted democratic reform of the political system. (One of its London leaders was William Cuffay, a Black tailor from Chatham, Kent.)

Tumultuous class conflict was not confined to Britain. Revolution would sweep across Europe within three years. Indeed the peoples of the British Empire were no less rebellious. Witness the Maori War of 1843–48 and the Sikh War of 1845–46 – state-of-the-art military technology versus crafted, hand-made weapons – directed against the indigenous peoples of New Zealand and the Punjab in India fighting the imposition of British sovereignty over their land.

What opinion Henry had on the unrest in Britain is unknown. Though he did speak out on religious issues. He confided to Moister that he was firmly opposed to public money being allocated to the Catholic Church by parliament. In chapels ranging from Southwark up to Edmonton, London, and down to Cowes, Isle of Wight, he may have included this topic in one of his numerous preaching engagements. Despite the fresh confidence of a man breaking new ground the prospect of facing a White congregation 'of intelligent pale faces and glistening eyes'[11] worried him. (Henry's association of intellect with colour carried an echo of Moister.)

After three months Henry was tired of the cloud, clamour and intensity of London and ready to leave. Just before he did so his sister – 'Mrs Fairclough' – brother-in-law and niece, Jane, visited Britain from their estate in Grenada; though they nearly missed each other, thinking Henry had left already for West Africa. They eventually crossed paths in Liverpool, the brother relieved to find his sister well after an illness.

The newly titled Reverend Henry Wharton had been booked passage to the Gold Coast by the WMS, on the schooner *Jane* sailing 17 May. Travelling with him was Thomas Birch Freeman, a Black Briton of African parents, who was General Superintendent of the Gold Coast Mission. He was a veteran of the tropics, having been in West Africa since 1838. From the establishment of the Mission in 1835, nine of the missionaries – out of less than 20 – had died, most within a year of their arrival, including Freeman's first wife.

Mr A.L. Jones, head of the Elder Dempster shipping line and West African merchant, felt 'West Africa has the wealth of the world. There is no other *country* (!) so rich'. Only the climate, he argued, prevented thorough commercial exploitation. Concern about tropical diseases and the inability of Europeans to withstand their attack led him to establish a school of tropical medicine at Liverpool University. While the knowledge gained should be harnessed to enhance imperial trade, the shipping magnate was scornful of the role of missionaries in this process. They spoil the natives by 'not teaching him how to use his hands and earn his daily bread. Circumstances in West Africa make the natives dishonest ... If we can remove these circumstances then the native labour is ample and excellent'.[12] Presumably these 'circumstances' included literacy and book learning generally.

Many, contrary to Jones, did see their work as missionaries, capitalists, colonial government administrators and officials as having broadly similar aims and objectives: to Europeanise indigenous peoples by preaching and teaching Christianity, create a commodity-based economy and construct a political system that would provide the legal and administrative framework necessary for the means of achieving social order, and in turn the success of the imperial project. This is not to deny that tensions existed between these various agencies. While their goals – to proselytise; to proletarianise; to subjugate – were theoretically compatible their implementation, at times, was not mutually complementary as Jones illustrates. Indeed, while in Kumase, capital of Asante, Henry complained how his task had been made more difficult by the 'pernicious' and 'immoral'[13] actions of European and American traders and mercenaries. Such tensions could only add to the burden of contradictions missionary Wharton encountered in the land of his antecedents. He, as a Grenadian Creole 'White man' recruiting among the Africans of the interior on behalf of his European employees, embodied possibly the most burdensome and inescapable contradiction of all.

The Gold Coast 'White man'

In his first letter to Moister after arrival Henry wrote that he 'felt perfectly happy and at home in Africa'. He had begun learning Fanti, but admitted that he would never be able to master the 'whistling, spitting language'.[14] (In this description we find an echo of Schlegel's denigration of guttural languages, which the philologist used as an instrument to devalue wholesale the wider culture for which these languages spoke.) After a short while in Cape Coast, an old slave trading fortress town with a population of about 5,000, and Anomabu, he went to the British quarter of Accra by the schooner on which he had arrived in West Africa. With the neighbouring settlement of Dutch Accra the total population was 7,000. Danish Accra, several miles east, had 4,000 inhabitants.

The shock of living amidst an alien, pagan culture transformed Wharton's enthusiastic, fresh evangelism to retreating indignation. He was offended by the licentious nature of the annual harvest celebrations at the three Accras. Festivities began on 30 August and continued for a week: feasts, sartorial parades, singing, playing music, dancing and drinking rum to prostrate dizziness. At Pram-pram, a day's journey from Accra, the obscenity he witnessed was almost unspeakable, should have been unwatchable and ought never to be replicated. What troubled the young missionary in particular was the locals' complete disregard for his status as a man doing God's work; and their own enslavement to fetish worship. The pagans needed to be Christianised. A generalised conversion would also have the benefit of eradicating the ongoing slave trade, which, he argued, was only fully extinguishable by the spread of the gospel.

It had been estimated by visitors to pre-colonial Africa that one-quarter to a half of the population were slaves, although the reliability of these guestimates has been questioned. Slave traders, whether European adventure capitalists, West African elites or North African Arab middlemen, saw the Christian missionaries as an obstacle to their accumulation of wealth.

Wharton was assigned the Kumase station – in effect, becoming chief missionary for Asante – at the District Meeting of the WMS at Cape Coast in January 1846. The population of Greater Asante was estimated at 3 million by the beginning of the twentieth century, when its boundary went beyond that of present-day Ghana. The capital of this vast empire – developed by forceful conquest and diplomacy over the preceding 200 years – was 150 miles deep into the tropical forest zone of the interior. To Europeans, the peoples had a martial reputation. By 1750 nearly 20 neighbouring kingdoms had been pacified. Asante military prowess even induced the European powers who occupied the coastal forts, such as Cape Coast Castle, to pay rent to the Asantehene (king). He commanded an empire rich in gold, with a relatively stable and mature pagan civilisation. Through the sale of gold, and slaves from defeated kingdoms, to Arab and European traders great wealth had been acquired by the monarchy and their patronised favourites. As a welcoming present from the king Wharton was given 2 sheep, 1 pig, 37 bunches of plantain, 6 yam, 300 eggs, 2 bushel of ground nuts and £4.10s (£4.50p) worth of gold dust. Was this extravagance a clever ploy to disarm with overwhelming hospitality a naive and irritating visitor?

European visitors to Kumase during the first decades of the nineteenth century were struck by the opulence of its elite and the eloquence and scale of much of the architecture. Bowdich, a merchant adventurer who visited in 1817, estimated the market place to be a mile in circumference. One of the main streets that ran through the city was 100 yards wide. Streets were swept daily, refuse collected. The wealthy had indoor toilets. Personal hygiene such as bathing regularly, cleaning teeth, shaving bodily hair and wearing clean clothes was a cultural sign of affluence and power. However, while the public grandeur was accessible to most, if only in passing, we should acknowledge this portrayal of civility as reflecting the lives of a small privileged elite, whose elevated status rested to large extent on the exploitation of slave labour, of which there were five categories. Those at the top of the pile were themselves allowed to own slaves. It could be argued that the standard of living of most Asante – the ahiato – while not luxurious by any standards, was superior to that of the Manchester proletariat described earlier by Engels. Subsistence agriculture, conducted through the family unit and characterised by a gender division of labour, was the daily practice of most. Because of its seasonal cycle this was sometimes combined with other occupations such as labouring, craft work, trading and mining. The spiritual life of the community was dominated by fetish worship.

Transgression of law and custom by the non-privileged majority was often met with harsh, publicly administered punishment with execution the consequence for many crimes. 'I have already witnessed several decapitations and I have seen as many as twelve headless corpses lying scattered in the public streets', wrote Wharton to his biographer. This judicial theatre expressed a number of warnings to its wider audience: deterrence; royal omnipotence; retribution. Human sacrifice at ritual occasions was normal – 'almost of daily occurrence'. He added a reflective, moralising overview 'never till that moment did I really feel myself to be in *miserable*, *degraded*, *pitiless* AFRICA'.[15]

To Wharton's mid-nineteenth century bourgeois eye such practices were barbaric and uncivilised. However, it would be wrong to let this moralistic interpretation pass without comment. Below is a description of the punishment of a regicide from eighteenth-century France. As the murderer of a feudal king, the hero is met with gratuitous ferocity.

> Flesh will be torn from his breasts, arms, thighs and carves with red hot pincers, his right hand holding the knife with which he committed the said parricide, burnt with sulphur, and, on those places where the flesh will be torn away, poured molten lead, boiling oil, burning resin, wax and sulphur melted together and then his body drawn and quartered by four horses and his limbs consumed by fire, reduced to ashes and his ashes thrown to the winds.[16]

In the event, they had to use six horses and still needed to hack off his limbs.

Such extreme devastation of the body, as public ritualised punishment on behalf of the monarch, was rare in both France and Asante. While in Britain the reorganisation of economic and social life caused by the Industrial Revolution exacted a daily harvest of the dead from those underground digging coal, navvying on canals and railways, operating the factory machines, in pestilential slums. And yet there was money to be made! Is it possible, therefore, to evaluate and compare disparate rituals in the task of elevating the worthiness of one culture over another?

The Fante, the dominant ethnic group of the coastal belt which included Cape Coast and Accra, were a people the Asante saw as a threat to their own pre-eminence in the region. Indeed, they had been at war with them in the 1870s. Many Fante had been converted to Christianity and had suffused indigenous ways and lifestyles with European cultural influences. Northern Ghanaians still joke that the Fante prefer bacon and eggs for breakfast to yam! In contrast, the Asante had historic contact with Arab traders who had brought Islam to the interior forest zone. These North Africans, because of the longevity of their presence, had a voice of sorts in the affairs of the Asante monarch. They did not like incursions by the agents of competitor religions. 'The Moors are up in arms against me',[17] wrote Wharton. The geographic location of Asante had previously acted as a natural defence against unwanted intrusions, and continued to play its part in restricting the growth of Methodist evangelism. The mission of conversion in Asante harvested little.

Wharton left Kumase in 1848. As leaving presents he was again given £4.10s.0d in gold dust, and a young boy whose subsequent fate is unknown. Though Henry felt he had failed his mission his experiences affirmed his belief in the rightness and necessity of his vocation. After being appointed to his next posting at the Domonasi station, some 30 miles north of Cape Coast in Fante territory, Henry married Annie Florence Grant. She had recently returned from an education in England. This union between a brown-skinned European-looking gentleman and the daughter of a Fante princess, placed Henry's feet firmly under the high table of the Gold Coast Euro-African elite. By 1850 the newly-weds were in Accra, as residents of the Mission House in James Town.

Three consecutive children died in their infancy during this decade. The James Town anti-government rebellion of 2,000 or so Africans in 1854 lasted two months, ending with bombardment by the Royal Navy warship HMS *Scourge* and the destruction of the towns of Christianborg, Teshi and Labodai. Many were killed by the shelling. These seismic events were terrible reminders of the hostility of both the political and physical climate. Yet while such profound traumas did wither the health and spirit of the Whartons the death of Henry's mother, his sister and the loss of his inheritance in Grenada smothered any longing to return to the Caribbean. In fact, more and more Wharton began to feel that England was his mother country 'in common with his fellow countrymen and British colonists generally',[18] while the Gold Coast was his adopted land. It was to England that he travelled with his two boys, Charles and Alfred early in July 1863. He was in bad health, suffering from an enlarged spleen and debilitated by periodic bouts of fever. The purpose of his journey was twofold: to place his boys at New Kingswood school, Bath, and to recuperate. Moister, on seeing his friend again after 20 years, remarked that he looked old and unwell. The possibility of any rejuvenation was quashed brutally and quickly by news from West Africa of the death of his youngest boy Henry – the fourth to die in infancy – on 8 July, just after he and his other boys had left for England. (The Whartons did not suffer unusually. Infant mortality in the Gold Coast was disproportionately high compared to other age groups.) Mother England was now actually hindering Henry's recovery. And, to compound his misery he got another dose of 'African' – malarial? – fever followed by diarrhoea. His doctor advised him not to return immediately, or travel and work while in the UK. It was not until 13 months later that Wharton returned, improved but not regenerated. Yet, cruelly, misfortune still slowed the pace of his journey home. He was delayed for three months at his disembarkation point of Cape Coast by a smallpox epidemic ravaging Accra. The death of the Whartons' youngest son was assuaged – can such grief ever be wholly relieved? – with the birth of Arthur on 28 October 1865, a little after nine months from the missionary's return to the Mission House at James Town.

Charles and Alfred returned home in 1866 having completed their studies at (the Wesleyan) Taunton College, after New Kingswood. At Taunton they may have been taught by S.G. Gwynne, later to become principal at Shoal Hill College, Cannock. In June 1870, Henry went to the UK for the fourth time to place Clara his only daughter, aged ten, in boarding school. Paying large expenses for the education of a daughter was unusual. The return would be cultural – marriage to a 'good', i.e. wealthy, family – rather than directly economic in the form of a well-paid career. Thus, a purely economic cost-benefit analysis argued against such an outlay. However, an important influence in favour of such an investment may well have been Annie's experience of British education. Whatever the intellectual rationale, the act itself was far-sighted. Travelling with Henry, Annie and Clara were the youngest boys – Arthur, 4, and William Moister, 3, the namesake of the Grenadian's biographer. As with his previous visit Henry – and Annie and the boys – was summoned home by yet another tragic death, of teenage Alfred, from fever. The Whartons were left with four surviving children. Those of us lucky enough to have access to protective medical and welfare programmes – still a minority of today's world – may find the frequent incursion of death into *any* family difficult to evaluate when trying to understand the emotional impact. Yet such thorough devastations were common to most nineteenth-century Gold Coasters and had to be overcome. Nevertheless, these weighty wrenchings of spirit and soul made the step heavier.

In 1872 the WMS broke with tradition and appointed Henry as General Superintendent of the Gold Coast District, the first time a non-British born Black man had been appointed. Thomas Birch Freeman had been the first man of colour to hold this post. Although the number of Black missionaries and agents of the WMS in Africa was increasing, the Society had not felt able in the past to entrust absolute control to colonial 'natives'. They preferred Europeans who they assumed would carry out their responsibilities more conscientiously. Unfortunately such prejudice cost lives. The two previous incumbents had died within ten months of each other. With the recent annual mortality rate of the post at something like 50 per cent, news of appointment to European office-holders may have been the signal to put all personal affairs in order before the final curtain. Henry, although a 'native', offered compromise with his hybrid, Euro-African ethnicity. Fully aware of the extra work that would ensue, he was stoical about the elevation. He already had enough to do. That year's transfer of Dutch settlements at Cape Coast to British control – bought in pursuance of the policy of enlargement in West Africa – had upped his workload by adding more territory and people to his district. (Henry accumulated further duties the following year when he was made chaplain to the Wesleyan troops in General Wolseley's Asante invasion force.) But there was more stress to come. If this steady incremental increase in work – on top of his grief – had not already brought more worry lines to Henry's brow, the jagged ruptures caused by the most serious earthquake in Wharton's experience – 11 shocks – etched them with fatal consequence. It devastated Accra and nearly entombed the whole family. The damage was multiplied by a tornado whipping up the debris, with repair further inhibited by incessant rain.

While the events of 1872 were momentous and burdensome the turmoil caused by the Anglo-Asante War of 1873–74 proved too much for Henry's withering physical and emotional constitution. Tension had been building between the Asantehene, his elders and advisers, and the British during the early years of the 1870s. In 1873 the Asante army invaded Fanteland and laid siege to Cape Coast, causing a disruptive influx of refugees into the town, leading to food shortage, starvation and an epidemic of disease. A colleague of Wharton's described the condition of Cape Coast at this vexed time.

> The rains, war, famine and pestilence seemed confederate to destroy. Most of our chapels were burnt down, and many of our converts slain ... The town was scarcely more than heaps of ruins,

> from the damage done by the heavy rains ... The crowds of human beings huddled together ... with their nakedness, want, diseases, and emaciated appearance, presented to the view an aspect of squalor and wretchedness shocking to look upon.[19]

As chaplain of the Methodist troops Henry would have come into daily contact with officers and men. What they thought of him, and he them, we can only guess. If, as seems probable, many of the rank and file British soldiers had internalised the view of the African(-Caribbean) as enunciated by the officers, Wharton's ministrations could not have been easy. General Wolseley, who was to receive honorary degrees from Oxford and Cambridge for overseeing the 'most horrible war I ever took part in', argued that Africans were intended to be White men's slaves. 'The Negroes are like so many monkeys; they are a lazy good-for-nothing race.'[20] The Black as beast of burden was classic Scientific Racism.

However, Wolseley's mediated version of this racism played itself out in a curious form. The fearful reputation of the climate of the Gold Coast was such that the British government was reluctant to commit White troops from the UK. A surgeon general of the army had put life expectancy of the British soldier in the Gold Coast at one month. Wolseley was therefore forced to recruit and did forcibly recruit, respectively, African-Caribbean troops of the West India regiment and local Fante and Hausa men and women. The majority of his conquistadores were thus mercenary or press-ganged.

Unknowingly, Henry left West Africa for the last time in September 1873. He arrived in the Madeiras, for recuperation and rest, on 10 October. He died at Reids Hotel, Funchal the next day. His last days in the Gold Coast had been characterised by war and its associated suffering. Such a state of affairs was to become commonplace in Africa over the next 25 years. Like most parts of the globe historically there had been tribal disagreements and conflict, but what made the violence and bloodied machinations of competing Europeans different was the scale. Their advanced technological power produced weapons with an hitherto unimaginable destructive power.

Imperial military campaigns like that of Wolseley's had oppressive social repercussions for the place of Euro-Africans in West Africa. As the presence of Europeans grew and became hegemonic, the metaphorical size of the African decreased. They and their history diminished, except of course in two respects: as tools of labour and as a comparative yardstick by which the superiority of European culture and civilisation could be measured. Henry, for his part, seemed to accept much of this Eurocentric arrogance. He was an active agent in the Europeanisation of the African through conversion; and went along with their proletarianisation. Yet he was deeply conscious of the 'pernicious' and 'immoral' side effects of this latter process if it was guided solely by the invisible hand of the market, untempered by God's intervention. Moister, too, commented upon the 'demoralising' and 'ungodly'[21] behaviour of many European traders in Africa and how the job of conversion had been made harder by the merchants' doings in Africa.

The variation of Anglo-Saxon cultural attitudes and practices towards ethnicity and 'race' experienced by the cosmopolitan Euro-African travelling between the metropolitan centre of empire and peripheral colonies, created a limbo world of moving and changing reference points: in the Africa of the African cultural distinctions were more important than an individual's colour; in the Africa of the European, colour and culture in that order become significant as determinants of social status; in the Europe of the European class – in terms of one's social relation to the means of production – was the primary determinant of political power and social status; in the Europe of the Black, colour was all. There were few distinctions made between different ethnic groups of colour. They were all literally tarred with the same brush as 'darkies', 'niggers' and – if the categoriser was feeling benevolent – 'noble savages'.

The social savagery of such labelling was compounded for Euro-Africans in the Gold Coast by British formalisation of separate laws governing Europeans and Africans/Euro-Africans that evolved after Anglo-Asante war of 1873–74. Europeans would be subject to the English legal code, administered by a government appointed judiciary; Africans, including Euro-Africans, by local African customary law dispensed by local chiefs and European district commissioners. Thus began an enforced legal equality between Africans and Euro-Africans whose historic bond was their ethnic African heritage but whose cultural and geo-political separation had also been long-standing. As is the case with many of the social processes wrought by capitalism, especially in its imperial form, this division brought with it the potential for unity and solidarity among those herded together in the face of a common enemy: those active in anti-colonial struggle were united by their politics rather than their ethnic origin.

For Arthur this process of Euro-African/African assimilation may have been eased through his possible knowledge of two Akan languages: Fante, from his mother; and Ga, as a result of his brief boyhood in Accra where it was commonly spoken. However, after the Anglo-Asante War, he spent just four years in the colony. It was not his identity and place within the Gold Coast that was problematical. Had he acted the script and returned home once his education in Britain had been completed, this role would have been relatively straightforward. Rather, as has been discussed, it was his ability – as an African at the centre of empire – to have a full and frank relationship with the colony.

NOTES

1. W.E.F. Ward, interview with author, Banstead, Surrey, 2 September 1993.
2. Reverend William Moister, *Memoir of the Rev. H. Wharton* (London 1875) p. 12.
3. Ibid., pp. 21–2.
4. Letter to Moister in Moister (1875) p. 102.
5. Moister (1875) op. cit., p. 26.
6. Ibid., p. 30.
7. Ibid., pp. 33 and41.
8. Ibid., pp. 89 and 42.
9. Ibid., p. 106.
10. Engels, *Condition of the Working Class in England in 1844* (Moscow 1973) p. 313.
11. Moister (1875) p. 61.
12. *African Review*, xx, 355 (9 September 1899).
13. Moister (1875) p. 192.
14. Ibid., p. 79.
15. Ibid., p. 107.
16. Michel Foucault, *Discipline and Punish* (London 1977) p. 3.
17. Moister (1875) pp. 109–10.
18. Ibid., p. 140.
19. Rev. Charles Rose in ibid., p. 193.
20. G. Arthur, 'The Letters of Lord and Lady Wolseley' (London 1922) p. 10, in Robert B. Edgerton, *The Fall of the Asante Empire* (London 1995) p. 110.
21. Moister (1875) p. 205.

13 *Class, ethnicity and memory: The selective approach to history*

Of princes

One of Arthur's sporting contemporaries was K.S. Ranjitsinhji, an Indian prince who used the cricket bat to produce fleeting moments of wonder and lasting memories of beauty. During the summer of 1899 he beat the scoring record of the legendary W.G. Grace by accumulating 3,000 runs over the season. In *Beyond a Boundary* Trinidadian Marxist C.L.R. James leaves the reader in no doubt as to the elevated status and place 'Ranji' held – and still holds – within the sport. He was revered by followers of cricket throughout the British Empire. He is irremovable from the pantheon of Great Names of Cricket.

Why has this not been so for Wharton with football? While his achievements in athletics do feature to a limited extent in the histories of that sport, the reasons for his absence in histories of football seems almost conspiratorial. A list of over 1,000 players in *Football Who's Who* for both 1900–1 and 1901–2 omit Wharton, as they do the Cother brothers, Fred Corbett of West Ham United and John Walker of Hearts and Lincoln City, all 'Coloured' players. The *Book of Football* (1906) focused on a number of leading clubs. In its treatment of PNE there is a section on goalkeepers which names four of those who either preceded or proceeded Arthur. But not the man himself. In separate discussions of 'Good Goalkeeping' and the longevity of career of some footballers in *Football and How to Play it* (1904) there is no mention of Wharton although he played professionally to 36 years of age. In the 'Table of Leading Goalkeepers 1872–1949' in *The Official FA Yearbook 1949–50* Wharton is absent because he failed to play for England, feature in an FA Cup Final or play for the Football League representative XI. Nick Hazlewood, the author of the most recent book devoted to goalkeepers *In the Way!* (1996), again did not find space to include Wharton. Other writers – Cashmore (1982); Hamilton (1982) and Woolnough (1983) – who dealt specifically with Black footballers and sportsmen – ignored or dealt with him in passing.

Both Ranjitsinhji and Wharton were labelled by British sports commentators as 'Coloured'. This is what united the two sportsmen: they were both the object of colour-coded – racialised – appraisal. However, racism took a variety of forms. The ethnicity and culture of the individual or group had also to be categorised. Once these three factors – colour, ethnicity and culture – had been dissected, the Asiatic – Yellow – peoples were placed at a more advanced position along the continuum of civilised/uncivilised than the African. According to this ordering of society as an ethnic Indian, 'Ranji' was of a less barbaric, more evolved culture. The justification for this assertion was premised on the view of the South Asian sub-continent as having had a history conveyed from generation to generation through the base language of Sanskrit. Since at least the eighteenth century some European scholars argued that Sanskrit, and the classical languages of Europe, Latin and Greek, had a common source. Indeed, some went as far as to propose that Sanskrit was the linguistic base from which all Indian and European languages had originated. This was the view of William Jones writing in 1786. A little later Friedrich Schlegel developed the notion of an ancient Indian 'Race' from which was constructed the concept of an Aryan 'Race'. The Aryans – Caucasians – had moved from their original territory of the Asian Caucasus and peopled Europe. For Schlegel, the Indian Aryans were responsible for the ancient civilisation of African Egypt. This interpretation of the past in effect de-Africanised Egypt. He felt that the physiological production of sound in a language betrayed the evolutional state of the people who spoke it. Indo-European languages were 'inflectional', noble languages able to transmit sophisticated thought; African 'guttural' languages were animalistic and unable to facilitate the transmission of civilised, progressive thought and ideas. Therefore Africans were the least evolved, most animalistic of humans. Arthur was a (sub-Saharan) African – or even worse, a hybrid – having no written language, so without history, having accumulated nothing of worth – only a void of Barbarism.

In respect of social class it could be argued that both Ranjitsinhji and Wharton came from aristocratic backgrounds, although the public perception of Wharton's class as a young athlete was that he was a 'gentleman', a bourgeois. This perceived difference is important. Ranjitsinhji was accepted by his peers, the public and the press as upper-class. He played as an amateur for Sussex. While Wharton, a resident of the industrial, proletarian North of England played football for working-class clubs and became a professional runner, the antithesis of the amateur 'gentleman' athlete.

It was much easier to forget Arthur because the communities in which he played his sport, lived and died did not have the means to ensure his posthumous survival. Working-class people and communities do not generally write their own histories, own printing presses, have editorial control within newspapers, commission art, erect statues, or have power over mediums of mass communication generally. While celebration of the defeat of enemies of the ruling class – Remembrance Sunday, in November, for instance – is seen almost as a social duty, working people do not in a similar manner collectively remember their victories, as a class, in a manner defined and constructed by themselves as a class. The Peasants Revolt 1381; Kett's Rebellion 1546; Tolpuddle Martyrs 1834; Chartists of the 1840s; 1919 Rebellions; Cable Street 1936; and the smashing of the National Front at Lewisham in 1977 are just a few examples of events, movements and battles that are not celebrated by the majority of workers in a carnival of joy. Where are the prominent statues, the physical representation of civic memory to honour these historic events of working-class action? Though this one-sided imbalance has token compensations: Winston Churchill has a prime site facing the Palace of Westminster. A constant stream of passers-by thus have a bird-arse view of the pigeons' colouring his pate white.

If momentous and inspiring working *class* acts are suppressed, erased or forgotten it is not surprising that the achievements of one individual are airbrushed out of the contested and congested space called 'History'. Wharton was made invisible because he *became* both Black and working-class. But what of 'Ranji'? Does not his indelibility in cricket history and folklore negate the theory that racism is to blame? Memory of him has proved durable to the withering corrosion of time. Well, he was an Indian, not an African. I have tried to offer an explanation as to why this difference of ethnicity and culture would affect his recognition.

The place – geographical situation – of their achievements is also important. Ranjitsinhji was an elite aristocratic cricketer who played at the southern heart of the empire. He was selected for England but did not *represent* England; rather just the glory of it – a cricketing colonial – as an imperial force. He was surrounded by individuals and institutions of enormous power. This included the power to produce Memory as a cultural commodity. Yet while Arthur was on the margins of influence and power his proletarianisation – the act of becoming working class – provides the essential clue to his erasure from collective memory. His career was fashioned and shaped by the paradox of opposing forces that at the same time raised and lowered him. He was elevated by his achievements on the sports field to the status of 'Celebrity'; while his occupational status as a professional runner, footballer and northern leagues cricketer lowered his social class. This is not a value judgement, just a description of fact brought about by his decision to become a professional sportsman, and through the blocking of alternative careers by others such as the Governor of the Gold Coast. 'Ranji' was remembered because of his talent and ability but as importantly because those with whom he mixed socially, of whom he was a part – the elite of cricket and society – also wrote. He also wrote a book on cricket from which C.L.R. James quotes. Wharton did not mix in such company. If he did put pen to paper his reminiscences have been lost, disappearing with all his other personal artefacts save a Bible and a small collection of photographs. Some of these came to the notice of Sheila Leeson via an individual collector who had bought an album disposed of by an elderly member of the Leeson family houseclearing on the death of a relative.

The 'Growing menace'

Yet the existence of both the South Asian cricketer and the Black African footballer alerts us to the reality of polychrome sport in late-Victorian – pre-first world war Britain. Other Black association footballers and runners have been mentioned already. In rugby James Peters, a Black man born in Manchester, played for England between 1906–1908; African-American racing cyclist Marshall Taylor beat British and continental opponents in 1902; in 1907 South African boxer Andrew Jeptha won a world title in London. Ex-slave Bobby Dobbs fought in Britain in 1898 and returned in 1902, staying for eight years.

People of colour were kitted up all over the place: at the crease; on the field; on the track; at the velodrome; and in the ring.

Boxing was the sport in which Black participation had been longest and most numerous. Because of its core elements – controlled aggression and muscled agility – and the personal qualities required to be successful – strength, character and durability – contests between Black and White had significance beyond the ring. Black prowess caused enormous problems for White supremacists. Peter Jackson, born at Fredericksted, Virgin Island in the Caribbean in 1861, won the Australian heavyweight championship in 1886 (a significant year!). Arthur Ashe (1993) cites Jackson as the first Black man to win an official national title. Shunned by White heavyweights in the USA he sailed to England for a match. On 11 November 1889 the Virgin Islander won the British heavyweight title from Jim Smith. He later returned to the USA and challenged James Corbett. After 61 rounds the fight was declared a draw. Corbett, who was to win the world championship from John L. Sullivan a year later, described Jackson as the best boxer he had met. The latter wanted a return against Corbett for the undisputed championship of the world in 1893. Corbett refused. There was a 'Race' to lose in defeat.

The whipping of White supremacist ideology by the triumphs of Black athletes, in particular boxers, vexed racists. Public appeals were made for the best sons of the White 'race' to come forward to defeat and subdue the animalist threat. The sports editor of the New York *Sun* was apoplectic.

> We are in the midst of a growing menace. The black man is rapidly forging to the front ranks in athletics, especially in the field of fisticuffs. We are in the midst of a black rise against white supremacy … Less than a year ago Peter Jackson could have whipped the world – Corbett, [Robert] Fitzsimmons, … but the white race is saved from having at the head of pugilism a Negro … There are two Negroes in the ring today who can thrash any white man in their respective classes … Wake up you pugilists of the white race! Are you going to permit yourself to be passed by the black race?[1]

The newspaper was widely read and influential. The open letter addressed to its (White) readers, expressing the sentiment that Black–White bouts were first and foremost racial – therefore political

– contests, was not received as the obscure ranting of an extreme and isolated crank. Ashe argues that it 'was the most provocative piece of racist sports journalism yet seen in America and caused a sensation that lasted for years afterward'.[2]

The success of African-American Jack Johnson in becoming the first world Black heavyweight champion in 1908 – he was forced to wrap the belt around him in Sydney, Australia, unable to find a venue in the United States – would no doubt have caused editor Charles Dana another paroxysm of racial fury. In fact the journalist's tirade merely lifted the lid – but with a public audience – on the latent prejudice that bubbled to the surface when notable White athletes were defeated by Blacks in significant sporting competition. The bruising caused by each jab, hook and upper-cut in Johnson's taunting, smiling demolition of White contenders was felt many times over by racist Whites, whose suffering was further intensified by the boxer's pride in himself and delight in his blood-spilling achievements. White hostility to Black prowess created an atmosphere in boxing – and other sports – of heightened racism. Johnson's win led to numerous lynchings and attacks upon Blacks throughout the United States. If the future of the White 'race' could not be assured in the ring, the futures of some Black men would be terminated outside it. The defeat of Johnson by a 'Great White Hope' became a burning passion. For others, such as the Reverend Meyer, the mere matching of Black and White was unfair. He campaigned to stop Johnson fighting 'Bombardier Billy' Wells in London in 1911.

> The present contest is not wholly one of skill, because on the one side there is added the instinctive passion of the Negro race, which is so differently constituted to our own, and in the present instance will be aroused to do the utmost that animal development can do to retain the championship, together with all the financial gain that would follow.[3]

Identified in Meyer's lay anthropology are three core concerns – biological, economic and political – of White supremacists: Black athletic success as symbolic expression of the degeneracy of the White 'race'; the consequent rewards of this success as a threat to White economic (and social) superiority; that the collective confidence and spiritual sustenance given to Black communities by Johnson as an heroic role model may inspire emulation. The champion was not only an Uppity Nigger who kicked White arses but he was also a rich 'un; and he sexually aroused, slept with and loved White women. Inevitably the giant Texan was stopped. He lost his title in Havana, Cuba, in 1915 to the 'Great White Hope' Jess Willard. The modern consensus is that the fight was fixed.

The central tenet in Meyer's explanation for Black success on the sports field – the animal in the Black – was to become the common feature in the apologies offered by the supremacists for defeats of Whites on track and field. The agility, physical dexterity, instinctive endurance and insentient durability of the Black athlete, derived from their animalism, made contests between Black and White unfair. The former would always be at an advantage when human competition included only the physical dimension. Thus it was because Whites were more evolved and civilised, at a more advanced stage of human development, that they were incapable of inflicting those kinds of comprehensive defeats in sport on Blacks that had been achieved – for the 'race' – in the economic, political and social spheres.

If the animalist thesis represents an attempt to discount Black athletic success by devaluing the victory – and, therefore, the social significance of defeat, unequal bodies in unequal contests – the method of ethnic cleansing used by the administrators of horse-racing in the USA to extinguish the economic competition posed by overwhelmingly successful Black jockeys illustrates how Black sportsmen were having to fight on many fronts. During the last quarter of the nineteenth century Black jockeys dominated flat racing. By the end of the first decade of the twentieth century riders were almost wholly White. The transformation had been brought about by a simple operation of the colour bar: Black jockeys were refused renewal of their licences to ride. In Britain a similar officially sanctioned colour bar operated in boxing. Black pugilists were not allowed to fight for British titles during much of the inter-war period. It was not until 1948 that a Black British boxer, middleweight Randolph Turpin, was allowed to contest a domestic title with a White Briton.

Black action – White script

Racism invested Black athletic achievement with great symbolic value. In such a politicised sports environment the erasure from collective memory of Black triumph was profound. For those Europeans and

Americans with an interest in maintaining the status quo, to accept Black success at face value would have undermined the crucial notion of biologically determined White superiority. If this ideological keystone was shifted, would not other ideas underpinning the hierarchical structure of society, such as those justifying class and gender inequality, also come crashing down? Of course, in reality, sporting contests between Black and White were anything but equal. The opportunity for most White athletes to develop their skill and talent was far in excess of that to Blacks. The operation of the colour bar, official and unofficial, whether in Britain, its empire or indeed any part of the globe dominated by Europeans, sustained inequalities across the board.

Martin Offiah, a Black rugby player for the England international team, is nicknamed 'Chariots' by his team-mates. It refers to the film *Chariots of Fire*, the last two words of the film's title having a phonetic harmony with the player's surname. It is the closest association any Black athlete has with the film about, among other things, athletics in the decade after the first world war. Yet one of the greatest sprinters in Britain in the first half of the 1920s was Harry Edward, born in British Guiana in 1895. An African-Caribbean who wore the vest of the Polytechnic Harriers club he first forced attention upon himself in central Europe in 1914 when he ran 200 metres in 21.7 seconds in Berlin in June, following this up with a time of 22 seconds for the same distance in Budapest in July. Though the outbreak of war shortened the duration of his career it did not dull his astonishing speed. In 1920 he won the AAA 100 yards title with a time of 10 seconds, also running the 220 yards in 21.6 seconds. At the Olympics of that year he won the bronze in 100 and 200 metres. It was said that his faltering start in the shorter distance deprived him of the gold (and silver). In 1921 he beat Harold Abrahams – a British Jew and one of the two central characters in the film – in both the 100 and 200 yards. At the 1922 AAA championship Edward won the 100, 200 and 440 yards titles *within an hour*. His outstanding performances won him the Harvey Memorial trophy, presented to the best athlete of the championship. Abrahams thought the young Guianan 'one of the most impressive sprinters I have ever seen'.[4] That the two runners featured – the other was Scot Eric Liddle – in *Chariots of Fire* came from ethnic minority backgrounds adds poignant irony to the exclusion of Edward. Furthermore, it was Sam Massabini's excellence in nurturing the talent of Edward that propelled

Abrahams to invite the part Arab-African, part Italian trainer to take him up. (Massabini also coached another Black runner, Jack London, who won the AAA 100 yards title in 1929 and was an Olympic silver medallist.)

The dramatisation, a romanticised and racialised portrayal of real sporting endeavour, was enormously popular and profitable. Both characters, Abrahams and Liddle, are brought together by their achievements on the track. Both had obstacles in the way of their pursuit of athletic excellence. For Abrahams it was anti-Semitic prejudice; for Liddle God – in particular the spiritual turmoil and conflict caused by his attempt to reconcile time spent running on the track with pursuit of a dialogue with God. The most well-remembered manifestation of this running battle was Liddle's refusal to compete on Sundays – the Sabbath. Paralleling the lives of these two athletes carried with it another sub-text proclaiming the egalitarian principles and practice at the heart of sport. Liddle and Abrahams evolve as personifications of the meritocratic ideal.

The opening dialogue 'Let us praise famous men and our fathers that begat us'[5] echoes two themes that have been central concerns of this book: memory and identity. Unfortunately the film commits to celluloid posterity a selective, arbitrary and orthodox interpretation of the social history of British athletics in the 1920s. The nation is White, overwhelmingly Anglo-Saxon and ruled by the fathers of God's children. The only perceived threat to this structured-by-nature supremacy comes from the Jewish Abrahams. (Liddle, though a Scot, is doing the work of God's chosen Englishmen as a missionary in China.) It won an Academy Award as 'best film of 1981'. On receiving the Oscar actor Colin Welland, involved in the making from the beginning, warned the Hollywood audience to beware, with words that had an unmistakable symmetry with the narrative of the film: more British winners were sure to follow. However, it was the picture's unspoken and missing dialogue – its silence – that was most eloquent. It pronounced British athletics in this inter-war 1920s to be a monochrome yet egalitarian sport where, upon the track, anti-Semitic racism could be pounded to dust underfoot. An early scene recalling Abrahams' induction to Gonville and Caius, his Cambridge college, reveals the contemporary texture of anti-Semitic prejudice through the mouth of a sneering porter. Later, at a dinner welcoming freshmen the master of the college pauses to solemnise the memory of those alumni who died in the first world war. 'They died for England, and all that England stood for.'[6] His Little Englander sentiment – drawn from the same bank of ideas as the prejudice of the porter – and character had been scripted as embodying the values of a disintegrating pre-war hierarchy.

Liddle, as a Christian sportsman, acts as a bridge between the old world and the new. Inhabitants of the former, such as the master and porter, with their highly racialised view of the nation, suffer its decline and degeneracy caused by the introduction of Universal Suffrage – the harbinger of bourgeois subordination to the inferior majority 'race' within. The most efficient system of rule – for all – was that premised on the concept of *noblesse oblige*: rule by the elite in the interest of all. Sport in this order of things had a specific social role. It was a muscular activity, exemplified by manliness, selflessness and hierarchy, and characterised by Godliness, sobriety, and patriotic duty. Sporting endeavour of this muscular Christian variety was a tool by which character was instilled and developed. This acquired character – that builds empire – forged through study of the Bible and exertions of the body was further customised by class. Elite participants at the public schools and Oxbridge would be equipped with the guiding principles necessary to rule. For the working class, it taught passive acceptance of higher authority from: the referee; the governing body of the sport; employers; and political masters.

C.L.R. James argued that cricket – the social and ethnic composition of its clubs and their style of play – was a looking-glass which 'at any particular period … reflects tendencies in national life'.[7] In *Chariots of Fire* these 'tendencies' are represented as pressures in both sport and society for progressive change away from the stifling know-your-place regime of old. Abrahams, as a Jewish student at Cambridge University, which had historically barred Semites from enrolling, was confidently making his place in the new order of things: you were what you did and you did what you wanted to do, unhindered by class or creed. This was – and should be – the measure of you; how you should be judged. The practised egalitarianism of Liddle and Abrahams, as sportsmen, stood as metaphor for the fresh easterlies – cleansing political winds blowing through from revolutionary Russia – that flavoured this inter-war period. The film's narrative spoke against a return to an ethos, in sport or society, that advocated the passive acceptance of inequality, hierarchy and elitism. Yet while addressing contemporary social and political tensions it did so in a timid, limited and monochrome style. Where was Harry Edward and Jack London? Indeed Liddle's record time of 9.7 for the 100 yards at the 1923 AAA championships broke, for the first time, Wharton's 'evens' set 37 years earlier. Incidentally, Liddle was buried in China, like Wharton far away from his birthplace, and was not honoured by a gravestone until after his resuscitation in *Chariots of Fire*.

One Black athlete whose career has not been forgotten, the detail reverberating through time and across cultures, is USA sprinter Jesse Owens. Hitler had intended the 1936 Berlin Olympics – the first to be televised – to be an athletic festival extolling the virtues of Nazism. But Owens packed his own script on leaving Ohio. He won four gold medals, blacking out the sunrays of Aryan success. His defeat of 'superior' German – and other White – runners (in an illusion of effortless grace) re-choreographed Hitler's intended dramatisation. According to Nazi ideology racial struggle was the motive force of history. Competition at its most naked was not over the control of material wealth and the means by which a society creates that wealth, but between 'races' for purity, survival and dominance. Only the unadulterated and non-miscegenised would endure. The salvation of the human 'race' – in effect, for Hitler, the biological struggle for Aryan pre-eminence – was only possible through the elimination of all other (sub-) species. Thus, the apparatus of racial oppression and destruction so characteristic of Nazism: official denigration of minorities; ethnic ghettoisation; forced and slave labour; concentration camps and the application of eugenic and ethnic cleansing genocidal in scale. Owens, as a Black 'auxiliary' of the United States was an 'Untermenschen', accorded the same racial status as Jews and Gypsies and the same social status as communists. All would be bound for the gas chamber upon the triumph of the Nazi will.

As triumphant Black sportsmen, Owens in 1936 and Wharton in 1886, are united by not only their ethnicity but the symbolic significance their excellence represented against a similarly racialised backdrop. Their athletic success semaphored comparable messages, rubbishing simplistic ideas of Black inferiority. In both Nazi Germany and late-Victorian Britain ideas about 'race' – in effect the relationship between physical appearance, behaviour and evolution – dominated and literally coloured any discussion of comparative national, social or cultural similarity and difference. 'Race' was used as an instrument to make social incisions: to divide the working class from uniting in pursuit of their objective material and political goal. It would be foolish to argue that the quality of life for minorities was similar in the two countries. An obvious difference was in the respective role of the state. While the ruling elite of the Nazis enforced a racial hierarchy through decrees of law and active brutality on the part of its militia, the British government did not force minorities and political opponents to shower in a gas chamber. What is argued is that the ruling class of both countries invested a great deal of worth in the concept of 'race'; it was pre-eminent in any discussion concerning the social health and well-being of The Nation. Both were highly racialised societies. This was how a Black resident in London at the turn of the century described the experience of a fellow Black.

> Recently, three white men, of gentlemanly appearance ... going in the opposite direction to that of a coloured man ... called the attention of his comrades to the presence of the coloured man, and then said 'Look at that thing' ... This laceration of the feelings of coloured people, which has now become a practice in England, is partly due to the fact that Englishmen, having adopted the notion that they are superior to coloured men, have found rudeness and incivility to be the best supports of the imposture.[8]

Yet there was a qualitative difference between the daily lives of ethnic minorities in Britain and Germany. Though in both countries 'race' – cloaked or naked – was a constantly recurring theme in much public debate, Wharton, while in Britain at least, was never fearful that the government would arbitrarily take his life in an effort to self-validate a racialised vision of how things should be.

At the time of Arthur's preparation for his win at the 1888 Sheffield Handicap the local *Daily Telegraph* reported a speech made by Sir John Lubbock to a

> meeting of working men at the Drill Hall, Bath. 'Our empire' said Lubbock 'contained representatives of almost every race of men, and every stage of human progress ... It is far from easy to understand savages, they naturally had much greater difficulty in understanding us ... Their modes of showing their feelings quite unlike ours.[9]

Lubbock's aim was to differentiate 'his' working men from those of a different colour who were separate not only in pigmentation but also in ideas, customs and, importantly, their ability to comprehend. Other Victorians argued there was a more fundamental cleavage. Among these were writer Charles Kingsley and social commentator Henry Mayhew. They spat repelling poison at the 'Dangerous Classes' – the bulk of the industrial working class – who were, like the savages of the Dark Continent, also a 'race' apart. (Kingsley considered Celts closer in evolution to Negroes than Anglo-Saxons.) In a society ordered by racial science everyone had to be colour coded. Such a categorisation would then act as a predictor of behaviour. The Nazis later attempted to universalise this racialised view of humanity and human development. The difference between the racial universe of Britain in the 1880s and 1990s and that of Germany in the 1930s was the degree to which the lesser 'races' were allowed a place in the New Order. Eugenics – effectively the science of racial purification – was a relatively new discipline in the 1880s. It reached an influential, genocidal maturity in Nazi Germany. Yet both societies were dominated by a ruling class that viewed themselves as a superior 'race'. Wharton and Owens confounded these ideas by their athletic skills. Although, as we have seen, the animalist theme was utilised by racial supremacists to escape from this contradiction.

The career of Owens after Berlin did not have the same uninterrupted angle of social descent that characterised Arthur's post-sport career. In 1950 he was named as 'Athlete of the Half-Century' by Associated Press. Twenty-two years later his old college awarded him an honorary doctorate. And in 1976 he received the Presidential Medal of Freedom, ranked as the highest civilian 'honour' in the USA. The reason for this is discernible. While Wharton's achievements had undermined the ruling ideas of the age of New Imperialism, in contrast Owens' four Olympic golds affirmed the meritocratic ideals at the heart of Democratic America. The symbolic message trumpeted to the German masses to the sound of the USA anthem, while Owens stood on his winner's podium, spoke of less inequality, less xenophobia and more individualism. Owens' success became wonderful propaganda material for the marketing forces of Liberal Democracy. Despite being a willing advocate of these ideals, especially in the post-1945 Cold War period, Owens was still considered a suspect Negro by J. Edgar Hoover and his FBI.

This was not the first time a sporting contest involving an American and German had been coated in numerous layers of ideological varnish. A few months earlier the world heavyweight boxing contest between the Max Schmeling and Joe Louis had been hyped up to King Kong proportions, particularly by Goebbels. (Louis was the first Black boxer able to fight for the title since Johnson.) The Nazis portrayed Schmeling as a teutonic superman; an Aryan colossus. He won by a knockout in the 12th round. The German magazine *Der Weltkampf* outlined the racial ramifications of this victory.

> The Negro is of a slave nature, but woe unto us if this slave nature is unbridled, for then arrogance and cruelty show themselves in the most bestial way … these three countries – France, England and white North America – cannot thank Schmeling enough for his victory, for he checked the arrogance of the Negro and clearly demonstrated to them the superiority of white intelligence.[10]

The Schmeling–Louis fight – and the return in 1938, which the 'Black Bomber' won inside a round – and Owens' experience in Berlin illustrate how the social and political context of sporting achievement determines the value that is placed on it. And it is not usually the self-evaluation of the sports man or woman that becomes hegemonic. The German boxer, heavyweight champion of the world between 1930 and 1932, was 'a decent, intelligent man … who found himself, to his own puzzlement, placed in a series of extraordinary situations owing to the history of his times'.[11] After the second world war he visited the USA and embraced Joe Louis. He also sent his former combatant money when Louis was destitute.

And destitution is no stranger to the Black heart of liberal America. (Although it should be pointed out that most poor North Americans are White.) This impoverishment has much to do with systemic racism. How else can we rationally explain the disproportionate number of dispossessed Blacks in the USA? Any examination of their lives – today and yesterday – ridicules the inference of progress towards ethnic equality suggested by apologists of liberal democracy on the back of Owens in Berlin. The college at which Owens built his pre-Olympic career, Ohio State, had during his freshman year, 1933, legalised its policy of segregating the accommodation of its Black and White students through the Ohio Supreme Court. Additionally, Black students were not allowed to live on campus. The job offered to Owens as part of his scholarship was goods-lift operator – Whites only being allowed to operate the passenger lift. Columbus, the town in which Ohio State was situated, was considered 'a cracker town just like Jackson Mississippi'[12] with its of history of racism. Owens was warned by Black newspapers and colleagues that the institution was no place for a Black man.

We write our own success: Sport and political struggle

Looking from the inside out – from the perspective of the runners as Black individuals – the major difference between Owens and Wharton was the public treatment their excellence attracted. Wharton's success was quickly forgotten because, paradoxically, of its symbolic importance. This is not to suggest a conspiracy of silence; many who have achieved – in all walks of life – have been forgotten: yet contrastingly many who have achieved little judged solely by their own efforts once the privilege of birth or wealth are factored out of the evaluation, are remembered. Historical memory is not arbitrary; this is recognised by those on the left in politics. Indeed, the key function of any socialist party is to act as the memory of the working class, celebrating confidence-inspiring victories and learning from defeat. With the theft of Africa continuing apace, it was not convenient to trumpet the deeds of a son of Africa conquering those sons of conquerors in their own backyard. The wider political significance of Arthur's achievements stood in contrast to the national/imperial events of the day. For Owens, it was the opposite. In many ways his Olympic success flowed with the prevailing current of international politics. The Nazis were an economic and imperial threat to the leading capitalist nations. This included state-capitalist USSR, the empire Hitler most wanted to destroy. Probably more than any other state in history, including the Soviet Union, Nazi Germany was a polity constructed around a particular body of ideas. As such it was vulnerable to practical refutations of its ideology by contradictory action and events. Owens should not have happened. His public denial of the nostrums of Nazism, on the track of the Nazis, and to their deepest embarrassment in front of thousands of Germans, provided immense propaganda material to the opponents of Fascism. These Defenders of Democracy – the USA, Britain, France –

conveniently and expediently put aside the racial inequality so obvious and profound in their own (enormous imperial and domestic) backyards – a contradiction analysed by George Orwell in his 1939 essay 'Not Counting Niggers' – to proclaim the success of Owens. His medals were held up to symbolise not so much a victory for ethnic equality – for this could have dangerous repercussions in house and yard – but rather a defeat for the particular variety of racialism as constructed, implemented and propagandised by the Nazis.

A generation later, Cassius Clay, as he was then known, replied to similar hypocrisy by throwing his Olympic gold medal into the river in his home state of Kentucky. His act pointed up the hollow weakness of symbolism-as-propaganda when confronted with a contrary reality: 'With my gold medal actually hanging around my neck I could not get a cheeseburger served to me in a downtown Louisville restaurant.'[13] This individual response to racism by one Black champion took a collective form eight years later at the 1968 Olympics. Against the background of growing Black anger and hostility to the war in Vietnam, where African-Americans were disproportionately filling the body-bags, Black athletes John Carlos and Tommie Smith black-fisted their way through the 200 metres medals ceremony. At the 400 metres equivalent their colleagues Larry James, Lee Evans and Ronald Freeman wore black berets, headgear of the revolutionary Black Panther movement. The lesson of Owens and Clay/Ali had been learnt. These Black athletes were determined not to allow their performances to be stolen from them. If they were to stand as metaphor, let them, the practitioners – the producers – be the transcribers, the evaluators.

> I wore a black right-hand and Carlos wore the left-hand glove of the same pair. My raised right hand stood for the power in black America. Carlos' raised left-hand stood for the unity of black America. Together they formed an arch of unity and power. The black scarf around my neck stood for black pride. The black socks with no shoes stood for black poverty in racist America. The totality of our effort was the regaining of black dignity.[14]

In this way does sport reflect global circumstances. It encapsulates both real and symbolic contest – sport and politics become intertwined and inseparable. While the geographical backdrop to Carlos, Smith, James, Evans and Freeman was the Estadio Olimpico, Mexico City, the political backdrop was one of Black revolutionary activism. (Interestingly, Rodney Pattison and Iain Macdonald, British winners of the Flying Dutchman yacht competition, also wore military caps and saluted when receiving their medals. Unlike Carlos and Smith they were not sent home.) Prior to the Olympics Black athletes in the United States had formed themselves into the Olympic Project for Human Rights. Carlos and Smith were both supporters of OPHR. The Project had originally intended a Black boycott of the Olympics. A revision of this plan saw the adoption of a policy that aimed to subvert the unthinking nationalism redolent of the Olympics as a whole. They were determined that the Stars and Stripes would not be wrapped around their bodies. While the dead Black soldier in Vietnam had no choice of what covered him, the athlete did. The conscript had been forced to give his life in service of the state. No such 'honour' would be forced upon Carlos and the others. Their wins were for 'Black America'. The Olympics was an opportunity to reinterpret the United in States and proclaim the virtues of Black consciousness. (These two occasions also provided an ideal platform upon which Black, USA athletes could vent their anger at the racist head of the USA Olympic Committee, Avery Brundage. The hostility of Black athletes towards the Chicago millionaire was historic, stemming from his fact-finding tour to Nazi Germany in 1935 when he returned empty-handed. He had been sent by the American Olympic Committee to assess the suitability of Berlin as the Olympic venue, and in particular the treatment of Jewish sports people. He could find no evidence of the mistreatment of Jewish athletes.)

The USA in 1968 was certainly not united. Many Blacks felt that the FBI had a hand in the killing of Martin Luther King in April. And in the death of Malcolm X in 1965. Rioting and rebellion by Black Americans in over 100 cities followed the murder of King: 39 were killed in the suppression, of whom 34 were Black. The struggle of African-Americans for liberty, justice and equality nearly 200 years after these principles had been inscribed in the constitution of the country was inextricably linked to their economic status. Along with systemic racism, poverty overshadowed most. It was this common enemy – with a common cause – that linked and united Black and White during the 'Poor People's March' on Washington in May, representing 30 million destitute Americans. It culminated in 'Resurrection City', an encampment put together by the marchers in the centre of the capital. After five days the leaders were imprisoned and the shanty town destroyed.

Mexico City itself was the site of an uprising by students and workers against the government of President Gustavo Diaz Ordaz in the months before the Olympics. Just a week before the opening ceremony soldiers with fixed bayonets charged a crowd of over 15,000. In the stabbing and shooting by the military that followed more than 40 protesters were killed. Indeed, 1968 was a year in which the oppressed in many different parts of the world took to the streets: in Ecuador, France, Brazil, Czechoslovakia to name some of those most prominent. The struggle for Black emancipation in the USA was at the forefront of a global phenomenon. The times really did seem to be changing.

While Arthur's known political activity was confined to small-scale political and economic conflicts – though he was a member of the Miners' Federation of Great Britain, forerunner of the NUM, during the General Strike in 1926 – his contribution, as a Black man, to the struggle of British labour for emancipation was not unique. There is a long history of political activity by Black Britons and Black residents of Britain: in 1780 Charlotte Gardiner was hanged for daring to confront the authorities through her part in the Gordon Riots; the same decade Olaudah Equiano began campaigning against slavery. His daughter, Anna Maria, is buried in the grounds of St Andrews Church, Chesterton, Cambridge. She died in 1797, aged four. (It is within shooting-over-the-bar-and-fetching distance of the home pitch of the Sunday League football team for which I play.) A plaque was erected on the outside wall. The words and the sentiment they express stand testament to a history of respect and tolerance of difference.

Should simple village rhymes attract thine eye,
Stranger, as thoughtfully thou passest by,
Know that there lies beside this humble stone
A child of colour haply not thine own.
Her father born of Afric's sun-burnt race,
Torn from his native fields, ah foul disgrace!
Through various toils at length to Britain came,
Espous'd, so Heaven ordain'd, an English dame,
And followed Christ; their hope two infants dear.
But one, a hapless orphan, slumbers here.
To bury her the village children came,

And dropp'd choice flowers, and lisp'd her early fame;
And some that lov'd her most as if unblest.
Bedew'd with tears the white wreaths on their breast;
But she is gone and dwells in that abode
Where some of every clime shall joy in God.

During the nineteenth century William Davidson, a Jamaican, was hanged in 1820 for his part in the Cato Street conspiracy. The conspirators were seeking revenge for the Peterloo Massacre of 1815 in which 11 demonstrators had been killed by the militia; William Cuffay was a leader of the Chartist movement in London; Henry Sylvester Williams formed the African Association in 1897, to encourage pan-African unity. (In 1900 the first ever Pan-African Conference was held in London. Its ultimate objective was the ending of colonialism.)

The black gloves and berets of 1968 were the African-American expression of a movement against oppression that had flowered with Toussaint Louverture's victorious slave rebellion in San Domingo – Haiti – in 1797. Yet from the anti-slavery campaigns of the eighteenth and nineteenth centuries to the Black Panthers of urban America and beyond, the primary characteristic feature has not been the ethnic exclusivity of the participants, but their common socio-economic background. Leader of the Panthers, Malcolm X, came to acknowledge the necessity of unity between peoples – after they had achieved unity amongst themselves – if any were to stand any chance of destroying capitalism.

> You have whites who are fed up, you have blacks who are fed up. The whites who are fed up can't come uptown [to Harlem] too easily because the people uptown are more fed up than anybody else, and they are so fed up it's not easy to come uptown ... when the day comes when the whites are really fed up with what is going on – and I don't mean those jive whites, who pose as liberals and who are not, but those who are fed up with what is going on – when they learn how to establish the proper type of communication with those uptown who are fed up, and they get some coordinated action going. You'll get some changes. And it will take both, it will take everything that you've got, it will take that.[15]

Arthur owed a debt, as do all sports people, to those who fought to improve the lives of Black and working people. Without pressure from below to change the lot of ordinary people, the small amount of leisure time and money for relative luxuries that did exist would not have. They forced those above, in parliament, in the boardroom, in the courtroom to change laws, working practices and conditions. In Britain it was activity by individuals and groups, such as the Chartists and trade unions in general, that won improved social and economic conditions which enabled men and to a much lesser extent, women, to pursue a living in sport. It was activists on the shop floor and on the street who created the space for Wharton to perform.

From 'Express Engine' to El Loco

The argument of Nick Hazlewood *In the Way! Goalkeepers: A Breed Apart?* is that you have to be a little crazy, unusual, demented, to want to play in that position. What other placing holds the prospect of getting your teeth kicked out with your first touch? Where you get the blame for defeat, but no praise in victory? I do not think Arthur was a jockstrap short of the full kit, but he would certainly fit the description to be included in Hazlewood's 'Breed'. He was extreme, brave, violent, vulnerable, mad. To my mind the first El Loco.

> Anyone who chose to play in goal in the 1880s–90s was considered brave, foolhardy and useless anywhere else. Anyone who was forced to play in goal lacked resolve, was useless anywhere else or both. The small boys, the duffers and the funk-sticks were the goalkeepers ... If any player who was playing out showed any sign of funk [cowardice] or failed to play up, he was packed off into goal at once, not only for the day, but as a lasting degradation.[16]

Goalkeepers were not formally acknowledged until 1871 when the FA inserted a rule that allowed those so designated to handle the ball anywhere in their half of the field. Though Sheffield Rules football had referred to the goalkeeper before this time, defining the position literally: anyone on the defending team who is nearest to his own goal. Until the 1890s a goalkeeper could be downed by one or more attackers (in an onside position), whether or not he had the ball. The more organised teams would use a rusher, a forward whose job it was to do just this. Any goalie foolish enough to catch a ball and hold onto it would almost certainly take a battering from any forwards within diving or lunging distance. All sides played with at least five forwards in the

1890s. This may explain Wharton's preference for fisting the ball away rather than catching it; and, in part, his reputation as the 'goalkeeper with the prodigious punch'. Despite his excellent timing and co-ordination, Arthur did not always connect with the ball!:

> Several times … [Bridgewater of Sheffield United] charged at Wharton [of Rotherham Town] as if he meant mischief. Stand-up fights because of these charges more than once seemed imminent, but the good sense of Wharton and the timely intervention of the referee prevented anything so discreditable.[17]

The position of goalkeeper suited Arthur's character. Despite the great risk of personal injury that in the 1880s would have threatened his potential as a sprinter, the potential for freedom of expression appealed to the extrovert in Arthur. Whether he could have played successfully in other positions is a moot point. He certainly could not have done with the same skill, agility, exuberance and longevity of professional career. As goalkeeper he had freedom to roam – to the half-way line, beyond even – and take shots at goal. This would not have been unusual. Only from 1912 were goalies restricted to handling the ball within the newly marked penalty area. Swinging from the bar, as has been noted, was another speciality. A letter writer to the *Sheffield Telegraph and Independent*, recalled (half a century after the event).

> In a match between Rotherham and [Sheffield] Wednesday at Olive Grove I saw Wharton jump, take hold of the cross bar, catch the ball between his legs, and cause three onrushing forwards – Billy Ingham, Clinks Mumford and Micky Bennett – to fall into the net. I have never seen a similar save since and I have been watching football for over fifty years.[18]

For some it was a cameo that said much about the nature of the player; for others a Black man hanging from the horizontal was second to their nature.

In summary

Once Arthur stopped playing football professionally in 1902, though his cricketing exploits continued to be publicised, little else about him was. So, there are many gaps in this study. What we can say is that his name is synonymous with numerous firsts, as: Black professional footballer; Black Football League player; 'gentleman' professional; 100 yards world record holder. The list could continue. However if his – if anybody's – life was reduced to a mere recitation of factual achievements it would, by its very nature, be incomplete.

His private relationship with Emma was left unresolved in the sense that the difficulties created out of living together and having separate lives – Arthur's being very public – was not underpinned by mutual love and respect. It was a journey neither would have chosen had they known the route beforehand. The birth of Minnie and Nora to sister-in-law Martha, assuming that they were Arthur's children, would have created unquenchable anguish for Emma, Martha and Arthur – for obviously different reasons. For all three the world may have acquired a surreal hue from 1893. Arthur, the nationally known celebrity ever willing to encourage adulation of him by others yet unable to give of himself fully to his most enduring fan, the woman with whom he had chosen to share his life. Public acclaim versus private grief. For a man so used to winning physical contests this covert emotional conflict may well have overshadowed his public triumphs with its tenacious, sustained impact. Once the door had been shut on the outside world, how much worth did his feats of time over distance, of combining agility and strength carry when faced with the complex emotions of his tumultuous marriage?

What of Martha and Arthur's anguish? Of lovers doomed from the moment their feelings awoke, enveloped and roused by a love procreative yet inevitably destructive; driven and haunted by the fallible, withering nature of its unsustainable secrecy. How did they cope with their public cloaking of their union; and the impossibility of accepting joint responsibility for the living embodiments of their affair? What was the burden of Emma and Arthur's barren marriage compared to Martha's life-long torment of dual denial: of being the mother to her children and partner of her lover?

For a man who was the focus of so much positive attention, who bought excitement into the lives of many, it was surely not lost on Arthur how negative his physicality could also be. Not only to those nearest to him, but to himself. (Can there be anyone closer?) Was not he also prevented from loving fully his children? And them from reciprocating?

While it could be argued that Arthur had a fair amount of power in determining the course of his personal relationships – marriage, his affair with Martha – he had little influence to deflect or duck the power of systemic, institutional racism and its proletarianising influence.[19] It can be assumed from his application to join the Gold Coast Government Service that he would have swapped his role as Northern Working-Class Hero with that of a nondescript West African civil servant. It is at this point that we find the consistent theme of paradox fusing the public and private dimensions of his life. His elevated status as sporting icon in Britain involved, as part of the Faustian pact, a denial of a return to West Africa on his own terms. As an anonymous official of the Colonial Office commented, his sporting excellence was 'inappropriate' training for the career of a bureaucrat. Thus his success, in the sweep of the hand of a pen-pushing official, becomes transformed into a handicap the burden of which is measured in years rather than yards. Though Arthur was not alone. To end a glittering sporting career in poverty is not unusual for working-class athletes, especially when they are Black. Joe Louis is a case in point. And Albert Johanneson, the South African winger for Leeds United who became the first Black African to play in an FA Cup final in 1965. Thirty years later for two days he lay dead in his Headingley flat unnoticed, broke and broken.

But racism in and of itself does not automatically cause destitution. Its impact is dependent upon the relation of power between the parties involved: the velocity and damage are dependent upon the social and economic relationship between the firer and the target. To illustrate it is worth recalling the career of another Black sportsman, Learie Constantine, who played cricket in Lancashire 20 years after Wharton. A Trinidadian and West Indies international he was invited, in 1928, to play professionally for Nelson in the Lancashire League. His family – his partner and their daughter Gloria – were later joined by another Trinidadian and family friend, C.L.R. James. According to James there was one other person of colour in the small cotton town, who collected refuse in a pushcart. After initial hostility the Trinidadians became accepted by the working-class community around them. No doubt Learie's success at the wicket – Nelson won the Lancashire League seven times in Constantine's nine seasons with the club – endeared him to the hearts – if not the minds – of most. James recalls one incident that Constantine interpreted as a sign of acceptance and belonging.

> Early one morning a friend turns up, has a chat and a cup of tea and rises to leave. 'Norma, I am just going to do my shopping. If

> you haven't done yours I'll do it for you.' Later Constantine said to me, 'You noticed?' I hadn't noticed anything. 'Look outside. It is a nasty day. She came so that Norma will not have to go out into the cold.'[20]

In 1943 Constantine booked rooms for himself and his family at the Imperial Hotel, Russell Square, London. He was in the capital playing for the West Indies against England at Lords. On arrival the manager, fearful of the effect of public expressions of prejudice from his other guests upon his trade, reluctantly agreed to honour Constantine's booking – for one night and no more. The family went immediately to another hotel and Learie sued the Imperial. He won £5 in damages. The hotel had chosen a public figure with a high profile, who had the economic means, social status as a civil servant and the social contacts to fight back 'against the revolting contrast between his first-class status as a cricketer and his third class status as a [Black] man'.[21]

The sports career of 'Darkie' – this epithet being applied to virtually all Black professional sportsmen in Britain up until the 1960s – Wharton was distinguished by two primary characteristics: his abilities as an athlete – skills that were the coalition of innate talent and toil; and the social reaction to his colour and ethnicity. In respect of the first characteristic, he achieved fame but no lasting material benefit for his physical prowess. In respect of the second the responses to his colour were conditioned by a national and imperial backdrop that held 'race' to be as important as social class in determining one's place in the world. Arthur's burden was not his colour but the dual identity forced upon him because he was a man of colour. He lived, as a sportsman, in two co-existing but different worlds: in one he was acclaimed and One of Us; in the other he was racialised and categorised as an Other. The *Athletic Journal* interview, 26 June 1888, told of two personaes, the public and the private. 'Arthur is a most sociable fellow when you know him, but you have to get to know him first … taken all-round he is a straight forward good natured chap.'

The words 'when you get to know him' can be rewritten as 'when you get to know him as a man, an individual' (albeit a social being). An unintended revelation that within the body of Arthur were two identities. It infers a discrepancy between the public and the private image but does not elaborate. Yet there was a distinction between Arthur the athlete and Arthur the 'Black Man', a racialised and racially determined Object. This political construction – an edifice of divide and rule and bulwark of the status quo – sought to devalue African civilisation and therefore the African. The images of noble and ignoble savage, central to any late nineteenth-century Euro-centric construction of the Negro, were for public consumption by the White masses. Yet the reporter appears to be saying that 'when you get to know him' as an individual, stripped of his racialised identity, 'he is a straight forward good natured chap'.

There is little doubt that the level of racism, whether it be the operation of the colour bar or personal abuse, was under-reported. C.L.R. James emphasises this point. 'Writers on sport ... automatically put what was unpleasant out of sight even if they had to sweep it under the carpet. The impression they created was one of almost perpetual sweetness and light.'[22] Constantine, a committed anti-racist who, somewhat contradictorily, ended his days among the political Establishment in the House of Lords, recognised the contrasting quality of his individual experience as a man among friends in Nelson, to his objective status as a Black man in White country.

> *Almost* the entire population of Britain really expect the coloured man to live in an inferior area ... devoted to coloured people ... Most British people would be quite unwilling for a black man to enter their homes, nor would they wish to work with one as a colleague, nor to stand shoulder to shoulder with one at a factory bench.[23]

For the last 15 years of his working life Arthur was a colliery haulage hand at Yorkshire Main Colliery, Edlington. He died on 12 December 1930 at Springwell House sanatorium near Edlington, Doncaster after a 'long and painful illness'.[24] He was buried four days later in a third-class grave in the municipal cemetery of the pit village. That Arthur finished his working days underground has poignant irony; there is an absurd symmetry between the slow but steady erasure of his achievements from collective memory and his days spent gathering coal-dust beneath the surface. During the writing of this book 'Football Unites – Racism Divides' launched the *Arthur Wharton Memorial Fund* to provide a headstone to mark Arthur's burial plot. Fittingly the largest donation came from the collective body of fellow professional footballers, the PFA. The headstone was laid in place on a rainy, overcast

Thursday, 8 May 1997. Among those present were his family; a long-time resident of Edlington – who knew nothing of Arthur – originally from Sierra Leone and a direct descendant of Sir Samuel Lewis, the first African to be knighted; professional footballers past and present, including Chris Dolby one of the few Asian professional footballers; the writer of the introduction to this book, Tony Whelan, who in laying flowers at the grave physically reaffirmed an honourable tradition of Black footballers that has struggled to fix for itself a foothold in the history of the sport; members of the Black communities in South Yorkshire; and workers from FURD, in particular Howard Holmes who has been instrumental in ensuring that Arthur is now visible to those who want to find him. The dust was again being kicked up from below.

NOTES

1. Charles A. Dana in Arthur Ashe Junior, *A Hard Road To Glory*, vol. 1 (1993 edition) p. 27.
2. Ashe, vol. 1(1993) p. 27.
3. Jeffrey P. Green, 'Boxing and the "Colour Question" in Edwardian Britain: The "White Problem" of 1911', in *International Journal of the History of Sport*, 5, 1 (1988).
4. Peter Lovesey, *The Official Centenary of the AAA* (1979) p. 75.
5. Ibid.
6. Ibid.
7. C.L.R. James, *Beyond a Boundary* (London 1996) p. 214.
8. Theophilus E. Samuel Scholes, 'Glimpses of the Ages: or the superior and inferior races, so-called discussed in the light of science and history' II, pp. 176, 177, 179, 237, in Fryer, *Staying Power* (1984) p. 439.
9. 12 September.
10. Ashe, vol. 2 (1993) p. 14.
11. Gerald Suster, *Champions of the Ring* (London 1994) p. 107.
12. William J. Baker, *Jesse Owens* (London 1986) p. 39.
13. Mike Marqusee, 'Sport and Stereotype: from role model to Muhammed Ali', in *Race and Class*, 36, 4 (1995) p. 10.
14. Ibid., p. 20.
15. George Breitman, 'The Last Year of Malcolm X' (New York 1967) pp. 206–7, in Kevin Ovenden, *Malcolm X. Socialism and Black Nationalism* (London 1992) p. 41.
16. Hazlewood (1996) p. 22.
17. *Rotherham Advertiser*, April 1891.
18. T.H. Smith, 12 January 1942.
19. Many skilled workers from the Caribbean migrating to Britain in the 1950s, found they were forced to take jobs requiring little special training or deployment of their skills. There are many works which cover racism as a means of proletarianisation. See, for example, Tony Bogues *et al.*, *Black Nationalism and Socialism* (London 1979); A. Sivanandan, *A Different Hunger: Writings on Black Resistance*, Chapter 3 (London 1983).

20. C.L.R. James (1996) p. 124.
21. C.L.R. James, *Beyond a Boundary* (London 1963) p. 110,.in Peter Fryer, *Staying Power: the History of Black People in Britain* (1984) p. 364.
22. C.L.R. James (1996) p. 112.
23. L. Constantine, 'Colour Bar' (1954) p. 67, in Peter Fryer (1984) p. 367.
24. *Sheffield Telegraph*, 16 December 1930.

Bibliography

Adi, Hakim, *The History of African and Caribbean Communities in Britain* (Hove 1995).

Alcock, C.W., *Book of Football* (London 1906).

Ali, Ahmed and Ali, Ibrahim, *The Black Celts* (Cardiff 1992).

Ashe, Arthur, *A Hard Road to Glory* (London 1993).

Akikiwe, Nmadi, *My Odyssey: An autobiography* (London 1970).

Baker, William J., *Jesse Owens* (London 1986).

Baker, W.J. and Mangan, James A. (eds), *Sport in Africa* (London 1987).

Bernal, Martin, *Black Athena* vol. 1 (London 1987).

Berry, Harry, *1887: A Sprinting Year* (Private n.d.).

Boahen, A. Adu (ed.), *General History of Africa: VII* (London 1990).

Bogues, Tony, Gordon, Kim and James, C.L.R., *Black Nationalism and Socialism* (London 1979).

Bolt, Christine, *Victorian Attitudes to Race* (London 1971).

Bose, Mihir, *The Sporting Alien* (Edinburgh 1996).

Bowley, Arthur L., *Wages in the United Kingdom* (Cambridge 1900).

Bredin, E.C., *Running and Training* (Northampton 1902).

British Biographical Index (London 1990).

Butler, Brian, *The Official History of the Football Association* (London 1991).

Cashmore, Ernest, *Black Sportsmen* (London 1982).

Champions of the Game, *Football and How to Play It* (Dundee 1904).

Cook, Chris and Stevenson, John, *The Longman Handbook of Modern British History 1714–1987* (London 1988).

Downer, Alf, *Running Recollections and How to Train* (London 1908).

Edgerton, Robert B., *The Fall of the Asante Empire* (London 1995).

Encyclopaedia Britannica (Cambridge 1884).

Encyclopaedia Britannica (Cambridge 1911).

Engels, Friedrich, *Condition of the Working Class in England in 1844* (Moscow 1973).

Fabian, A.H. and Green, Geoffrey (eds), *Association Football* (London 1960).

Farnsworth, Keith, *Sheffield Football: A History 1857–1961* (Sheffield 1995).

Farnsworth, Keith, *Sheffield Wednesday: A Complete Record 1867–1967* (Derby 1987).
Finney, Richard (ed.), *100 Years of Football in Rotherham* (Rotherham n.d.).
Football Association, *The Official FA Year Book 1949–50* (London 1949?).
Football Who's Who 1900–1901.
Football Who's Who 1901–1902.
Foucault, Michel, *Discipline and Punish* (London 1977).
Fryer, Peter, *Staying Power: The History of Black People in Britain* (London 1984).
Golesworthy, Maurice, *Encyclopaedia of Association Football* (London 1973).
Goodall, John, *Association Football* (London 1898).
Green, Geoffrey, *The Official History of the FA Cup* (London 1960).
Hamilton, Al, *Black Pearls* (London 1982).
Harding, John, *For the Good of the Game: The Official History of the Professional Footballers' Association* (London 1991).
Hargreaves, J.D., *Decolonization in Africa* (London 1991).
Hazlewood, Nick, *In the Way! Goalkeepers: A Breed Apart?* (Edinburgh 1996).
Hill, Robert H. (ed.), *The Year Book 1969* (London 1969).
Hilton, Rodney, *Bond Men Made Free* London 1986).
Hobsbawm, Eric, *The Age of Capital* (London 1995).
Hobsbawm, Eric, *The Age of Empire* (London 1995).
Hobsbawm, Eric, *The Age of Revolution* (London 1995).
Hopcraft, Arthur, *The Football Man* (Harmondsworth 1971).
Hopkins, A.G., *An Economic History of West Africa* (London 1988).
Illingworth, E., *A Short History of the Northern Counties Athletic Association 1879–1979* (Leeds n.d.).
Information on Ireland, *Nothing But the Same Old Story* (London 1986).
International Dictionary of Medicine and Biology vol.1 (New York 1986).
Jackson, N. Lane, *Sporting Ways and Sporting Days* (London 1932).
James, C.L.R., *Beyond a Boundary* (London 1996).
Jamieson, D.A., *Powderhall and Pedestrianism* (Edinburgh 1943).
Kelly's Directory of Cheshire (London 1902).
Kelly's Directory of Lancashire (London 1901).
Killingray, David (ed.), *Africans in Britain* (London 1994).
Lenin, V.I., *Imperialism, The Highest Stage of Capitalism* (Peking 1975).
Lorimer, Douglas, *Colour, Class and the Victorians* (Leicester 1978).
Lovesey, Peter, *The Official Centenary of the AAA* (London 1979).
Malik, Kenan, *The Meaning of Race* (London 1996).
Mangan, J.A. (ed.), *The Games Ethic and Imperialism* (London 1986).
Mangan, J.A. (ed.), *The Cultural Bond: Sport, Empire, Society* (London 1993).
Marx, Karl and Engels, Friedrich, *Articles on Britain* (Moscow 1971).
Mason, Tony, *Association Football and English Society 1863–1915* (Brighton 1980).

Mason, Tony, *Passion of the People? Football in South America* (London 1995).
Mason, Tony (ed.), *Sport in Britain* (Cambridge 1989).
Moister, Reverend William, *Memoir of the Rev. H. Wharton* (London 1875).
Nawrat, Chris and Hutchings, Steve, *The Sunday Times Illustrated History of Football* (London 1996).
Needham, Ernest, *Association Football* (London 1900–1).
Ovenden, Kevin, *Malcolm X. Socialism and Black Nationalism* (London 1992).
Packenham, Thomas, *The Scramble for Africa* (London 1992).
Parker, G.A. (ed.), *South African Sports: An Official Handbook* (London 1897).
Pelling, Henry, *A History of British Trade Unionism* (London 1987).
Plumb, Philip W. (ed.), *The 1970 Clipper Annual of Football Facts* (London 1969).
Quercetani, R.L., *A World History of Track and Field Athletics* (London 1964).
Ranjitsihnji, Prince, *Jubilee Book of Cricket* (London 1912).
Royle, Edward, *Chartism* (London 1980).
Scholes, Theophilus E. Samuel, *Glimpses of the Ages vol. 2* (London 1908).
Scott, D. and Bent, Chris, *Borrowed Time: A Social History of Running* (1984).
Shearman, Montague, *Athletics and Football* (London 1887).
Sivanandan, A., *A Different Hunger: Writings on Black Resistance* (London 1983).
Soar, Phil, *Hamlyn A–Z of British Football Records* (London 1981).
Sumerton, Gerry, *Now We Are United: the Official History of Rotherham United* (Harefield 1995).
Suster, Gerald, *Champions of the Ring* (London 1994).
Sutcliffe, C.E. and Hargreaves, F. (eds), *History of the Lancashire Football Association 1878–1928* (Middlesex 1992).
Taylor, Rogan and Ward, Andrew, *Kicking and Screaming: An Oral History of Football in England* (London 1995).
Taylor, Rogan, *Football and its Fans* (Leicester 1992).
Thabe, G.A.L. and Mutloatse, M., *It's a Goal: 50 Years of Sweat, Tears and Drama in Black Soccer* (Johannesburg 1983).
Twydell, Dave, *Rejected FC: Vol. 1* (Middlesex 1992).
Watman, Melvyn, *An Encyclopaedia of Athletics* (London 1967).
Watman, Melvyn, *History of British Athletics* (London 1968).
Williams, Graham, *The Code War: English Football under the Historical Spotlight* (Middlesex 1994).
Woolnough, Brian, *Black Magic: England's Black Footballers* (London 1983).

Newspapers

Ashton Herald
Athletic Journal
Athletic News

Cannock Advertiser
Cheltenham Press
Cheshire Daily Echo
Darlington and Stockton Times
Doncaster Chronicle
Football Echo and Sports Gazette (Southampton)
Football News and Athletic Journal
Gold Coast Times
Heckmondwike Reporter
Illustrated Sporting and Dramatic News
Manchester Guardian
Newcastle Evening Chronicle
Newcastle Weekly Chronicle
Northern Echo
Rotherham Advertiser
Sheffield Daily Telegraph
Sheffield and Rotherham Independent
Sheffield Sports Special (The Green 'Un)
Sheffield Telegraph and Independent
Socialist Worker
Sporting Chronicle
Sporting Life
Sporting Man (Newcastle)

Journals and Articles

African Review, xx, 355 (9 September 1899).

Black Cultural Archives, *Black History Month 1993* (London 1993).

Berry, Harry 'The Kaffirs Tour 1899–1900', *Association of Football Statisticians – Report 41* (March 1985).

Calder, Angus, *The Careers of Learie Constantine* (unpublished 1996).

Green, Jeffrey P., 'Boxing and the "Colour Question" in Edwardian Britain', *International Journal of the History of Sport*, 5, 118 (1988).

Jenkins, Ray, 'Salvation for the Fittest? A West African Sportsman in Britain in the Age of New Imperialism', *International Journal of the History of Sport*, 7, 1 (May 1990).

Jenkins, Ray, 'Sportsman Extraordinaire', *West Africa* (5 June 1985).

Jenkins, Ray, 'Gold Coasters Overseas, 1880–1919', *Immigrants and Minorities*, 4, 3 (November 1985).

Jenkins, Ray, 'Wonder Wharton: Forgotten Hero', *South* (December 1987).

Keller, T., 'See Why They Ran', *Guardian* (9 March 1985).

Kirk-Greene, Anthony, 'Imperial Administration and the Athletic Imperative', in Baker W.J. and Mangan, J. (eds), *Sport in Africa* (London 1987).

Lewis, R.W., 'Football Hooliganism in England before 1914', *International Journal of the History of Sport*, 13, 3 (December 1996).

Lewis, R.W., 'The Genesis of Professional Football: Bolton-Blackburn-Darwen, the Centre of Innovation', *International Journal of the History of Sport*, 14, 1 (April 1997).

Marqusee, Mike, 'Sport and Stereotype: from role model to Muhammad Ali', *Race and Class*, 36, 4 (1995).

Metcalfe, Alan, 'Organised Sport in the Mining Communities of South Northumberland 1800–1889', *Victorian Studies*, 25, 4 (Summer 1982).

Neale, Steve, 'Chariots of Fire', 'Images of Men', *Screen* (September–October 1982).

Stoddart, Brian, 'Sport, Cultural Imperialism and Colonial Responses in the British Empire', *British Society of Sports History: Proceedings of the Fourth Annual Conference* (July 1986).

Transactions of the Aborigenes Protection Society 1890–96, 4, 1.

Turnbull, Simon, 'Wharton the Evens Favourite', *Northern Echo* (11 July 1993).

Vasili, Phil, 'The Right Kind of Fellows: Nigerian Football Tourists as Agents of Europeanisation', *International Journal of the History of Sport*, 11, 2 (August 1994).

Vasili, Phil, 'Walter Daniel Tull 1888–1918: soldier, footballer, Black', *Race and Class*, 38, 2 (1996).

Public Documents

Colonial Office Papers.

Swinton Papers, Churchill College, Cambridge.

Theses

Stuart, Osmond Wesley, *'Good Boys', Footballers and Strikes: African Social Change in Bulowayo 1935–53* (unpublished), School of African and Oriental Studies, University of London (1989).

Tyas, Michael D., *Rotherham United FC: An analysis of its origin and development in the period 1870–1914* (unpublished), North Staffordshire Polytechnic (1987).

Private Collections

Jenkins Papers.

Leeson Papers.

Index

Titles of Related Interest

FRANCE AND THE 1998 WORLD CUP

The National Impact of a World Sporting Event

Hugh Dauncey and **Geoff Hare**, both at the University of Newcastle (Eds)

This book examines France's hosting of the soccer World Cup, held in ten cities in summer 1998. It covers the major socio-economic, political, cultural and sporting dimensions of this global sports event, including bidding for and organizing the Finals, the improvement of sporting and transport infrastructures, marketing, merchandizing and media coverage, policing and security during the month-long competition and building a national team. The analysis of France '98 is set within the sporting context of the recent history and organization of French football (the links between football, money and politics; the sporting public) and more broadly within the French tradition of using major cultural and sporting events to focus world attention of France as a leader in the international community. The book concludes with an evocation of the day-to-day impact of four weeks of sporting festivities, and the lessons to be drawn concerning sport and national identity in an era of increasing economic, political, cultural and sporting globalization.

212 pages 1999
0 7146 4887 6 cloth 0 7146 4438 2 paper
Sport in the Global Society No. 7
A special issue of the journal Culture, Sport, Society

FRANK CASS PUBLISHERS
Newbury House, 900 Eastern Avenue, Newbury Park, Ilford, Essex IG2 7HH
Tel: +44 (0)181 599 8866 Fax: +44 (0)181 599 0984 E-mail: info@frankcass.com.
NORTH AMERICA
c/o ISBS, 5804 NE Hassalo Street, Portland, OR 97213 3644, USA
Tel: 800 944 6190 Fax: 503 280 8832 E-mail: cass@isbs.com
Website: http://www.frankcass.com

SCORING FOR BRITAIN

International Football and International Politics, 1900–1939

P J Beck, Kingston University

Despite traditional images regarding the separation of politics and sport in Britain, the history of British international football illuminates the emerging use of sport as an instrument of British foreign policy, most notably, in terms of complementing the government s cultural propaganda programme.

This study considers the nature and development of linkages between international football and politics in Britain between 1900 and 1939. It provides also a history of international football in Britain. Beck examines how the growing politicization of sport in other countries, encouraged British governments to interpret sport as offering an instrument of policy supportive of British interests in the wider world. He points out that association football, Britain's major sport, came to be seen as a means of projecting favourable images of Britain as a 'great nation' to a large and often responsive overseas audience. The British government's intervention in international football is examined. Throughout this study football is viewed alongside other types of international sport, including the Olympics. Other themes highlighted include the official attitudes towards professional sport and the ongoing debate about international sport as a potential cause of international co-operation or conflict. It is based on British government records, private papers, the press as well as the archives of FIFA and the four British football associations.

272 pages 1999
0 7146 4899 X cloth 0 7146 4454 4 paper
Sport in the Global Society No. 9

FRANK CASS PUBLISHERS
Newbury House, 900 Eastern Avenue, Newbury Park, Ilford, Essex IG2 7HH
Tel: +44 (0)181 599 8866 Fax: +44 (0)181 599 0984 E-mail: info@frankcass.com.
NORTH AMERICA
c/o ISBS, 5804 NE Hassalo Street, Portland, OR 97213 3644, USA
Tel: 800 944 6190 Fax: 503 280 8832 E-mail: cass@isbs.com
Website: http://www.frankcass.com

SPORTING NATIONALISMS

Identity, Ethnicity, Immigration and Assimilation

David Mayall and **Michael Cronin** both at Sheffield Hallam University (Eds)

This volume examines the ways in which sport shapes the experiences of various immigrant and minority groups and, in particular, looks at the relationship between sport, ethnic identity and ethnic relations. The articles in this volume are concerned primarily with British, American and Australian sporting traditions and the themes covered include the consolidation of ethnic identity in host societies through participation immigrant sports and exclusive sporting organizations, assimilation into 'host' societies through participation in indigenous, national sports, and the construction by outsiders of separate ethnic identities according to sporting criteria.

160 pages 1998
07146 44896 5 cloth 07146 4449 8 paper
A special issue of the journal Immigrants and Minorities
Sport in the Global Society No. 6

THE RACE GAME

Sport and Politics in South Africa

Douglas Booth, University of Otago, New Zealand

In this book Douglas Booth takes a fresh look at the role of sport in the fostering of a new national identity in South Africa. It looks at the thirty-year course and the changes in the objectives of the sports boycott of South Africa. Black South Africans initially proposed the boycott as a strategy to integrate sport, and Western governments and international sporting federations such as the International Olympic Committee later applied the boycott with similar intentions. At first, South Africa's ruling National Party dismissed all demands either to integrate sport or to extend political rights to blacks, but prolonged international isolation forced it to make concessions, and by the mid-1980s the government had accepted integrated sport. The international sporting community readmitted South Africa to competition in the early 1980s in acknowledgement of state president F W de Klerk's political initiatives and commitment to a universal franchise. Sport remains an integral element of post-apartheid politics. State president Nelson Mandela and his government believe that sport can unite black and white South Africans and contribute to social and political change. Indeed there have been moments, such as South Africa's victory in the 1995 World Rugby Cup, when unity through sport seemed possible. But through careful analysis Booth argues that sport will never unite South Africans except in the most fleeting and superficial manner.

280 pages illus. 1998
0 7146 4799 3 cloth 0 7146 4354 8 paper
Sport in the Global Society No. 4

THE RUGBY WORLD

Race, Gender, Commerce and Rugby Union

Timothy J L Chandler, Kent State University and
John Nauright, University of Queensland (Eds)

This book explores the expansion of rugby from its imperial and amateur upper-class white male core into other contexts throughout the late nineteenth and twentieth centuries. The development of rugby in the racially divided communities of the setter empire and how this was viewed are explored initially. Then the editors turn to four case studies of rugby's expansion beyond the bounds of the British Empire (France, Italy, Japan and the USA). The role of women in rugby is examined and the subsequent development of women's rugby as one of the fastest growing sports for women in Europe, North America and Australasia in the 1980s and 1990s.

256 pages 1999
0 7146 4853 1 cloth 0 7146 4411 0 paper
Sport in the Global Society No. 10

MAKING MEN

Rugby and Masculine Identity

John Nauright, University of Queensland, and
Timothy J L Chandler, Kent State University, Ohio (Eds)

This collection of essays charts the development of rugby football from its origins in the English public schools and ancient universities to its acceptance in the farthest reaches of the empire. As the authors show, central to an understanding of the place of rugby in all these settings is evidence demonstrating that the game was a form of both hegemonic masculinity and homosocial behaviour, as well as a means of promoting nationalism and social control.
A major aim of the editors has been to highlight the changes and continuities which the game of rugby and its traditions of manliness and masculinity have undergone due to the effects of both time and place. The book concludes with a discussion on the current state and future of rugby, particularly of the impact of the World Cup, professionalism and commercialism on this still 'gendered' sport.

260 pages illus. 1996 repr. 1998
0 7146 4637 7 cloth 0 7146 4156 1 paper

KENYAN RUNNING

Movement Culture, Geography and Global Change

John Bale and **Joe Sang**, both at Keele University

Winner of the British Sports History Prize for Best Book, 1997

> *'An excellent monograph on the phenomenal success of Kenyan middle distance running which will be of interest to a wide readership including everyone with a serious interest in athletics from all over the world, scholars with a specialist interest in socio-cultural studies of sport and specialists in African Studies. Provides an exemplar for future scholarly work in comparative studies of sport and studies of the sports globalisation process.'*
>
> *African Affairs*

The record-breaking achievements of Kenyan athletes have caught the imagination of the world of sport. How significant really is Kenya in the world of sports? This book, the first to look in detail at the evolution and significance of a single sport in an African country, seeks to answer these and many other questions. *Kenyan Running* blends history, geography, sociology and anthropology in its quest to describe the emergence of Kenyan athletics from its pre-colonial traditions to its position in the modern world of globalized sport. The authors show the qualities of stamina and long distance running were recognized by early twentieth century travellers in east Africa and how modern running was imposed by colonial administrators and school teachers as a means of social control to replace the indigenous fold traditions.

228 pages illus. 1996 repr. 1998
0 7146 4684 9 cloth 0 7146 4218 5 paper